POLITICAL PHILOSOPHY NOW

Chief Editor of the Series:
Howard Williams, Aberystwyth University, Wales

Associate Editors:
Wolfgang Kersting, University of Kiel, Germany
Steven B. Smith, Yale University, USA
Peter Nicholson, University of York, England
Renato Cristi, Wilfrid Laurier University, Waterloo, Canada

Political Philosophy Now is a series which deals with authors, topics and periods in political philosophy from the perspective of their relevance to current debates. The series presents a spread of subjects and points of view from various traditions which include European and New World debates in political philosophy.

Also in series
Hegel and Marx: After the Fall of Communism
David MacGregor

Politics and Teleology in Kant
Edited by Paul Formosa, Avery Goldman and Tatiana Patrone

Identity, Politics and the Novel: The Aesthetic Moment
Ian Fraser

Kant on Sublimity and Morality
Joshua Rayman

Politics and Metaphysics in Kant
Edited by Sorin Baiasu, Sami Pihlstrom and Howard Williams

Nietzsche and Napoleon: The Dionysian Conspiracy
Don Dombowsky

Nietzsche On Theognis of Megara
Renato Cristi and Oscar Velásquez

Francis Fukuyama and the end of history
Howard Williams, David Sullivan and E. Gwynn Matthews

POLITICAL PHILOSOPHY NOW

Kant's Political Legacy
Human Rights, Peace, Progress

Luigi Caranti

UNIVERSITY OF WALES PRESS

© Luigi Caranti, 2019

First edition published in hardback, 2017

All rights reserved. No part of this book may be reproduced in any material form (including photocopying or storing it in any medium by electronic means and whether or not transiently or incidentally to some other use of this publication) without the written permission of the copyright owner except in accordance with the provisions of the Copyright, Designs and Patents Act 1988. Applications for the copyright owner's written permission to reproduce any part of this publication should be addressed to the University of Wales Press, University Registry, King Edward VII Avenue, Cardiff CF10 3NS.

www.uwp.co.uk

British Library Cataloguing-in-Publication Data
A catalogue record for this book is available from the British Library.

ISBN 978-1-78683-431-7
eISBN 978-1-78316-980-1

The right of Luigi Caranti to be identified as author of this work has been asserted in accordance with sections 77, 78 and 79 of the Copyright, Designs and Patents Act 1988.

Typeset by Marie Doherty
Printed by CPI Antony Rowe, Melksham

Contents

Acknowledgements	vii
List of Abbreviations	ix
Introduction	1
Part I: Human Rights	**15**
1 Kant's Theory of Human Rights	17
2 Human Rights: the Contemporary Debate	40
3 The Foundation of Human Rights: The Dignity Approach	57
Part II: Peace	**105**
4 The Kantian Model	107
5 Democratic Peace Theory	160
6 The Two Models Compared	195
Part III: Progress	**207**
7 Kant's Early Teleology in *Idea*	209
8 *To Perpetual Peace*: A Secular Guarantee of Progress?	218
9 Progress and Political Agency	235
Notes	257
Bibliography	279
Index	299

Acknowledgements

I owe gratitude to many friends and colleagues for this book, and those cited here are a small subset of the people whose help should be acknowledged. Sebastiano Maffettone, Alessandro Ferarra, Allen Buchanan, John Tasioulas and others offered valuable critical comments on part I. Michael Doyle, Bruce Russett, Daniele Archibugi, Pauline Kleingeld, Paul Guyer, Massimo Mori, Thomas Pogge and, again, many others contributed to the chapters collected in part II. In particular, I greatly profited from the criticisms I received from Joshua Cohen and his students at the Stanford Political Science Workshop. Alessandro Pinzani deserves a special mention for his help not only with part III, but for reading and commenting on the whole book, providing precious challenges to my reading on Kant when we disagreed and extra reasons to strengthen the points where we shared similar views. All the guests and participants of the Colloquium on Philosophy and Global Affairs at the University of Catania indirectly helped to shape single theses defended in the book, whose preparatory work began, perhaps not accidentally, when the Colloquium was born (2010). In a similar fashion, I profited from the discussions with Kant scholars on occasion of the various editions of the Multilateral Kant – Colloquium and of the Clélia Martins Kant – Colloquium held in Marilia (São Paulo, Brazil). I would also like to thank some of my students, at LUISS and at the University of Catania, who attended my graduate seminar on human rights. Special gratitude goes to my PhD student Nunzio Alì who followed and supported the development of my work. Immense gratitude goes to my family for the multiform emotional support and for the time they concede me to follow my interests.

Besides people, I owe gratitude to institutions, in particular to the European Commission that enabled two years of study for part II at Columbia University through a Marie Curie Global Fellowship.

Some of the chapters of this book appeared in different form in previous publications. A shortened version of chapter 1 appeared in the *Routledge Handbook for Human Rights* (Taylor & Francis 2011), some of the theses offered in part II appeared recently in a paper published in the *Journal of Political Philosophy* (many thanks, incidentally, to its anonymous referees) and in my book *La pace fraintesa* (Rubbettino 2012), while chapter 8 appeared in the collective volume *Politics and Teleology in Kant* (UWP 2014) edited by Paul Formosa, Avery Goldman and Tatiana Patrone. Thanks to all publishers for their permission to reprint.

List of Abbreviations

References to Kant's works follow the *Akademie* pagination. The list of abbreviation is provided below. The translation of Kant's political writings used in this book is that of H. B. Nisbet in H. Reiss (ed.), *Kant, Political Writings* (New York, 1991). For the parts not covered by Reiss's edition, I use the Cambridge edition of the works of Immanuel Kant.

Anth	Anthropologie in pragmatischer Hinsicht (AA 07). *Anthropology from a Pragmatic Point of View*. Translated by R. B. Louden in CE: Kant, I. (2007) *Anthropology, History, and Education*, G. Zöller and R. B. Louden, eds. (Cambridge: Cambridge University Press).
Br	Briefe (AA 10–13). *Correspondence*. A selection from these volumes is translated by A. Zweig in CE: Kant, I. (1999) *Correspondence*, A. Zweig, ed. (Cambridge: Cambridge University Press).
EaD	Das Ende aller Dinge (AA 08). *The End of All Things*. Translated by A. W. Wood in CE: Kant, I. (1996) *Religion and Rational Theology*, A. W. Wood and G. di Giovanni, eds. (Cambridge: Cambridge University Press).
EEKU	Erste Einleitung in die Kritik der Urteilskraft (AA 20). *First Introduction to the Critique of the Power of Judgment*. Translated by P. Guyer and E. Matthews in CE: Kant, I. (2000) *Critique of the Power of Judgment*, P. Guyer, ed. (Cambridge: Cambridge University Press).
GMS	Grundlegung zur Metaphysik der Sitten (AA 04). *Groundwork of the Metatphysiocs of Morals*. Translated by M. J. Gregor in CE: Kant, I. (1996) *Practical Philosophy*, M. J. Gregor, ed. (Cambridge: Cambridge University Press).

GSE	Beobachtungen über das Gefühl des Schönen und Erhabenen (AA 02). *Observations on the Feeling of the Beautiful and Sublime.* Translated by P. Guyer in CE: *Anthropology, History, and Education.*
IaG	Idee zu einer allgemeinen Geschichte in weltbürgerlicher Absicht (AA 08). 'Idea for a Universal History with a Cosmopolitan Aim'. Translated by A. W. Wood in CE: *Anthropology, History, and Education.*
KpV	Kritik der praktischen Vernunft (AA 05). *Critique of Practical Reason.* Translated by M. J. Gregor in CE: *Practical Philosophy.*
KrV	Kritik der reinen Vernunft. *Critique of Pure Reason.* Translated by Norman Kemp Smith (1965) (New York: Saint Martin's Press).
KU	Kritik der Urteilskraft (AA 05). *Critique of the Power of Judgment.* Translated by P. Guyer and E. Matthews in CE: *Critique of the Power of Judgment.*
Log	Logik (AA 09). *The Jäsche Logic.* Translated by J. M. Young in CE: Kant, I. (1992) *Lectures on Logic,* J. M. Young, ed. (Cambridge: Cambridge University Press).
MAM	Mutmaßlicher Anfang der Menschheitsgeschichte (AA 08). *Conjectural Beginning of Human History.* Translated by A. W. Wood in CE: *Anthropology, History, and Education.*
MS	Die Metaphysik der Sitten (AA 06). *The Metaphysics of Morals.* Translated by M. J. Gregor in CE: *Practical Philosophy.*
RL	Metaphysische Anfangsgründe der Rechtslehre (AA 06). *Metaphysical First Principles of the Doctrine of Right.*
TL	Metaphysische Anfangsgründe der Tugendlehre (AA 06). *Metaphysical First Principles of the Doctrine of Virtue.*
Nach	*Nachschrift zu Christian Gottlieb Mielckes Littauisch- deutschem und deutsch-littauischem*

	Wörterbuch (AA 08). *Postscript to Christian Gottlieb Mielcke's Lithauanian-German and German-Lithuanian Dictionary.* Translated by G. Zöller in CE: *Anthropology, History, and Education.*
Päd	Pädagogik (AA 09). *Lectures on Pedagogy.* Translated by R. B. Louden in CE: *Anthropology, History, and Education.*
Refl	Reflexion (AA 14–19). *Reflections.* A selection from these volumes is translated by C. Bowman, P. Guyer and F. Rauscher in CE: Kant, I. (2005) *Notes and Fragments*, P. Guyer, ed. (Cambridge: Cambridge University Press).
RezHufeland	Recension von Gottlieb Hufeland's Versuch über den Grundsatz des Naturrechts (AA 08). *Review of Gottlieb Hufeland's Essay on the Principles of Natural Right.* Translated by A. W. Wood in CE: *Practical Philosophy.*
RGV	Die Religion innerhalb der Grenzen der bloßen Vernunft (AA 06). *Religion within the Boundaries of Mere Reason.* Translated by G. di Giovanni in CE: *Religion and Rational Theology.*
SF	Der Streit der Fakultäten (AA 07). *The Conflict of the Faculties.* Translated by M. J. Gregor and R. Anchor in CE: *Religion and Rational Theology.*
TP	Über den Gemeinspruch: Das mag in der Theorie richtig sein, taugt aber nicht für die Praxis (AA 08). *On the Common Saying: That may be correct in theory, but it is of no use in practice.* Translated by M. J. Gregor in CE: *Practical Philosophy.*
ÜGTP	Über den Gebrauch teleologischer Principien in der Philosophie (AA 08). *On the use of Teleological Principles in Philosophy.* Translated by G. Zöller in CE: *Anthropology, History, and Education.*
VAMS	Vorarbeit zur Metaphysik der Sitten (AA 23). *Preliminary notes for Metaphysics of Morals.*

VAZeF	Vorarbeiten zu Zum ewigen Frieden (AA 23). *Preliminary notes for Toward Perpetual Peace.*
V-Anth/Fried	Vorlesungen Wintersemester 1775/1776 Friedländer (AA 25). *Anthropolgy Friedländer (1775–1776).* Translated by G. Felicitas Munzel in CE: Kant, I. (2012) *Lectures on Anthropology*, A. W. Wood and R. B. Louden, eds (Cambridge: Cambridge University Press).
V-Anth/Mensch	Vorlesungen Wintersemester 1781/1782 Menschenkunde, Petersburg (AA 25). *Menschenkunde (1781–1782).* Excerpts translated by R. B. Louden in CE: *Lectures on Anthropology.*
V-Lo/Dohna	Logik Dohna-Wundlacken (AA 24). *The Dohna-Wundlacken Logic.* Translated by J. M. Young in CE: *Lectures on Logic.*
V-Lo/Wiener	Wiener Logik (AA 24). *The Vienna Logic.* Translated J. M. Young in CE: *Lectures on Logic.*
V-Mo/Mron	Moral Mrongovius (AA 27). *Morality: Mrongovius's Lecture Notes.*
V-Mo/Collins	Moralphilosophie Collins (AA 27). *Moral Philosophy: Collins's Lecture Notes.* Translated by P. Heath in CE: Kant, I. (1997) *Lectures on Ethics*, P. Heath and J. B. Schneewind, eds (Cambridge: Cambridge University Press).
WA	Beantwortung der Frage: Was ist Aufklärung? (AA 08). *An Answer to the Question: What is Enlightenment?* Translated by M. J. Gregor in CE: *Practical Philosophy.*
ZeF	Zum ewigen Frieden (AA 08). *Toward Perpetual Peace.* Translated by M. J. Gregor in CE: *Practical Philosophy.*

To Chiara, Matilde and Marcello

Introduction

Kant's political thought has recently received considerable attention, often and interestingly beyond the relatively narrow circle of the usual interpreters. In addition to the obvious and direct influence Kant had on the early and late Rawls – hence on contemporary political philosophy as a whole – his views have had a profound impact on one of the major research programmes in the social sciences of our times, the so-called democratic peace theory, as well as on the latest developments of the philosophical foundation of human rights. Similarly, one can safely argue that all broadly liberal accounts of global justice, ranging from the moderate, state-centred approaches of Thomas Nagel (and again Rawls) to the more radical proposals of cosmopolitan democracy, are indebted to the critical philosophy. A good portion of the reflection on domestic, international and global justice, as well as peace studies, is thus inspired by one part or another of Kant's legacy.

This is hardly surprising if one reflects that the Königsberg philosopher has often been used when humanity found itself in need of reconstructing a horizon of sense and a perspective for political action after devastations of various sorts. Kant inspired the reconstruction of values and fundamental moral principles after the First and Second World Wars, served as model for war-averting institutions such as the United Nations and the European Union, and inspired the major documents of human rights, thereby contributing to the definition of a normative language used, more or less in good faith, by virtually all countries and peoples around the globe. We currently live at a historical moment of profound restructuring of the political world we inherited from the cold war. An unexpected long recession, the erosion of national sovereignty, faltering regional governance (for instance the EU), a lack of adequate international regulation needed for global problems such as climate change, terrorism, dangerous socio-economic inequalities – these characterize a political reality of unprecedented complexity. It seems that the world is in need, perhaps more than ever, of a philosophical project with a clear indication at least of the direction to take. The project offered by Kant still seems one of the best at our disposal.

But what part of Kant's lesson has been received? What version of his thought taken up? Despite the central role Kant's thought has played in contemporary politics, one cannot help noticing how scholars have been interested either in debating specific hermeneutical issues or in isolating very broad moral and political principles to use them (often reshaped according to need) for their own theories. Hermeneutical work has thus been carried out without much attention to the thorniest issues of our world – at least those that could be treated through Kantian lenses with reasonable hope of intellectual and practical progress. Conversely, those who have focused on these concrete issues using Kant as a guide, have done so with very scant hermeneutical care. Rarely is it ever highlighted how Kant, properly understood, can do more than propose abstract norms. His concrete guidance for political action has remained underappreciated.

Among many, three major political issues of our times seem to be particularly apt to be dealt with through Kantian lenses: the foundation of human rights; the promotion of peace in an insecure and war-prone world; the definition of what political actors should do to reform the world, how they should do it and why there are grounds to believe that such efforts will not be vain. We start with a thorough reconstruction of Kant's view of our innate right to freedom, which is used for defining what a Kantian theory of human rights would look like. After a review of current philosophical approaches to human rights, we focus on Kant's linking of autonomy with human dignity to suggest the skeleton of a new foundation of these rights. We then deal with Kant's theory of peace, in particular, with the way in which Kant's 'recipe' has been interpreted and at times seriously misunderstood by contemporary scholars working in the democratic peace research programme. We measure the distance between Kant's original model and its contemporary reinterpretation, assess normatively the two models, and show how the original turns out to be more convincing and promising than the copy. Finally, we deal with two closely interdependent parts of Kant's thought that have proved to be indigestible for the contemporary reader: his view that there is a natural progress in human affairs; and his closely related theory of political action. Despite appearances, what Kant says on why we incline to a better future has very little to do with providential or, broadly speaking, metaphysical views. Purged of any dogmatic element, his teleology offers a compelling argument for believing that the system of human affairs has a tendency to evolve towards a less unjust and violent future. Moreover, Kant has something interesting to say on the right balance that politicians seriously interested in furthering justice should strike between moral demands and the concrete reality in which political action takes place. Balancing vision and pragmatism is for Kant not only a moral obligation, but also the most challenging and difficult task facing a politician. It is the essence of (good) politics and, in analogy with the Aristotelian mean in morality, it is a sort of golden middle way between fanaticism and conservation. Unlike the Aristotelian mean, however, practical wisdom is a necessary but not sufficient instrument to be on the right track. The political life for Kant is more difficult than the moral life, and politicians cannot be merely good men endowed with good sense plus some experience of the world. They also need to be on top of the best social science available, because they cannot afford to ignore the consequences of their actions to the same extent allowed to the moral person. At a time in which people have grown suspicious of the Enlightenment promise that the human race is progressing, even if non-linearly, towards a better, more just future, the present work is intended as an antidote to this too realist posture.

A few extra words on each of the three parts that constitute the book will allow the reader to see the direction we have taken in this study and to assess its relevance for contemporary politics.

Human rights. There is little need to argue at length for the importance of human rights in today's international politics. If we look at their role in 1948, when they were first officially introduced by the Universal Declaration of Human Rights (UDHR), and compare it with the role they play today in various contexts, one can easily realize that their impact has increased beyond anything the drafters in 1948 could have hoped or imagined. Human rights today are not merely the official normative language that most politicians speak around the world (not always in good faith, of course). They are standards that determine (a) the conditions of legitimate sovereignty; (b) whether the international community has a right to intervene (in different forms, up to military actions) against governments or power groups that violate them massively and systematically; (c) whether countries are eligible to enter the European Union; (d) the accountability of the forty-seven governments that are members of the Council of Europe (including Russia, Turkey, Hungary) to an international tribunal such as the European Court of Human Rights, which delivers binding judgements often leading to an alteration of national legislation; (e) the backbone and *raison d'être* of a number of international institutions (e.g., the UN High Commission) and influential NGOs; (f) a source of inspiration for millions of activists around the world, providing them with a common language and a shared basis of political initiative. Quite simply, and independently of how often human rights are violated, these standards have long since ceased to be mere occasions of moral outrage and protest; they have become standards of political decency with concrete repercussions.

If human rights today have an impact on politics far greater than in the past – a point that even the most cynical observer can hardly deny – the philosophical reflection that surrounds them has had a less fortunate history. It is doubtful that we are today in a better position than in 1948 to answer any of the following questions: Why are human rights *rights*? Why are they *human* rights? How are they different from moral rights? Are they merely political rights? Are they an extension of the traditional natural rights or are they fundamentally different? What human goods, liberties or prerogatives should they protect? What is the relation between democracy and human rights? Is democracy a human right? Are human rights inherently Western standards? Do they have a legitimate application in contexts *not* infused with a liberal-democratic public culture? And finally, and perhaps crucially, what is their foundation, i.e. why are they standards – of whatever sort – that we should obey or at least take seriously?

An academic, an activist or simply an ordinary inquirer wanting to dig into these questions, and in particular the last one, would hardly find clear, let alone unanimous, accounts in the literature. Allen Buchanan (2010) calls this state of affairs the justification deficit, that is, the gap between the growingly important role human rights play today and our inability to have a shared view on their foundation. What we have today is a philosophical menu that offers three approaches profoundly different from one another.

The first identifies human rights with standards that have a binding normativity simply because we need the benefits they protect. More precisely, but still very roughly, interest-based approaches argue that human rights are binding because without them societies can barely flourish, or flourish as much as they could. Thus, human rights do not protect any intrinsic dignity of human beings. They rather protect and serve fundamental human *needs* and are to be taken seriously as long as we care about humans' well-being.

Another school of thought, authoritatively represented by Rawls and Raz, would rather tell our reader that human rights are binding because they have come to play a role in international politics. Since, as a matter of fact, they define the boundaries of a government's authority over its territory, they *ipso facto* are to be taken seriously. If you ask whether human rights have any warrant to perform such a crucial role, this school would probably look down on you and suspect that you are an old-fashioned metaphysician dangerously attempting to undermine what practice has already established. There is no need for a philosophical foundation for human rights because they already have a de facto foundation. They are preconditions of legitimate sovereignty and, if violated, they generate widely accepted grounds for intervention by the international community in the internal affairs of a state. And this is pretty much all that needs to be said about their 'foundation'.

Finally, there are scholars of a more orthodox or traditional orientation (e.g. Kamm and to a certain extent Tasioulas) who would try to salvage the idea that human rights are legitimate and binding standards because humans have an intrinsic dignity that institutions, and perhaps even private individuals, are bound to respect. This more traditional school would capitalize on and expand the often heard line that humans have certain rights 'by virtue of their humanity' by finding in the notion of humanity some positive feature that human rights are supposed to protect. Needless to say, in the attempt to prove that humanity is intrinsically valuable, much depends on how convincing the reasons are to which this sort of orthodoxy appeals.

Why throw Kant into this foundational debate and use his thought as a source of inspiration? After all, when Kant talks of humans' innate right to freedom, it is not clear whether such a right can safely be considered equivalent to a 'human right' as we now conceive of it. Moreover, Kant's ethics is perceived as distant from the attempt, recommended by nearly all experts on human rights, to find some non-metaphysical basis to which representatives of different cultures and traditions can give their assent. Finally, Kant's account of our dignity seems to rest on his controversial doctrine of our belonging not only to the phenomenal world but also to the noumenal one, a very metaphysical tenet indeed.

Notwithstanding these difficulties, Kant has much to say to philosophers of human rights, no matter how this lesson has been surprisingly ignored or misunderstood. To begin with, on our interpretation not only does Kant challenge the current instrumental and political foundations of human rights, something hardly surprising given his deontological orientation. More interestingly, he cuts deeper than non-instrumental foundations as they are currently practised (Nagel 1995; Kamm 2007; Tasioulas 2015) because Kant does not *start* from the intuition that humans are inviolable or from the assumption that they have 'dignity'. Quite simply, Kant explains *why* that is the case, which – I think – is not of secondary importance in the economy of a foundation. Take Nagel as an authoritative example of non-instrumentalism. After asserting that humans have dignity, Nagel stops any further inquiry by arguing that '[a]ny attempt to render more intelligible a fundamental moral idea will inevitably consist in looking at [the] same thing in a different way' (1995: 92). Kant does not stop there, and attempts to spell out why we owe respect to any human being. The ultimate Kantian reason is obviously our 'awe-inspiring' capacity for moral agency. Beyond Kant, our task will be to construe this notion of moral agency in a manner broad enough to 'buy in' traditions and cultures very different from the Kantian or, more broadly, the Western.

Another reason to use Kant and his account of basic rights is that he manages to combine rigidity on certain universal standards (in particular freedom and equality) with flexibility concerning the implementation of these standards in the face of the moral pluralities of our world. Kant would condemn the tendency, popular among Rawlsians, to water down the universals of justice, and consider any violation of the *perfectly* equal right to freedom as inexcusable for cultural or religious reasons (a position that virtually no theoretician today would dare embrace). At the same time, he would also condemn the contemporary tendency to force these *minima moralia* on individuals and peoples – a prudence that many think incompatible with a commitment to universal standards. Kant does not deflect from considering maximum liberty for each individual and perfect formal equality as rights inherently human, but allows great flexibility to each society in its progress towards the implementation of these standards, and grants *no* permission to outsiders to impose them in a crusade-like style. This combination of rigidity about principles and flexibility about the times and modes of their implementation deserves more attention than is usually conceded. It is at this point that the first part of this book intersects with the third, where we deal with the strategy a good politician is supposed to adopt to advance justice.

Once having reconstructed what an authentically Kantian theory of human rights looks like (chapter 1), and having compared it with the three major approaches distinguished above (chapter 2), in the third chapter we shall offer a foundational argument largely inspired by Kant, but different from his at a couple of crucial points. While we exploit Kant's link between autonomy and dignity to offer a foundation profoundly different from the one centred on Griffin's notion of personhood, as well as distanced from Tasioulas's and others' non-instrumentalist accounts, we hold against Kant that autonomous agency need not be only agency performed under the auspices of the Categorical Imperative. We shall argue that authentic, duty-based moral agency occurs even when people act under different moral imperatives including the Golden Rule. Also, probably even more against Kant, we deny that autonomous agency is a peculiarity of human animals, siding with the weaker thesis that humans are merely capable of this form of agency *to the highest degree of development* in the animal world.

Peace. In the definitive articles of *To Perpetual Peace* (1795), Kant advocated three main institutional reforms to eliminate the greatest self-inflicted tragedy of humanity, that is, war. Kant thought that if national governments could become 'republican' (roughly, but only roughly, what we would now call liberal democracies) and an international federation of states (along the lines of the UN or the EU) could be established, and a certain degree of permeability between states to allow visits by foreigners ('the right to visit') could be ensured, everlasting peace among nations would eventually follow. In the 1980s, Michael Doyle (1983a and b) interpreted a 200-year absence of conflicts between democracies – a historical fact whose significance is challenged by only a handful of scholars (Spiro 1996; Archibugi 1997; Gowa 1999; Henderson 2002) – as a striking piece of evidence in favour of Kant's theory. Doyle's claim sparked one of the most important research programmes in the social sciences of our times – the Democratic Peace Theory (DPT) – a programme at the intersection of political philosophy, political science and international relations.

Currently there is a general consensus that democracies have rarely fought each other – what Doyle called their 'separate peace' (1983a). Scholars, however, are far from proposing a shared explanation for this regularity. Those of a liberal orientation view it as evidence that Kant's project is both sound and in the process of being implemented. Others deny or strongly reduce the significance of each of the three Kantian claims. Ever since Doyle's seminal writings, this debate shows no sign of decline in size and intensity; indeed, it has reached a level of sophistication that makes it a textbook example of Kuhnian 'normal science'. Needless to say, there are many scholars who believe that there is something profoundly misconceived in the very essence of the 'separate peace' theory and, more generally, in the approach that does not see the international scene as a table in which power politics is the only factor that counts. Not only exponents of the realist school, though, have found Doyle's rejuvenation of Kant's political project hopelessly wrong-headed. In a powerful and coherent criticism Sebastian Rosato identified a number of 'logics' underpinning DPT and showed that none of them stands either the proof of logic or the proof of facts. And doubts remain whether the replies offered by DPT scholars (Kinsella 2005; Doyle 2005) are fully convincing.

In light of significant disagreements among supporters of DPT and well-grounded criticisms from sceptics, the second part of this book offers the opportunity to rethink one of the most promising research programmes of our times. It does so in three steps. To begin with, chapter 4 contains a thorough and systematic study of Kant's original theory of peace, which is intended as both a term of comparison for assessing the latest versions of DPT as well as a theoretical instrument to propose patterns of solution to DPT's main difficulties. Chapter 5 reconstructs the origins and developments of DPT without passing over its major controversial points. In particular, we will see that even the most refined version of DPT still fails to exploit the full potential of the original Kantian model.

Chapter 6 focuses on this last point and shows how the Kantian model is both quite different from and normatively superior to DPT, even in its best guise. The final character of part II, however, is far from being merely dismissive of DPT. The goal is rather to reinvigorate DPT by showing a Kantian path that may help in overcoming its stumbling blocks. With its enormous potential for the transformation of our world, a strengthening of DPT is quite likely to be worth the effort.

In a nutshell, the reinvigoration we propose moves from a reading of Kant's three definitive articles profoundly different from the one assumed by DPT. First of all, we draw a distinction, ignored by DPT scholars, between a liberal democracy and a republic. It is one thing to say that liberal democracies are the best approximation to the Kantian republic that history has so far experienced. It is quite a different thing to hold, as DPT scholars do, that they are identical in all relevant aspects. Only if the distinction is clear can one attempt to explain why liberal democracies at times 'misbehave' in the international arena, by using force when neither their security nor human rights are at stake. Equally important is the removal of a misunderstanding that surrounds the second definitive article. While DPT scholars have interpreted the League Kant recommended as open to republics only, this was never Kant's intention. No matter how popular this 'restricted access' reading is, it is demonstrably wrong as an interpretation of Kant and very dubious as a normative prescription for improving world security. Finally, the reduction of the significance of cosmopolitan right[1] (the gist of Kant's third definitive article) to a recommendation to trade internationally as much as possible, will be similarly assessed and rejected, both as an adequate reading of Kant and as a promising normative recommendation. Kant's 'right to visit', it will be argued, extends far beyond the securing of the conditions that enable international trade. Cosmopolitan right establishes a standard of respect for human beings which is thought a crucial peace-promoting factor in its own right. Only derivatively is it thought to enable another peace factor, that is, economic interdependence. Moreover, although Kant is not explicit about it, he seems to hold that economic interdependence promotes peace only if it rests on fair terms of cooperation between the parties. Not only has DPT advanced a limited reading of cosmopolitan right, but even that little part of Kant's third definitive article that did capture the attention of DPT scholars – the one on the 'spirit of commerce' as incompatible with war – has been misunderstood. By no means every form of international trade generates peace, as abundant evidence shows. Only *fair* international trade does, quite independently of whether it is practised between democracies and under the framework of a common intergovernmental organization (IGO).

Progress. Closely connected to Kant's theory of human rights and peace is his progressive view of history. Kant thought that the world is not inhospitable to our efforts to transform it into something peaceful and just. Unfortunately, his arguments to prove that we are progressing (perhaps even *bound* to progress) towards that happy ending are intrinsically controversial and generally regarded with suspicion. No matter how controversial, Kant's teleology has come to be recognized more and more as a constitutive, non-dispensable part of his entire political thought, whose main thrust can and should be defended if one is interested in extracting from Kant a convincing theory of political agency. The last three chapters explore the evolution of Kant's intuitions on the issue of progress. Chapter 7 deals with the first formal appearance of a progressive teleology in the 1784 essay *Idea for a Universal History with a Cosmopolitan Purpose*. It will be argued that, as presented in *Idea*, Kant's progressive view can be salvaged only if the mechanism of social unsociability is (a) detached from the – by contemporary standards – hardly defensible notion of 'natural dispositions', and (b) understood in conjunction with general premises about human nature and the world that Kant takes as self-evidently true. Seen in this light, Kant's teleology is reduced to the affirmation that, given certain constant features of human beings (mainly a measure of benevolence and the ability to see their best interests through experience), as well as relatively constant objective circumstances of the world (resources scarce yet indefinitely expandable through production and commerce), an approximation of human affairs towards the 'cosmopolitan constitution' is more likely than any other outcome. Contrary to all previous interpretations of *Idea*, it will be argued that the status of this thesis extends beyond the merely regulative function of guiding our historical research towards some unity. The chapter affirms that Kant's goal in *Idea* is more ambitious: the goal is that of providing epistemic reasons to believe that non-linear progress towards the cosmopolitan constitution, rather than regress or stagnation, is the most likely development of human affairs.

The same hermeneutic approach will be used to deal with the (in)famous Guarantee Thesis as presented in later essays, in particular in *To Perpetual Peace*. Here Kant (aptly) altogether abandons the talk of 'natural dispositions' and expands the best strategy at his disposal, namely the mechanism of unsocial sociability. Chapter 8 shall argue that this strategy, properly understood, is sufficient to rebut three main objections that contemporary scholars have mounted against the plausibility of the Guarantee Thesis, in particular from an epistemological, anthropological and moral point of view. The overall hope is to show that Kant's teleology is far from being a naive piece of Enlightenment optimism or faith in the benevolence of God. It is rather a systemic view on the mechanisms governing human actions. This may fail to produce conviction that progress is inevitable, or even merely that tragedy is ruled out for the human race, but will suffice to show how our efforts to bring about a better world are both meaningful and obligatory.

With Kant's progressive view of history clarified and (to the extent possible) defended, the book ends with a detailed discussion of Kant's view of the proper way in which political actors interested in progress should direct their efforts. How should 'moral politicians' act in order to maximize their contribution to progress towards a peaceful and just world? How is Kantian rigour in moral life compatible with a form of agency – politics – that always require compromises? Kant has a very interesting theory on how politicians can and should conceive of their agency as inspired by moral law and yet be by no means reducible to a mechanical application of preformed precepts. The first goal of chapter 9 is to clarify how Kant reserves for politics a space of action with relative autonomy from law and morality. The specific question of the autonomy of politics will be approached with an eye to the general question whether Kant is successful in producing a consistent and convincing theory of political agency.

Defining the exact limits of the domain of politics in relation to the domains of law and morality is a difficult task because Kant himself is not always consistent on this point. Many contemporary misunderstandings are in fact generated by oscillations and paradoxes for which Kant himself bears some responsibility. We aim to reconstruct a theory of political agency that is both inherently consistent and harmonious with the rest of Kant's philosophy. Key for our interpretation will be a close analysis of the Kantian 'characters' of the 'moral politician' with the more or less negative counterparts, the 'political moralist' and the 'moralizing politician'.

By offering a systematic reconstruction of Kant's theory of politics, the last part of the book pursues a second goal: it bridges the gap between Kant's philosophy and political action concerned with human rights protection and peace. Kant's analysis of the 'best practices' of the 'moral politician', as well as his decrying of the dangers implicit in the initiatives of political moralists, moralizing politicians and moral fanatics, offers, if properly understood, valuable guidance to responsible political actors to maximize the impact of their efforts, and a tool to identify and possibly defuse counterproductive initiatives by a vast and diverse array of false prophets, masked lovers of the status quo, self-interested pessimists. The last part of the book thus complements the first two by focusing on how a wise activism in favour of human rights and peace should be pursued. Not only was Kant able to define with clarity the general principles on which our political action should rest. He was also capable of saying illuminating things on how such principles have to be translated into concrete actions. The fact that this part of his thought has attracted significantly less attention than is devoted to the definition of the principles does not make it less crucial.

As we said, the three parts of Kant's political legacy we focused on are strongly interrelated. A clear view of why humans are worthy creatures will reinforce not only our commitment to human rights but also our willingness to engage in political action leading to a more peaceful world. Conversely, a more peaceful world will reinforce reciprocal understanding and respect among peoples, ultimately leading to a greater respect for human rights. Moreover, both goals can be meaningfully pursued only if we have some cogent theoretical reasons to believe that the world is not structurally inhospitable to our well-meaning political initiatives, if not loaded in favour of them. Finally, political action concerned with human rights protection and peace needs guidelines. In particular, a clear view of the role of politics as subordinated and yet not reducible to morality should help to avoid the equally disastrous attitudes of the moral fanatic and of the cynical or self-seeking defender of the status quo.

INTRODUCTION

This book highlights and reinterprets those parts of Kant's political legacy that are particularly important for the lives of individuals in the twenty-first century. The leading assumption is that if this legacy is taken seriously, one can understand better why human rights are important, what we need to do to make the world less violent and why there is grounded hope that our efforts to improve things will not be vain. My goal was not to write a book of interest to specialists only, because Kant's thought should be discussed and properly understood outside philosophical circles, let alone the small circle I belong to, that of Kant scholars. The attempt to reach out to a broad audience explains and – I hope – partly excuses my treatment of classical points in Kant scholarship without the completeness they would otherwise deserve. Certainly an objective this book did not have was that of providing a thorough discussion of the interpretative work that past and present specialists have done on Kant's view of basic rights, peace and progress. My ambition was to write a book that may be of interest to Kantians but also to educated readers with scant familiarity with Kant's philosophy or even with philosophy in general.

When the potential audience is so large, the risk of displeasing almost everybody is high. Some readers will find the book too academic in manner and too slow in treating subtle hermeneutical issues. Some, I am sure, will find it too casual in touching interpretative problems so long debated among Kant scholars. Some will find it almost naive in its attempt to defend theses, e.g. that the system of human affairs is bound to progress or the idea that a durable peace is within our reach, that appear too big to be addressed properly as parts of a monograph. Still, if the book promotes an understanding of Kant's political legacy at least free of common misperceptions and dangerous misappropriations, we shall be content to displease. Kant has still a lot to say to guide us to a better understanding of our dignity, to a sharper view of the reforms we need if we are to make our world less violent, unstable and unjust and to a perspective on our future less burdened by the all too common belief that nothing ever changes. It was my impression when I started the preparatory work for the book that Kant's lesson had been at times forgotten, more often quickly dismissed as indefensibly metaphysical, even more often greatly misunderstood, especially in research programmes with a great impact on how liberal democracies see their role in the twenty-first century.

At the end of this journey that impression has grown stronger. This gives me confidence that I have not fought with imaginary adversaries, although I am less sure I have overcome them.

Ultimately this book will have reached its main objective if readers find in it at least a coherent vision of what we can hope for in our future and what we can do to care effectively for the political world we inhabit. John Rawls famously thought that the evil humans suffer is mainly the outcome of political injustice (Rawls 1999: 6–7). He was – I hope my readers will agree with me on this at least – correct. We inherit from Kant a model for reducing injustice that after more than two centuries shows no sign of obsolescence – as long as it is handled with care and exploited to its full potential.

Part I:
Human Rights

1 • Kant's Theory of Human Rights

Some philosophical accounts of human rights are currently presented as Kantian or strongly influenced by Kant's intuition that human beings have a peculiar, fundamental characteristic which, properly understood, can serve to ground the kind of respect human rights promise to guarantee. Other accounts, probably the majority on the contemporary philosophical menu, are fashionably announced as anti-Kantian, or at least post-Kantian, for their firm refusal to adopt allegedly parochial standards of normativity. Despite this array of positive and negative references, scholars have devoted relatively little attention to precisely understanding Kant's account of innate natural rights as a first step towards the identification of what would be an authentically Kantian theory of human rights. To be sure, we have at our disposal sophisticated interpretations of Kant's theory of justice (*Recht*), of rights in general, of cosmopolitan law, of humanity and personality, and of many other concepts that are relevant to any theory of human rights. Yet, with the exception of a recent systematic attempt by Otfried Höffe (2010), no one has ever read Kant's moral and political thought to find in it what we would call today a theory of human rights.[1]

There are mainly two motives for this gap in the literature. First of all, Kant uses the expression 'human rights' in the plural (*Rechte der Menschen* or *Rechte der Menschheit*) only twice in his published works (*RGV*, 69 and *WA*, 39) and few other times in the Reflexionen, mainly when he is commenting on the position of natural law theorists (*Refl*, 6785, 7308, 7594). Most of the time, he speaks in the singular – of one right of humanity (*Recht der Menschen* or *Recht der Menschheit*).[2] This is the innate right to freedom that humans have 'by virtue of their humanity'. It is not clear, however, whether this thought is sufficiently similar to the central intuition behind the culture of human rights, according to which certain rights are bestowed on humans merely by virtue of their membership of the species. In fact, as we shall see,

Kant means by humanity our capacity to set ends for ourselves. It is dubious that drafters of human rights documents and activists around the world have in mind this technical notion when they invoke certain rights as pertaining to humans as such.

On a more profound level, Kant's ethics is perceived as diametrically opposed to the effort, recommended by virtually *every* expert on human rights, to find some intercultural, non-parochial, possibly non-metaphysical, basis to which representatives of profoundly different cultures and traditions can give their assent. Two features of Kant's account of basic rights seem to run counter to this pluralism-sensitive approach. First, Kant's notion of humans' inherent worth depends on a controversial belief that we are transcendentally free, i.e. not accountable in our behaviour, through the laws of the natural world. Moreover, Kant's assumption that individual freedom is the central moral value is questioned by alternative, non-Western approaches that give priority to the group or to the received tradition over the individual, as exemplified by the so-called East Asian and Islamic challenges to human rights. As a result, there are very few thinkers today who venture to use Kant's practical philosophy as a basis for establishing a philosophical foundation of human rights. Even the recent proposal by James Griffin (2008) has a Kantian flavour in its focus on 'purposive agency' or 'personhood', but substantially differs from Kant's, as Griffin himself is keen to clarify.

Although the reasons that keep contemporary philosophers far from Kant are plausible, it appears odd that on the rich philosophical menu at our disposal today a Kantian theory of human rights fails to have some space. This is particularly true if one realizes that Kant succeeds in combining rigidity on certain universal standards (in particular freedom and equality) with a surprising flexibility concerning the implementation of these standards vis-à-vis the moral pluralities of our world. Kant would condemn the tendency to water down the universals of justice, and consider the worldwide violations of the right to freedom and *perfect* formal equality as inexcusable for cultural or religious reasons.[3] At the same time, however, he would also condemn the contemporary tendency to impose these *minima moralia* – a prudence that many think incompatible with a commitment to universal standards. Kant allows great flexibility to each society in its progress towards the implementation of these standards. This combination of rigidity about the principles with flexibility about the times and manners of implementation deserves more attention than is usually conceded.

The present chapter offers only the first step towards a Kantian foundation of human rights. Our main ambition is the identification of the material from which such a theory may be developed. The chapter will analyse, in the first part, Kant's idea that we have an innate right to freedom 'by virtue of our humanity'. In the second part the focus will be on our 'capacity to set ourselves ends', which Kant considers definitional of our 'humanity'. In particular, we will deal with the question whether this 'capacity' is best understood as practical freedom or rather as autonomy, two kinds of freedom quite different in Kant. In the third part we will argue that it is autonomy – our ability to be *moral* agents, not mere spontaneity – that for Kant serves as the ultimate ground on which the innate rights to external freedom and formal equality rest. In the attempt to spell out precisely how autonomy grounds these rights, we will propose an argument bridging two conceptual gaps: from being autonomous to being worthy of a certain kind of respect; and from being worthy of respect to the kind of protection which human rights promise. The last section focuses on two very recent interpretations, by Katrin Flikshuh and Andrea Sangionvanni, sceptical of the idea to use Kant's innate of right to external freedom as a basis for a plausible theory of human rights.

1. 'There is only one innate right'

Probably the text where Kant comes closest to expressing a theory of human rights, as we would understand it today, is to be found in the *Metaphysics of Morals*, in particular in the section devoted to the General Division of Rights. There Kant suggests two ways in which rights can be divided, depending on whether one assumes the perspective of the science of right or looks at rights as moral entitlements. If one makes reference to the science of right, the division is that between natural rights based on a priori principles, and positive rights, those created by a legislator. If one makes reference to rights understood as (moral) entitlements, the distinction is between innate and acquired rights. The former originate from – obviously inborn – moral capacities 'independently of any act that would establish a right' (*MS*, 6:237), that is, prior to the commonwealth, while the latter presuppose the act of establishment of a civil condition.

Given this general division, Kant then quite abruptly claims that 'There is Only One Innate Right' (*MS*, 6:237), which is freedom, understood as 'independence from being constrained by another's choice' (*MS*, 6:237).[4] And he briefly explains that we have this right 'by virtue of our humanity' (*MS*, 6:237). In order to clarify and spell out this extremely concise argument (almost a sheer assertion), it is useful to approach the issue with the division among rights just introduced. From Kant's taxonomy, we can infer the following. Our innate right to negative (or external) freedom has three main features: (a) it is a natural right that, as such, rests on a priori principles; (b) we are entitled to it before the establishment of a commonwealth (even if a state may be required to enforce it); and (c) it stems from a moral capacity. Kant does not make it explicit that the right to freedom is a natural one, but the fact that acquired rights presuppose the will of the legislator, while the right to freedom, as innate, precedes the commonwealth, entails that this is what he means. Features (b) and (c) seem to be logically linked in such a way that (c) grounds (b). It is precisely because this right 'stems from a moral capacity' that humans possess it even before the establishment of the commonwealth.[5] But, ultimately, even (a) rests on (c). Otherwise, one could hardly understand why humans possess this natural right 'a priori'. It follows that, in order to understand our right to external freedom, it is crucial to explain the moral capacity on which it rests.

This is confirmed by Kant's quick reference to the reason why we have a right to external freedom. He claims, as we have said, that each human has it 'by virtue of his humanity'. In the *Metaphysics of Morals* and elsewhere, Kant construes humanity as the capacity 'by which he [the human being] alone is capable of setting himself ends' (*MS*, 6:387). More explicitly, Kant says that 'the capacity to set oneself an end – any end whatsoever – is what characterizes humanity (as distinguished from animality)' (*MS*, 6:392). Such a capacity is thus the ground on which our right to freedom rests.

The analysis of this crucial capacity and of its alleged potential to ground the sole innate right is the object of the next paragraph. For the moment, let us notice that Kant interestingly infers from our sole innate right, in a way that seems to be analytical, four more innate rights among which, importantly, is the right to perfect formal equality. He claims:

> This principle of innate freedom already involves the following authorizations, which are not really distinct from it (as if they were members of the division of some higher concept of right): innate equality, that is, independence from being bound by others to more than one can in turn bind them; hence a human being's quality of being *his own master* (*sui iuris*), as well as being a human being *beyond reproach* (*iusti*), since before he performs any act affecting rights [*rechtlischen Akt*] he has done no wrong to anyone; and finally, his being authorized to do to others anything that does not in itself diminish what is theirs, even if they do not want to accept it. (*MS*, 6:237–8)[6]

Kant considers the derivation of these 'four implicit human rights' (Höffe 2010: 87) from the right to freedom as analytical ('they are not really distinct from it'). This is why he claims that they are not like species of a higher genus ('as if they were members of the division of some higher concept of right'). In fact this would imply that each of these four rights has a feature that differentiates it from the genus (the right to freedom). In the right to freedom – Kant thinks – we already find the features we need to spell out these extra four rights. Let us see why.

Regarding equality, the explanation is simple. Each individual has a right to a sphere of freedom whose extension is limited only by the condition that such freedom be compatible with that of all others according to a general rule. Since whatever arguments I may have to limit your freedom are also *ipso facto* arguments that you may use to limit my freedom (the force of the condition that these freedoms be limited according to a *general* rule), it follows that all individual spheres are equal. Otherwise we would be adding some extra condition besides that of compatibility. This is of crucial importance because it establishes that no a priori discrimination between individuals is allowed. Kant does not specify very well what this right to equality consists of, whether only to equal treatment before the law, or to some sort of equal access to necessary means of subsistence, or merely to the opportunity to obtain such means. Nonetheless it is quite clear that he has in mind a prohibition to discriminate between individuals for reasons that fail to take into account their equal status *as human beings*.

No religious or cultural factor can justify the assignment of larger shares of freedom to some citizens to the detriment of others. To give an obvious example, Rawls's decent people (Rawls 1999) would therefore be considered violators of human rights.[7]

We then have the three remaining rights. As Höffe (2010: 89) correctly notices, the right to be one's own master follows ('hence') from the right to equality. Here the reasoning seems to be that if we are all equal, nobody is authorized to rule over me and – the Rousseauian principle – no individual or group has the right to impose on me civil laws to which I have not given my consent. Almost *en passant*, Kant here extracts from equality a principle that makes his natural right far more ambitious than contemporary philosophers are today ready to accept. Both within the society and the family, and in the relation between the state and individuals, human beings are entities to which nothing can be done without their explicit or implicit consent. No constitutional system that is not based on this fundamental principle is therefore justified from the perspective of natural right.

Also the right to be 'beyond reproach', at least before one has performed any legal act [*vor allem rechtlischen Akt*], follows from the right to equality. Höffe argues that Kant here expresses the basic principle that a moral wrongdoing (e.g. failure to help the needy) cannot be turned *ipso facto* into a legal wrongdoing. Another possible reading, perhaps less sophisticated, is that 'before one has performed any legal act' is to be read as referring to the condition before the establishment of the commonwealth, namely as characterizing the state of nature. Here everyone is beyond reproach not because there are no moral obligations (this is where Kant departs from Hobbes) but because these obligations, what is mine and yours in general, cannot be impartially adjudicated.

Finally, we have the right to act as we please, even if this displeases someone, as long as this does not curtail the rights of other equal fellow humans. Thus one can legitimately lie and provide false information, because others still have the liberty to believe or not believe these statements. But one's lies cannot infringe the equal rights of others. It is one thing to lie to someone and even about someone in a non-consequential way. It is a different thing to defame a competing actor. No matter how hard it is to draw in real life, Kant appeals here to a common-sense distinction. From the perspective of human rights, separating *Ius* from ethics is highly significant. Through this distinction, Kant rules out any legal system geared to the promotion of a particular comprehensive view. Although natural right is a pre-legal, moral right, it yields no 'ethical state', that is to say, a government which, by virtue of some substantive ethical perspective, limits individuals' freedoms more than is necessary to guarantee their compatibility. It rather commands the construction of a commonwealth defending our equal spheres of freedom while avoiding the use of coercion to promote specific worldviews.

2. 'By virtue of his humanity'

So far, we have merely introduced what Kant thought is our sole human right and why he thinks that one can analytically infer from it four additional rights. It is now time to go back to the central question. What is the ground on which our right to freedom rests? As we said, the only indication Kant provides is that each human being has this right 'by virtue of his humanity [*kraft seiner Menschheit*]'.[8] We also saw that Kant means by 'humanity' a capacity, and that key to the correct understanding of Kant's entire doctrine is the exact determination of this capacity. In the *Metaphysics of Morals* and elsewhere, Kant construes humanity as the capacity 'by which he [the human being] alone is capable of setting himself ends' (*MS*, 6:387). More explicitly, 'the capacity to set oneself an end – any end whatsoever – is what characterizes humanity (as distinguished from animality)' (*MS*, 6:392). In the section following the one devoted to the innate right to freedom, Kant also says that humanity is a human being's 'capacity for freedom, which is wholly supersensible' (*MS*, 6:239).

Thus we have an innate right to freedom (and to the other four subrights) because we are capable of setting ourselves ends. What does that mean? How is it that the exclusive possession of a mere ability to set ends entitles me to anything? If I am capable of killing for futile motives or for securing goods very distant in time (as only humans can do), this certainly does not entitle me to any right, moral claim or the like. Why, then, does Kant believe that the capacity to set ends for themselves entitle humans to a right to external freedom? The expression 'capacity to set ends', as it stands, evokes two different capacities, both present in Kant's system: practical freedom and autonomy. In a sense that will be explained shortly, both are 'wholly supersensible', as Kant says in the definition of humanity quoted above, at least if this means that they cannot be captured by a naturalistic account of human beings. Depending on which of the two kinds of freedom one reads into this 'capacity to set oneself ends', Kant's argument for the foundation of our sole innate right will look very different. It is therefore incumbent on us to introduce the two kinds of freedom in their bare essentials and then to decide which of the two Kant means in this context.

3. Two Kinds of Freedom

Famously, for Kant human actions are not fully determined by the sensuous inclinations that normally motivate us. Rather, given any inclinations, no matter how strong, it is always up to the individual to 'endorse' them or to resist them. With the fairly obvious exception of non-voluntary responses to stimuli (such as the familiar knee coming up on a hammer strike), Kant thinks that human behaviour as a whole is subject to free rational deliberation. This means that all voluntary actions stem from the individual's free evaluation of a certain subjective rule of action, or maxim, as Kant calls it. Thus humans scrutinize through their reason the opportunity (moral or prudential) of a certain maxim and are free to adopt it or reject it. Kant at times expresses this crucial point with reference to the notion of an *arbitrium liberum*, distinguished from the *arbitrium brutum* typical of animals (*KrV*, A533–4/B561–2). Humans, on this theory, set the ends of their life for themselves without being driven or fully determined by desires and needs. At most, desires and needs *suggest* a course of action. A free decision on the part of the actor to endorse such a course, thereby making it one's own end, is, however, always necessary. This explains the force of the reflexive clause ('capable of setting *himself* ends') that appears in the formula above. Humans set ends *for themselves*. These ends are in no way imposed on them by external forces or internal passions. Humans enjoy what Kant at times calls 'freedom in the practical sense' (*KpV*, 5:562).

The Kantian notion of practical freedom comes very close to what one would call rational agency. This agency can be described by means of two essential characteristics: (a) independence from pathological necessitation, and (b) capacity to act on the basis of imperatives (rules of action) in the pursuit of a given goal. Thus humans are rational because they select the rule that guides their behaviour (they do not act randomly) and they are free to select such a rule. To give an obvious example, if I am thirsty, and I see no reasons why I should resist or delay the satisfaction arising from the extinguishing of my thirst, I can freely select the maxim: 'Any time an agent X is thirsty, she should drink.' As emphasized by Allison (1990), although apparently plain, this account of rational agency is already highly controversial in that it expresses an incompatibilist account of human freedom. In fact, for Kant the decision to drink is not fully determined by my inclination, nor is it determined by a more sophisticated pleasure calculus or the like. The decision to endorse the maxim in question is irreducible to one of the many natural causes we experience in the sensible world (in us or outside us). The decision is a radically free act on the part of the subject. As Kant sometimes puts it, it is only on this condition that I can say that *I* perform any action, as opposed to 'something in me led me to act' or 'that particular objective state of affairs evolved in a certain direction.'

In a nutshell, this is the theory of freedom Kant presents in the first critique and that in about 1781 he thought sufficient for the sake of morality. In the *Groundwork* (1785), however, we are present at the grand *entrée* of the concept of autonomy, which makes Kant's theory of freedom even more problematic for the sensitivity of contemporary philosophers. Autonomy, as defined in the *Groundwork* and in the *Critique of Practical Reason*, entails more than independence of pathological necessitation, a feature underlying all kinds of rational behaviour and equivalent to the notion of *arbitrium liberum*. It entails more than the ability to distance ourselves from our contingent inclinations in favour of some distant yet still empirically motivated end (e.g. I resist my desire to smoke in view of the higher goal of avoiding cancer). For the mature Kant, an agent whose freedom is limited to this ability is free but irremediably heteronomous. The agent is free because her inclinations (no matter how strong) do not exhaust the causal story behind her actions (it always takes a free rational act of endorsement), yet the agent is heteronomous because inclinations are a necessary component of the motivational story behind any action she performs.

On the contrary, being autonomous for Kant entails the ability to act in *complete* independence from inclinations. Positively expressed, this means being able to find sufficiently strong motivation in a very special kind of non-empirical interest, which is respect for the moral law. The ability to be governed by the authoritative force of morality is what autonomy consists in. As Allison puts it, a 'will with the property of autonomy is one for which there are (or can be) reasons to act that are logically independent of the agent's needs as a sensuous being' (Allison 1990: 97). An autonomous agent does not merely give herself the rule of her action (this is spontaneity or practical freedom). She does so independently of *any* inclination. This is what Kant expresses in slightly different language in one of the official definitions of autonomy in the *Groundwork* where this form of freedom is introduced as 'the property of the will by which it is a law to itself (independently of any property of the objects of volition)' (*GMS*, 4:440). While the human will is always a law to itself, because even heteronomous behaviour presupposes that one makes a certain sensuously motivated maxim *one's own* maxim,[9] namely that one gives a law to oneself, it is only in autonomous agency that this law is self-imposed *without sensuous influences*. This is the force of the parenthetical clause in the above definition of autonomy.[10]

Thus for Kant humans display two kinds of freedom. Through practical freedom, they set ends for themselves and do it without being fully determined by inclinations, even if the motivational package that leads to action is sensibly influenced. Through autonomy, they set ends for themselves independently of any empirical motive. Since for Kant any form of agency, including moral agency, presupposes that the agent is moved by some interest, this means that moral/autonomous agency will be motivated by the only form of *pure* (that is, non-empirical) interest open to humans, that is, respect of the moral law.[11] On this reconstruction, autonomous behaviour is equivalent to moral behaviour, although, obviously, moral behaviour is only a subset of free behaviour (which includes heteronomous actions). Now, the crucial question for us is: which of these two forms of freedom is alluded to in the definition of 'humanity' as 'the capacity to set oneself an end – any end whatsoever'?

4. Autonomy as the Basis of the Right to External Freedom

Both practical freedom and autonomy appear respectable candidates to serve as the basis of our innate right to freedom because both are peculiar to human beings and satisfy Kant's definition of humanity.[12] The reference to '*any* end whatsoever' in this definition suggests that Kant means practical freedom, because even immoral ends seem to be contemplated. Other considerations, however, of a systematic and textual nature, lead us much more convincingly in the opposite direction. Starting from the systematic reasons, the fact that a certain capacity is peculiar to a species hardly grounds any right of that species. As we said above, the human species is arguably the sole one capable of killing in cold blood or even for amusement, but this hardly grounds any right, let alone a human right to kill in this mood. Thus, the nerve of the argument cannot be the exclusive possession of an ability, but its intrinsic worth. Kant's argument must be that freedom, as a property of our will, displays something intrinsically good about humans, something that grounds human dignity and, a fortiori, lays the foundation for our right to external freedom. This something, as any student of Kant knows, is precisely autonomy, understood as a property necessary and sufficient for a will to be a good will, that is, the only thing in the world that is 'good without qualification' and that, like a jewel, shines 'by itself, as something that has its full worth in itself' (*GMS*, 4:394). Practical freedom at most displays our nature of rational beings, a feature that in a sense already positions us above the natural world. Practical freedom, however, does not establish our greater worth compared to any entity of the sensible world. For this, the ability to follow the moral law even to the detriment of any empirical interest (including our survival) is required. While practical freedom makes us kings and queens of the sensible world, autonomy makes us demigods, inhabitants of this world, but at the same time qualified members, or, perhaps more modestly, qualified applicants to another kingdom.

Moving to the textual reasons, Kant affirms that the sheer capacity to set ends for themselves makes humans extrinsically more valuable than animals or things, but not superior to them as for their intrinsic, unconditioned value. He writes:

> In the system of nature, a human being (*homo phaenomenon, animal rationale*) is a being of slight importance and shares with the rest of animals, as offspring of the earth, an ordinary value (*pretium vulgare*). Although a human being has, in his understanding, something more than they and can set himself ends, even this gives him only extrinsic value for his usefulness (*pretium usus*); that is to say, it gives one man a higher value than another, that is a *price* as of a commodity in exchange with these animals as things, though he still has lower value than the universal medium of exchange, money, the value of which can therefore be called preeminent (*pretium eminens*).
>
> But a human being regarded as a *person*, that is, as the subject of morally practical reason, is exalted above any price; for as a person (*homo noumenon*) he is not to be valued merely as a means to the ends of others or even to his own ends, but as an end in himself, that is, he possesses a *dignity* (an absolute inner worth) by which he *exacts* respect for himself from all other rational beings in the world. He can measure himself with every other being of this kind and value himself on a footing of equality with them. (*MS*, 6:434–5)

Kant denies explicitly that practical freedom confers an unconditioned value to humans. At most, understanding and practical freedom make humans particularly efficient and functional entities, goods more valuable than any other in the world, yet inescapably mere goods. To the contrary, considered as subjects of a morally practical reason, that is, as autonomous, humans elevate themselves above any price, become ends in themselves, and legitimately demand respect from similar creatures. Kant re-emphasizes the point when he claims: 'Humanity in his person is the object of the respect which he [man] can demand from every other human being' (*MS*, 6:435). Humanity as the basis for the only innate right to external freedom is ultimately our being subject to the moral law, our being autonomous.[13]

5. From Autonomy to Human Rights via Equal Respect

At this point, it remains to be explained how precisely our humanity, understood as autonomy, is supposed to ground our right to external freedom, and its four sub-rights, which, it will be remembered, are the closest things we have in Kant resembling what we call today human rights. The inference is less direct and clear than one may think, and things are complicated by the fact that we intersect with here a classical problem in Kant studies. The problem is that of the relation between ethics and law. In fact, the move from our capacity for moral agency (autonomy) to our right to external freedom is precisely an inference from morality to law. From the fact that humans are autonomous beings, their worth can be easily inferred. But how can we infer from this worth the right to external freedom and the other four innate rights we saw before? Some interpreters argue that one can do it through a transcendental argument, as if external freedom were a condition of the possibility of autonomy. Others hold that the right to external freedom can be grounded without any reference to autonomy and morality, and that this was in fact Kant's intention. As we said, the division between these two groups is reminiscent of and overlaps to some extent with another division, classical by now in Kant scholarship, between scholars who read in Kant a relation of dependence, more or less qualified, between ethics and right (the normativity of the universal principle of right as dependent on that of the categorical imperative), among which Habermas (1990), Guyer (2002), Ludwig (2002), and others such as Willaschek (1997), Wood (2002), Pogge (2002) and Baiasu (2016), who assert an independence, again more or less qualified, between the two realms. After all, the divide under consideration is nothing but a special case of the broader divide just introduced. Whether a right to external freedom can be derived from our autonomy in fact amounts to asking whether a fundamental juridical norm has its source in the moral law (or better in its enabling condition).

Starting from the first group, Mary Gregor claims that a right to external freedom is presupposed in the very concept of autonomy. For humans to be autonomous, Gregor thinks, it is necessary for them to be given the possibility to choose between alternative courses of action (Gregor 1963: 7). This interpretation has been endorsed by a number of commentators who insist on the necessary link between autonomy and external freedom, the latter explicitly construed as a condition of the possibility of the former (Molholland 1990: 402f.; Weinrib 1992: 27; Carr 1989: 719–31; Bielefeld 1997: 524–58).[14]

Moving to the second group, Thomas Pogge for example argues in favour of the possibility and opportunity to separate ethics from politics in Kant and, a fortiori, to keep the right to external freedom (as expressed in the universal principle of right) as logically independent of autonomy. As textual evidence in favour of this reading, Pogge cites a passage from the Introduction to the Doctrine of Right in which Kant affirms that the universal principle of right does not require that I conform to it 'just for the sake of this obligation' (*MS*, 6:231). As Kant puts it: 'reason says only that freedom *is* limited in its idea to those conditions [the universal principle of right] and that it may be actively limited by others; and it says it as a postulate that is incapable of further proof' (*MS*, 6:231).[15] Far from limiting himself to the familiar thesis that, unlike moral duties, legal duties (and of course the principle of right that grounds them all) do not require that agents act 'from them', for Pogge Kant would here be severing the bonds between the Categorical Imperative and the universal principle of right altogether, by stating that the 'bindingness' of the latter does not depend in any way on that of the former. The obligation to conform our actions to the universal principle of right would follow *from the very idea of freedom* ('in its idea'), because this idea already contains the restriction that the freedom of one be compatible with that of all others. The main task of the *Rechtslehre* would thus be to come up with a set of rules enabling the 'coexistence game' of equal citizens, under the specified restriction. Such a restriction, however – and this is the crucial point – is already contained in the definition of the game and is not imported from external sources (Pogge 2002: 141–2).

Recently, Gunnar Beck has reached a similar conclusion. Beck advances two fundamental objections to the traditional interpretation. On the one hand, he claims that it has scant textual evidence. On the other, that it is not evident why one needs external freedom to be autonomous. An individual can be autonomous even if she is deprived of external freedom. Think of the case of a slave. As Beck puts it:

> As long as the agent possesses a morally good will, no external force can obstruct his internal state of autonomy, even though restrictions on his external liberty may prevent the agent from exercising or acting upon his autonomy, i.e., to act in accordance with what he nevertheless accepts as his duty and wills to act on.[16] (Beck 2006: 383)

Which of the two groups of interpreters is on the right track? The general impression is that there are pieces of truth scattered in both hermeneutical schools, but the first group seems closer, *pace* Beck and Pogge, to Kant's spirit and text. To begin with, although Kant does not justify humans' right to external freedom through an *explicit* reference to autonomy, it is sufficient to investigate his notion of 'humanity' to find autonomy around the corner. As we saw, humanity is the explicit ground Kant offers for our right to external freedom. Humans have that right 'by virtue of [their] humanity', says Kant. Our reconstruction of Kant's argument showed that the essence and worth of our humanity consists of our capacity to conform to the moral law. That is: it consists of our autonomy. Analogously, Pogge's sterilized, freestanding reading of the *Rechtslehre*, and of Kant's liberalism in general, is certainly wrong if it is meant as a reading of Kant's intentions, i.e. as a reading of the way Kant himself saw the relation between moral normativity and legal normativity. Again, we saw that it is our worth as autonomous beings that grounds an equal right to external freedom for all consociates, which is nothing but the universal principle of right in an embryonic form. Moreover, Pogge's reading seems to be hardly compatible with Kant's rejection of Hobbes's account of how individuals leave the state of nature and enter the civil condition. While for Hobbes these are mainly prudential reasons, for Kant they are moral ones, and ultimately refer to the equal moral status and dignity humans already possess in the state of nature. Thus, when Pogge suggests that free rational agents facing the problem of organizing their coexistence would choose the principle of right as their supreme principle he seems to be conceptualizing the exit from the state of nature as Hobbes does. But again, this is a conceptualization that Kant explicitly rejects. As pointed out by Bernd Ludwig (2006), Pogge cannot give an authentically Kantian reason why these free individuals should play the *Rechtslehre* game while leaving the state of nature.

The bit of truth to be found in the second orientation, and in particular in Beck's reading, is that external freedom does not really seem to be a condition of the possibility of autonomy. This is the main problem with the first group of interpreters. They rightly view external freedom as dependent on our autonomy; they err when they construe the former as a condition of the possibility of the latter. As in the case of the slave, one can remain an autonomous individual even if deprived of external freedom. Autonomy, as a property of our will, can always be exercised, even when our external freedom is most compressed. It is something, so to speak, nobody – individual, state or even yourself – can take away from you.[17] This does not mean, however, that autonomy does not play any role in the foundation of our right to external freedom. It means merely that we have to abandon the hope of finding a transcendental argument that makes external freedom necessary for autonomy. More modestly, we have to investigate the presuppositions, not directly of autonomy, but of the peculiar respect we are entitled to by virtue of being autonomous. The argument, in a very sketchy form, would be this:

1. Humans are autonomous (in the Kantian sense).
2. This property expresses an intrinsic worth, exalts humans 'above any price', dignifies them and therefore entitles them to respect, understood as a guarantee not to be treated as mere means.
3. Any arbitrary limitation of the external freedom of human beings amounts to treating them as mere means, that is, a failure to respect them in the required manner.
4. External freedom may be limited only to make the external freedom of one compatible with that of all others.
5. Any individual has a (pre-political, inborn) right to the largest amount of freedom compatible with the same freedom of all others.
6. All humans have a pre-political, inborn right to external freedom (and formal equality).

Dignity here bridges the logical gap, generally unnoticed by the first group of interpreters, between autonomy and external freedom.[18] From dignity originates respect, and from respect originates the prohibition to limit arbitrarily, not autonomy itself, which is, strictly speaking, immune from restriction, but external freedom. Without a reference to dignity and to the equal respect it generates, however – and this is the problem with the second group – at best humans can be said to have good prudential reasons to attribute to themselves equal spheres of external freedom, but not a *right* to that freedom.

Even if this reading appears closer to Kant's spirit and text, it should be granted that a foundation of human rights along the lines suggested faces two main difficulties. On the one hand, it renders the argument dependent on Kant's proof of the reality (even if 'from the practical point of view' only) of our autonomy. Since both the arguments offered in the *Groundwork* and those of the second critique are controversial, to say the least, the price to pay is considerable. On the other hand, even granting that these or other similar arguments succeed, the problem of the significance of autonomy in non-Western cultures remains untouched. If we are proved to be autonomous, but being autonomous is not seen as the sole or even as the main source of human worth, then Kant's argument seems to be a non-starter for an intercultural consensus on human rights. A foundation to be considered as compelling outside the circles of Kantians needs to do more than offer a charitable reconstruction of the logic of Kant's argument. A confrontation with the alternative foundations offered by the contemporary debate on human rights as well as an open confrontation with the two difficulties just mentioned is necessary. These are in fact the goals of the two following chapters. Before moving on, however, we need to discuss the recent work of two Kant scholars who put in question the very idea of using Kant as a reliable guide for a better understanding of human rights.

6. Flikschuh and Sangiovanni: can there really be a Kantian theory of human rights?

Katrin Flikschuh and Andrea Sangiovanni have recently proposed two accounts that run in a direction diametrically opposed to the one defended so far. On the one hand, Flikschuh denies that Kant's innate right to freedom, by virtue of its lack of determinateness, can serve as the basis of a plausible theory of human rights, at least if by human rights we understand the rather determined juridical standards we find in current documents and treaties. On the other hand, Sangiovanni argues even more radically that there cannot be any 'truly' Kantian theory of human rights, that is a theory that remains faithful both to central tenets of Kant's philosophy and to the common understanding of human rights. As he puts it, 'Any careful reading of Kant will reveal him to be not just indifferent to human rights claims but actively skeptical of them' (Sangiovanni 2015: 671). Needless to say, if any of these two readings is correct, the argument offered in the preceding section needs to be seriously revised, to say the least.

Flikschuh's main reason to discard the innate right to freedom as a basis for a theory of human rights is the fact that it is 'beyond legislation', which means that it cannot be the 'object of any positive law making' (Flikschuh 2015: 660). Kant's innate right and its four sub-rights seem to be too indeterminate and formal to be translated into substantive claims on others. Moreover, even if such a translation could be possible and we could infer specific legal constraints on others from it, its formulation would presuppose, like acquired rights, the existence of a civil condition. But if the latter is the case, then human rights specified from the innate right to freedom could not function, like human rights should, as pre-political constraints on legislation.

The reason why this reading is dubious has been shown by the other sceptic we need to discuss. Sangiovanni actually endorses Flikschuh's idea that the innate right to external freedom cannot be the basis for a theory of rights, but rejects the reasons she offers for that conclusion. Like the universal principle of right, innate right can function as the main moral, pre-political constraint on constitutional and ordinary law-making. And how the constraining would proceed is nicely exemplified by Sangionvanni.

> We know that to be in accordance with innate right, all positive rights must be granted on equal terms to all (such as no one may be bound by others to more than one can in turn bind them), and be consistent with each person's original independence (such that no one be forced, through no choice of their own, to be subject of another's choice – as in, say, feudal relations between lord and serf). From such higher-level implications of innate right one could then derive a list of (lower-level) human rights. (Sangiovanni 2015: 674)

Which specific lower-level human rights are inferred from these general constraints may vary. Sangionvanni cites as examples a right to independence, a right not to be born a slave, a right not to be economically independent to the point that one needs to beg and so on. Moreover, from a lower level right not to be born a slave one may derive a human right of orphans to receive protection from the state or from the right to independence one may derive a right to freedom of the press and so on. Going beyond Sangiovanni, we could add that the specific human rights to be inferred – at whatever level of specificity – depend on a variety of factors, including where a balance between different world traditions is found. A balance, needless to say, that need not be reached once and for all but that can legitimately vary in turn depending on a variety of factors, including the cogency of the philosophical reasons we find to prefer one lower-level right over another or the evolution of the same traditions that need to concur to this specification. As we said at the beginning of the chapter, what is attractive about Kant for a theory of human rights is that he appears to be able to combine rigidity on certain universal standards (the general constraints above) with flexibility on the specific ways in which those standards are translated in legal norms. In sum, the innate right to external freedom may not itself be a human right, but can easily generate general constraints (including but perhaps not limited to the four 'sub-rights' Kant himself spells out) that set limits of acceptability on potential human rights properly understood.

Let us then move to Sangiovanni's alternative reasons to reach pretty much the same negative conclusion of Flikschuh. In his view, the innate right to freedom 'cannot be a basis for human rights because human rights must be directly and externally imposeable in a way that innate right (or those rights derived directly from innate right) cannot be' (Sangiovanni 2015: 675). Human rights need to be able to license coercive actions against a violating state even if the violator does not agree with this action. In other words, human rights license *unilateral* action by third parties with respect to the victim and the alleged violators, and in general external to the state where the violations occur. But such license, continues Sangiovanni, conflicts irremediably with Kant's idea that no unilateral use of force is legitimate. This tenet in Kant is evident when he introduces a moral duty to leave the state of nature. Famously, for Kant the problem of this state is that there is no authorized third entity that can adjudicate potential conflicts among individuals as to what is 'mine or yours'. In other words, before a civil condition is created, any attempt to defend what one *thinks* is his or hers would be irremediably unilateral, hence no different than violence.

This contains an important lesson for seeing why Kant's innate right to freedom is unfit as a basis for human rights. Once a state is created through the united will of the people and therefore a civil constitution is established, any external defender of human rights would be no different than the unilateral defender of his or hers in the state of nature. And Sangiovanni thinks that this is the deep philosophical reason that explains Kant's condemnation of external interference in internal affairs of a sovereign state. Kant's fifth preliminary article of *To Perpetual Peace*, on which more will be said in chapter 4, in fact affirms that there is no way states can forcibly interfere in the internal affairs of a sovereign state, even if the latter's constitution is scandalous. The same point also accounts for Kant's denial of a right to revolution. The will of the rebels, no matter how morally well grounded their claims are, would still count as unilateral. Therefore, revolution is always illegitimate. Finally, the very same point explains Kant's idea that sovereignty is indivisible. If a state alienates part of its sovereignty to a supranational body (say the European Union or the UN only for matters of human rights protection) and a dispute arises whether the state in question has violated human rights, any verdict of the supranational body against the state, no matter how well grounded in evident moral reasons, will count as a unilateral act of force. Only an undivided sovereignty that rules without internal or external limits can legitimately make use of force.

Sangiovanni also offers an argument regarding Kant's notion of dignity as equally unfit to serve as a basis for human rights, but let us deal first with his point about the unilateral will. The weakness of this argument is not Sangiovanni's use of the theses he correctly reads in Kant. The problem is with his conception of human rights. He seems to take for granted that for a normative constraint to count as a human right it must license coercive force by an entity external to the state. This is problematic for three main reasons. To begin with, Sangionvanni ignores here the distinction between human rights and international human rights. Only about the latter can one say that they intrinsically license international interference. But international human rights are not meant to remove human rights understood, as Buchanan does (2010), as those rights that we may find appealing independently of international recognition and protection. Secondly, as we shall see in detail in the following chapter, only one of the three major schools in the current philosophy of human rights, the so called practice-based or political view, sees the permission to interfere in the internal affairs of a state as a defining feature of human rights. Orthodox and interest-based approaches can and often do conceive of human rights independently of the whole question of enforceability. For example, James Nickel – an exponent of the interest-based approach – laments that Rawls's idea of identifying human rights with 'grounds for interference' is misguided and leads him to a counterintuitive minimalism. As Nickel puts it, 'leaving out any protection for equality and democracy is a high price to pay for assigning human rights the role of making international intervention permissible when they are seriously violated' (Nickel 2003). For many scholars, there are things we might want to call 'human rights' for a series of philosophical or non-philosophical reasons that do not license any form of interference other than the soft practice of 'naming and shaming'. And it would certainly be bizarre if this kind of interference, given Kant's defence of the freedom to criticize publicly one's own government (the freedom of the pen), were to be considered as incompatible with Kant's principles. Thirdly, these schools even have room for calling something a human right that does not even appear in the official documents at our disposal, even before the whole question of enforceability arises. No matter how plausible it is to think that an essential feature of human rights is their ability to license coercive actions from external observers (from economic sanctions up to military intervention), this Rawlsian intuition is not necessarily correct. Certainly, it is not universally endorsed. As such it can hardly be used as a premise from which an argument about the (in)compatibility between Kant and human rights starts.

What about Sangiovanni's argument against the idea, a version of which will be presented in chapter 3, of using the Kantian notion of dignity as a foundation of human rights? The problem seems to lie in the fact that dignity is an inherently *moral* notion. As such it is pervasive and full of impact in the realm of ethics, but allegedly irrelevant and impotent in the realm of right. What are Sangiovanni's reasons to believe that dignity is a normative notion with consequences only in the first realm and not in the second? He notices that the term dignity (at least in the appropriate sense of a status humans are entitled to) never occurs in Kant's political or legal writings (*Doctrine of Right, To Perpetual Peace* and so on) but only in the moral ones (*Critique of Practical Reason, Groundwork, Doctrine of Virtue* and so on). Sangionvanni thinks this absence is not accidental because dignity sets limits to the way

I can treat myself and others in the relations that are the concern of morality, not those that interest right. As an example, Sangiovanni cites the familiar example of lying. Kant thinks that lying 'annihilates his [a human being's] dignity' (*MS* 6: 429) but entails no infringement of right. It would appear to follow that dignity concerns how we should treat each other morally, not the way right prescribes that we treat our external relations.

There are two main problems with this argument. To begin with, while it is true that Kant does not mention dignity in the Doctrine of Right, he talks there about humanity, for example when he explains why we have an inner right to external freedom. Remember the clause 'in virtue of one's humanity' we discussed above. If our reading is correct, the notion of humanity relates to our autonomy, and autonomy relates to dignity because the former is the ground of the latter. Thus dignity is crucial in the Doctrine of Right even if Kant does not mention it. Moreover, there is a very straightforward way of explaining why Kant does not feel obliged to mention, let alone discuss dignity, in the Doctrine of Right and in the other political writings. The reason may be, not that dignity is irrelevant, but that Kant has already secured the reality of dignity in other places of the system, not accidentally more foundational, that is, *Critique of Practical Reason* and *Groundwork*. Ultimately, Sangionvanni's irrelevance thesis is another version of the independentist thesis we mentioned above. Not accidentally, he mentions as support for his view an allegedly growing number of scholars who believe that the normativity of right in Kant stands in full independence of the ethical normativity (Sangiovanni 2015: 689). There is no space available here to add much to what we just said about dignity and its role in the system of Kant's practical philosophy. One thing, though, could be mentioned. While it is obvious that right is fully detached from a preoccupation with the motivation with which we follow our duties (juridical or ethical), Sangionvanni seems to omit that even independentists conceive of right as nothing but the application of Kant's overarching normative principle that we are all free, autonomous individuals to the business of how individuals should interact in their external relations.[19] It is in virtue of that status as free and autonomous individuals that we deserve to have perfectly equal spheres of external freedom, as opposed to, say, live in a feudal state. It is in virtue of that status that we have the whole set of juridical duties.

As Kant quite explicitly puts it *in* the *Doctrine of Right*, 'we can know our own freedom (*from which all moral laws, and so all rights and duties proceed*), only through the moral imperative, which is a proposition commanding duty, from which the capacity for putting others under obligation, that is the concept of right, can afterwards be explicated [*entwickelt*]' (*MS* 6: 239, my emphasis).

Secondly, the example of lying does not show that dignity is relevant only in the realm of ethics. *Pace* Sangionvanni, it merely shows that it is relevant in circumstances that are not the business of right. This is perfectly compatible with the possibility that dignity is relevant for both right and ethics. Human dignity may be the ground of all ethical precepts *and* of all juridical precepts, even if the two sets do not coincide. In fact, on our reading dignity rests on autonomy which is the ground of both all moral duties and of our innate right to external freedom. This right entails that each individual has an equal sphere of freedom, which is the exact content of the universal principle of right. It follows that human dignity is not only relevant, but the very essence of the doctrine of right. It is the ultimate normative ground on which its main principle rests.

2 • Human Rights: the Contemporary Debate

1. Human Rights Today

Human rights play a crucial role in contemporary politics: they are a lingua franca that allows representatives of different worldviews to have a common basis of shared values, and they inspire activism around the world and set limits to the sovereignty of states. Their importance has many reasons, one of which is particularly intriguing. They are an authentic novelty in the history of human reflection on the universal rules that should govern each and every agent. In fact, no earlier attempt to turn moral claims into norms governing politics even resembles what human rights are doing in our world. Certainly, a tendency towards universal acceptance was built into all major metaphysical and religious worldviews – think of the universal element built into the very etymology of 'Catholicism' or of the inborn tendency of all major religions to speak *the* truth about fundamental matters. Nonetheless, no preceding set of ideas has aspired to become the common normative language of mankind *independently* of the metaphysical or religious substratum on which it rested. Human rights today are the hope that we can start from very different assumptions about the ultimate truth and still reach common norms to govern the way we should treat each other. Even if our religious, philosophical and moral views vary significantly and have the potential to lead to conflict, we can still resort to the language of human rights to find agreement, or at any rate a shared basis for dialogue.

By virtue of this ambition, human rights perform the function that made them vital even outside the relatively small circles of academics and politicians. This was imposing a limit on national sovereignty and giving the 'international community', as it is called, authority to intervene in countries' domestic affairs. All major occurrences of political violence after the fall of the Berlin wall – from Rwanda to Syria, and Afghanistan, Iraq, Sudan, Libya and Mali – have been conceptualized in the language of human rights violations, triggering a demand for action by national and international bodies, through the intervention of single external states or by a coalition, with or without the endorsement of the UN. Since virtually all states accept the authority of human rights (at least on paper), this is hardly surprising. More or less serious forms of interference in domestic affairs by the 'international community' have *ipso facto* been legitimized. Even governments that were barely sincere in their homage to human rights regretted binding themselves to such abstract norms. Vice paid a high price to virtue in those cases.

Another feature of human rights is worth mentioning. They limit the right each people has to give laws to itself. Although one hardly hears this point in academic discussions, it should be clear that human rights compete with the dominant value of our times, that is, democracy. If we take human rights seriously, communities do not have an unlimited right to self-determination.[1] They have this right – and specific human rights protect just that possibility – but with well-defined limits not democratically determined.

2. The Benthamian Curse: Human Rights Without Foundations

Given the fundamental role human rights play in politics (and for the lives of millions of people around the world), it is hardly surprising that not only scholars, but also politicians and common citizens still feel the need to reflect on what grounds their normativity. How have philosophers responded to this burgeoning request for clarification? What arguments have they offered – at least recently – to those who believe in human rights but would like to get a better grasp on the reasons why we have them? More importantly, how did they respond to those who are not convinced that human rights should be the ultimate tribunal of what a people can or cannot do? Well, this is more or less the state of play. Philosophers have reached no unified account, but this is hardly a problem, even less a surprise. What is more worrying is that while the culture of human rights around the world gains momentum and proves that common people accept these universal standards, it is unclear that these improvements have come by virtue of the philosophical work done so far. In other words, it is unclear that any sceptic of human rights has become less sceptical because philosophy has provided a good account of the normative force of these rights. And if you think that philosophy should not change the minds of sceptics around the world, there is nonetheless room to say that philosophy has not even clarified the terms of the discussion. The confusion has reached so high a peak that a leading scholar in the field, James Griffin, has recently felt the need to step back from substantive questions to reach a meta-perspective. He asks, 'What are we philosophers, political theorists, and jurisprudents trying to do?' (Griffin 2012: 3) when talking about human rights. Similarly, Allen Buchanan recently asked 'What is a Philosophical Theory of Human Rights?' (Buchanan 2010: 680). Not to mention Joseph Raz (2010) who thinks, quite simply, that human rights have no foundations.

Thus the main question about human rights is still before us in its full force: how do we know that human rights are not simply the invention of well-meaning minds shocked by the brutality of the Second World War and the horrors of totalitarian regimes? How do we know that they are what they promise to be – ultimate standards with cross-cultural, universal validity? And how do we know whether the list of human rights we have in the main documents (the UDHR, treaties and so on) is the correct list, namely it includes those rights that are to be considered as *human* rights? Maybe we should have a shorter list. Is it really the case that everyone has a human right to rest and leisure, including holidays with pay, as famously stated by Article 24 of the Universal Declaration of Human Rights? And what about a human right to the 'highest attainable standard of physical and mental well-being', as declared by Article 12, section 1 of the International Covenant on Economic, Social, and Cultural Rights? And what about less famous cases of ambitious rights such as article 27, first paragraph, of the UDHR which reads, 'Everyone has the right freely to participate in the cultural life of the community, to enjoy the arts and to share in scientific advancement and its benefits'?

Questions about the proper list and nature of human rights are logically distinct from the foundational question. Let us assume that you have a compelling argument that shows (a) that humans have dignity and (b) that they are entitled to certain rights by virtue of that dignity. These results are going to influence what you say about the proper list and nature of human rights; but obviously more philosophical work needs to be done to come up with an account of which rights should be conceived as an essential protection of human dignity and to answer the question about the nature of human rights. Still, the foundational answer one adopts is going to impact greatly on the other two issues. More importantly, it enjoys a logical priority over them. While it is conceivable, as in the example above, that one comes up with an answer to the foundational question while still remaining non-committal with the regard to the other two, it would be bizarre to submit an account of the nature and the proper list of human rights, and remain fully non-committal on why human rights are not a sheer invention. Both for reasons of space and for its logical priority, in what follows we are going to focus on the foundational question. In the remaining part of this chapter we are going to reconstruct the contemporary foundational debate, highlighting strengths and weaknesses of the three main orientations currently available. In the following chapter, we shall submit the essential elements of a foundation alternative to the accounts available today which, in our view, avoids most of their impasses.

3. The Foundational Debate: Three Main Orientations

The 'justification deficit' is so acutely felt among philosophers that a voluminous publication devoted to the foundational problem has recently appeared (Cruft et al. 2015) with contributions by the most authoritative scholars. Here the different accounts are divided into three main groups that by and large overlap an earlier tripartition by Tasioulas in Reductive, Orthodox, and Political views (Tasioulas 2012). We now have (a) instrumental justifications, (b) non-instrumental justifications and (c) practice-based justifications. Let us introduce the essentials of the three approaches with a few critical notes that should suffice to explain why in our opinion none of them provides a convincing foundation.

3.1 Instrumental/Reductive Foundations

Instrumentalists (let us call them this) think of human rights as useful means to realize certain features of human lives that are taken as self-evidently valuable and worthy of protection. When it comes to specify what these features are, three different answers are suggested. Some think that *agency* is the feature in question.

Others deny that one single good can be the basis of human rights and opt for a plurality of goods central to human life. Thirdly, the capability approach developed by Sen and Nussbaum insists on human rights' point of securing capabilities, i.e. real opportunities for individuals to realize certain functions, like mental and bodily health, central to a good life. Let us start with the first kind of instrumentalism.

Agency, the capacity to act on self-imposed ends, is both something that humans tend to value highly and something that distinguishes us from other animal species, at least in terms of degree. Few would in fact deny that even if some animals are capable of purposive agency, they are so to a considerably lesser extent than human beings. The most authoritative exponent of this orientation is James Griffin (2008). Griffin thinks that human rights protect human dignity by affording humans the means necessary to exercise their capacity for agency.

No matter how appealing agency-based justifications of human rights, they encounter serious difficulties. The major problem, already noticed by Danto (1984) in his critique of a similar foundation proposed by Gewirth (1984), is that slaves have agency, and agency to a certain degree of development, enriched by education and skills, otherwise they would be worthless to a master. But obviously slaves have their human rights violated; hence agency cannot be the foundation of human rights. And if by agency Griffin means more than the minimum education and resources slaves have, then setting in a non-arbitrary way the amount of goods sufficient to meet the requirements of agency becomes difficult. Intuitively, human rights are not rights to a good life, but to a decent one. But who is to say what decency for an entity endowed with agency requires? Another problem with agency-based accounts is that when we think that torture violates human rights, we do not think that the wrong done to the victim has exclusively and perhaps even primarily to do with the deprivation of her agency. We think that part of the wrong has to do with the pain that the victim suffers. Finally, agency-based accounts seem to be committed to the bizarre view that children or mentally impaired people are not entitled to human rights. Since their capacity for purposive action is either not yet developed or permanently lost, it seems to follow that they do not have human rights. That is certainly an unwelcome conclusion, because both morality and the law attribute human rights to these people.

An alternative instrumentalist account suggests that a plurality of goods, not only one, as in the agency-based account, lies at the foundation of human rights. John Finnis (1980) suggested an allegedly objective list of human goods: life, knowledge, play, aesthetic experience, sociability (friendship), practical reasonableness, religion (*sic*). On his account, human rights are justified to the extent in which they further these goods. Similarly James Nickel adopts a pluralist perspective and argues that human rights secure (and are thereby justified by) four goods: life, the steering of one's life, avoidance of cruel and degrading treatment, avoidance of severely unfair treatment (quite apart from the degree to which it is degrading).

Cruft et al. (2015: 13) include in the instrumentalist family also the position of John Tasioulas who in fact expands the list of goods protected by human rights to an indeterminate and open-ended list of things that benefit humans, with the sole constraint that establishing a human right to X does not impose excessive burdens on corresponding duty-bearers. Classifying Tasioulas in the instrumentalist camp is controversial, because he explicitly rejects the idea that his pluralist approach 'dispenses with any reliance on the controversial notion of human dignity' (Tasioulas 2015: 53). Tasioulas thinks – quite orthodoxically – that human rights and our entitlement to the plural goods they are meant to secure ultimately rest on the 'intrinsically valuable status equally possessed by all human beings' (2015: 53). Thus he concludes: 'human dignity and human interests are equally fundamental grounds of human rights' (2015: 53–4).

Unfortunately, both pillars on which this double-source justification rests are rather shaky. When it comes to explaining the intrinsically valuable status humans have, not to mention their *equal* status, in fact when it comes to addressing the question one would think any foundation should address, Tasioulas only gives us a list of the features that contribute to a 'non-metaphysical, changing definition of human nature'. The 'ontological basis' of human dignity, we are told, is that we are characterized by 'capacities for language-use, for registering a diverse range of normative considerations (including evaluative considerations, prudential, moral, aesthetic, and others besides), and for aligning one's judgments, emotions and actions with those considerations' (Tasioulas 2015: 54). On the question why these capacities generate any 'dignity' for humans Tasioulas does not say much. Unfortunately, if we are doing foundational work, this is *the* question. And it is even more so for an approach, like the one under scrutiny, that sees dignity as an essential ingredient in a foundation.[2]

The major problem with the other pillar is that the interests that generate human rights are potentially infinite. In fact, on Tasioulas's account, any universal human interest that (a) could be protected through the introduction of a corresponding human right and (b) does not impose excessive burdens on duty bearers should generate a corresponding human right. Thus, for example, if people could avoid getting bored in the workplace (perhaps by rotating the most boring functions), and if we could invent a social scheme in which this can be done without imposing too high costs on duty bearers, then there should be a human right not to get bored in the workplace. A rather strange conclusion, given the broadly shared intuition that human rights are about setting minimum standards, as opposed to promoting the good life.

Finally, as pointed out by O'Neill (2015: 76–8), most of the time, and in particular regarding positive human rights to goods and services, Tasioulas's idea that duties corresponding to human rights must be dischargeable by duty bearers (in particular, with no harm to the human rights of the latter) presupposes that duty bearers are easily identifiable, but it does not say much about how this identification should take place. Precisely who, for example, should give resources to alleviate global extreme poverty? Rich individuals? Rich governments? Both? And in any event, how rich do they have to be to become the legitimate target of a human rights obligation?[3]

A foundation somewhat similar to Tasioulas's insists on universal human needs as the basis for human rights. Henry Shue (1997) first, and David Miller (2012) more recently, argue that there is a set of basic needs all humans have independently of their conception of the good life. Needs for food, water and air, but also for a minimum degree of social interaction and recognition are the first that come to mind. While perhaps this approach avoids the underinclusion of the agency-based approach and the overinclusion of the argument just discussed, it still faces at least two problems. On the one hand, the determination of the 'golden mean' seems to be quite arbitrary. Who decides how basic a need is to be included among those generating human rights? On the other hand, quintessential human rights such as first-generation civil and political rights can be traced back to basic human needs only by some stretching. It is possible that our access to food and our psychological health will be at risk in a society where civil and political rights are denied. Sen's famous thesis that freedom of the press averts famine could here be used as authoritative support (Sen 1999). But proponents of this approach tend to take it for granted that one can easily reconstruct similar causal connections between all civic and political rights and those basic needs. This should be proved instead of taken for granted.

Finally, the capability approach developed by Sen and Nussbaum suggests a direct link between human rights and capabilities, that is, real opportunities for individuals to realize their life plan (Sen 1984, 2004; Nussbaum 2001, 2011). Nussbaum lists ten basic human capabilities (life, bodily health and integrity, senses, imagination and thought, emotions, practical reason, affiliation, relations to other species (!), play and control over one's environment) and thinks that all human beings are entitled to these things as a matter of (human) rights. One problem this approach shares with most of the instrumentalist positions so far discussed is quite simply the conflation of needs, goods, capabilities on the one hand, and rights on the other. To say it in Joseph Raz's terms (2010), the fact that something is very important for me (and for all other human beings) is not a sufficient reason to turn that thing into something I have a right to. Arguably being loved is among the most important things in human life, but would it make sense to say that I have a right to be loved?

This last problem teaches perhaps the general lesson to be learned about instrumental justifications. To put it crudely, instrumental justifications do not justify any *right*. They simply reinforce the importance for human lives of certain things, with variations as to what those things are. They hardly provide an argument to move from the importance of the goods to the claim that we are *entitled* to them. To be sure, not all positions discussed share this problem in the same manner. Tasioulas, for example, is well aware of the good/right gap. We have already noticed that his inclusion in the instrumentalist camp could be contested. Still, his solution to the good/right gap is to rely on a pre-given and, as it stands, merely stipulated equal dignity of all humans, which leaves us with a disturbing impression of question begging.

3.2 Non-Instrumental/Orthodox Foundations

While instrumentalism starts with the identification of some more or less objective human goods and then moves (quite magically) to their transformation into things we have rights to, non-instrumentalism relies on the intrinsic worth human beings supposedly have. The point of human rights is not that of protecting the interests of humans but of protecting a status humans possess. It is by virtue of this status that the interests humans have acquire normative force. As Kamm puts it:

> [F]undamental human rights [...] are not concerned with protecting a person's interests, but with expressing his nature as a being of a certain sort, one whose interests are worth protecting. They express the worth of the person rather than the worth of what is in the interests of that person. (Kamm 2007: 271, cited in Cruft et al. 2015: 17)

Thomas Nagel (1995) endorses Kamm's intuition about persons' worth as the basic ground of human rights. And, like Kamm, he does not think it necessary to justify that status. Nagel stops any further inquiry by arguing that '[a]ny attempt to render more intelligible a fundamental moral idea will inevitably consist in looking at the same thing in a different way, rather than in deriving it from another idea which seems at the outset completely independent' (Nagel 1995: 92).

Allen Buchanan (2010) also thinks that human rights cannot be grounded by appealing only to the goods they secure and protect. He argues in favour of this conclusion by using an illuminating example. Let us imagine a female chief executive. She is well paid for the top position she occupies, and therefore has a good life. Let us further imagine, however, that for the same job she is paid slightly less than a male top executive merely because she is a woman. Our intuitions strongly suggest that we have here a clear violation of human rights, even if none of the goods the woman needs for a decent or even good life are put at risk by the lower compensation. This illustrates how human rights have to do with the protection of a status, of an *equal* status to be precise, quite independently of whether and how they promote human well-being. A deontological element seems to be irreducible in any convincing account of rights in general and of human rights in particular.

Cruft, Liao and Renzo (Cruft et al. 2015: 17–18) think that the adoption of non-instrumentalism does not imply the rejection of the idea that human rights are grounded on the plurality of goods they protect. Human rights could be grounded both on human status/dignity as well on their ability to promote/further/protect certain objective human goods, such as agency, freedoms, capabilities and so on. They also think, with Tasioulas (2015), Nickel (2002, 2005, 2015), Wenar (2005) and others, that there are good reasons to think that relying on moral status only will never deliver the list of human rights we are accustomed to. With absolutely no idea of what matters to humans, and left with the bare notion that they possess a status, these authors think that we will never be able to cover the numerous areas of human interest protected by human rights, from civil and political liberties to access to food, shelter, bodily integrity and so on.

This is an important point that needs careful scrutiny. Much could be said against this syncretic approach that combines instrumentalism and deontology. As we will be explaining in some detail later, the main problem is that this position conflates two levels in a foundation of human rights that should be kept clearly distinguished. On one level, there is the question of what provides normative force to the idea that humans have a status that entitles them to certain basic rights. Let us call this the foundation *stricto sensu*. On a less profound level, there is the question of what goods need to be secured for having a life compatible with that status. The second is mainly a technical question that depends on the level of our social and psychological knowledge, on historical circumstances, on the average welfare of a given society and on many other variables that should *not* be made part of a normative justification. In short, the second question, despite appearances, is not part of a foundation at all.

Two other non-instrumentalist positions are worth mentioning. The first is that proposed by Alan Gewirth (1984). Gewirth proposes a 'transcendental' argument in which one starts from the idea that we are all purposive agents (we all act for some good that we consider as worth pursuing). Since freedom and well-being are necessary conditions for the pursuit of any end, it follows that we are constrained to want freedom and well-being, which is equivalent to say that we want the freedom and well-being of all to be protected through human rights. The second position has been recently proposed by Katrin Flikschuh (2015) and has a similar transcendental flavour. She thinks that human rights are constraints we cannot help embracing if we accept the task of designing rules for others whom we have no permission to coerce. Both positions have serious weaknesses. We have already noticed how appealing to agency and to the conditions of its possibility will never take us even close to what we usually include in human rights, as shown by the example of the slave as a fully purposive agent. As for Flikschuh, she begs the whole foundational question by assuming that legislators ought to deliver laws under the constraints she imagines. The whole point of a foundation of human rights is to explain *why* legislators have those constraints, that is, why any law that does not respect the equal status of human beings violates something that has normative force. Flikschuh is led to this strategy by her dubious interpretation of Kant's theory of the innate right to external freedom in the *Metaphysics of Morals*. Since she refuses to accept both the role that Kant himself assigns to this right, that is, as foundational of the entire *Metaphysics of Morals* (Flikschuh 2015: 662) and the justification Kant gives of that very right, that is that we have it 'by virtue of our humanity', the result is that in a foundation of human rights presented as 'Kantian' the resources Kant himself provides for the enterprise are ignored.[4] The foundational argument that this project intends to submit does just the opposite, as we shall explain in due course.

3.3. Practice-based/Political Foundations

An increasing number of leading scholars, including John Rawls (1999), Joseph Raz (2010, 2015), Charles Beitz (2009), Allen Buchanan (2013, 2015), Samantha Besson (2015) and perhaps Thomas Pogge (2002, 2008) think that the essence of human rights is to be found in the role that they have come to play in the practice of international politics.[5] In particular, human rights define the limits of states' sovereignty and, as a consequence, identify the cases in which the international community (under whatever institutional form it presents itself) has the right to intervene to protect individuals from national authorities. Most of these scholars are non-committal regarding the possibility of having a moral foundation of human rights similar to the one defended by non-instrumentalism. However, they believe that nothing essential is left out if we justify human rights by looking at the role that they have come to play in international practice. Their nature is thus that of defining the limits of sovereignty and their foundation (assuming that this is a distinct question) is the de facto acceptance of these limits by institutions around the world. In the succinct definition by Rawls, human rights 'restrict the justifying reasons for war and its conduct, and they specify limits to a regime's internal autonomy' (Rawls 1999: 79).

There are obviously different practice-based justifications. For example Tasioulas (2012) distinguishes between a subset view and a *sui generis* view. The subset view holds that the political, sovereignty-limiting dimension of human rights is just the necessary complement to whatever normative force human rights already have from other sources (say by virtue of human dignity). The sovereignty-limiting dimension would be a component of human rights' normativity that the orthodox view overlooked. The stronger *sui generis* view, defended by Beitz (2009), holds that the normative essence of human rights is *exhausted* by that political function, and any reference to an underlying layer of universal moral rights is at best superfluous if not misleading.

Subspecies types of the political view do not pose much of a challenge to the traditional or orthodox view. In fact, they simply add one dimension to the essence of human rights – the state sovereignty-limiting dimension – that the orthodox view allegedly overlooks. They do not seem, however, to deny that the normativity of human rights depends also on something other than this political function. And if this is the case, subspecies views are parasitic on other foundations of human rights, orthodox or not. Hence, in order to assess the political view we must concentrate on the *sui generis* type. For the sake of argument, let us imagine its most defensible form. This would hold something like the following. We do not know, and do not need to know, whether human rights rest on some underlying set of universal moral rights or on some fundamental respect-conferring feature humans possess. And we do not need to commit ourselves to the assertion of a link between human rights and an alleged intrinsic dignity of human beings. Their normativity is already demonstrated if one looks at the function they have come to play in contemporary international politics.

One way to counter this view is to point out how it makes human rights dependent on the existence of the state system. The most serious problem for the political view, however, is the fact that it violates what Joshua Cohen (2006) called the 'fidelity condition'. This condition demands that any philosophical account of human rights must be faithful to (or at least not too distant from) (a) the way in which human rights are introduced in official documents and (b) the way in which activists use them around the world. The political view is particularly bound to this constraint because it construes the normativity of human rights by looking at the *practice* of human rights. Now, it is highly dubious that the very idea of *reducing* the normativity of human rights to the function they play in international politics is compatible with their 'practice'. The main human rights documents, from the UDHR on, all introduce human rights as the expression of the intrinsic dignity of the human being. Keeping the central intuition of natural law and natural rights (the ancestors of human rights), those documents construe the normativity of rights as fully independent of states, institutions and established patterns of international politics. Precisely because of this independence, they are thought capable of limiting the authority of states and of critically assessing politics as traditionally practised. It thus seems that the political justifications are turning the normativity game upside down, making the obligatory force of human rights dependent on the existence of the status quo instead of having the authority of the latter (including the sovereignty of states) dependent on a pre-existing normativity of certain rights.

An alternative way of seeing the main problem is the following. Human rights have certainly come to have the function on which practice-based accounts insist. What remains obscure is why human rights are to be conceived as *nothing but* that specific political function. If the answer is that this is what practice has made of them, then we need to be very clear about what we mean by 'practice'. Certainly this reduction is neither the way in which human rights are presented in official documents, nor the way in which they are usually understood by activists around the world, who see in them the expression of an intrinsic dignity of the human being for which action is required. The culture of human rights is permeated by reference to our dignity and can hardly be reduced to a legalistic appeal to abstract norms, no matter how well established.

Defenders of the political view could at this point draw a distinction between the culture of human rights and the contemporary practice of conceding that the former may be at odds with the political view while the latter actually establishes and justifies it. Drafters of human rights documents, activists and orthodox philosophers may have thought that human rights have a fundamental moral dimension on which their political role rests, but the practice of human rights suggests otherwise. Today people (ordinary citizens or officials) identify certain rights as human rights *simply* by checking whether they perform the sovereignty limitation role we discussed. In other words, the practice of human rights has introduced the following existence condition: a right is a human right when it is widely accepted that its violation justifies interference in domestic affairs. Nothing more is required. This is what Raz (2010) calls the 'ordinary face of human rights', and it is by virtue of considerations of this sort that he can conclude that the use of the term 'human rights' in legal and political practice and advocacy 'either relies on the legal recognition of human rights as limiting state sovereignty, or claims that should be so recognized'.

The problem with this line of thought, that comes close to the last-resort argument left to the political view, is twofold. On the one hand, in acknowledging its distance from the culture of human rights, it concedes that it violates the fidelity condition. On the other hand, in focusing exclusively on the practice (narrowly defined to include only the current patterns of international politics, the 'ordinary face of human rights'), it renders human rights too dependent on the status quo and on the contingent circumstances that led to whatever de facto consensus is now available. Should the international system fall back to a Westphalian stage, would we say that ethnic cleansing perpetrated by a government against its citizens is no longer a violation of human rights because the international community now thinks of it as a strictly domestic issue?

It could be argued that proponents of the political view do not need to rely on the consensus currently and contingently available but on a 'principled distinction between matters that *may* or *should be* of international concern (such as torture) and matters that *may* or *should not be* of international concern (such as marital fidelity)' (Cruft et al. 2015: 20). But how could we draw that distinction if (a) practice *ex hypothesi* cannot be a guidance and (b) appeal to external moral grounds to identity those matters serious enough to fall appropriately in the category of the 'international concern' would seem to betray the very 'political' nature of the approach?

There is another path open to proponents of the political view to avoid a reduction of their position to a sort of positivistic stance for which anything already contained either in the practice or in the culture of HR is *ipso facto* valid. They could argue that human rights are the object of an overlapping consensus between cultures or comprehensive doctrines. Like Rawls's overlapping consensus within liberal polities, this international consensus would not be a mere modus vivendi, but a principled adherence to political principles. Every moral and religious tradition of the world would find some comprehensive reasons to converge.

Translated in terms of an appeal to global public reason, we will discuss and reject this approach in the next chapter. For the moment, it is worth reporting a preliminary difficulty of the present strategy noticed by Cruft, Liao and Renzo (Cruft et al. 2015). The overlapping consensus approach seems to run into a dilemma. If it is meant as an agreement between *all* cultures and traditions, then it is at odds with reality because – quite simply – not all moral stances represented in the world are compatible with human rights. But if the idea is that of finding a consensus among all *reasonable* traditions and cultures, or among charitable interpretations of them, then it looks that the real normative work is done by a prior standard of reasonableness, not by consensus itself.

The difficulties of the political view all seem to stem from the dubious belief that the normativity of human rights must remain fully *within* the practice. More promising appears the idea, on which we shall return, to look for a reflective equilibrium, to use again a Rawlsian concept, between external reasons, mainly derived from moral philosophy, possibly applied to the central question of why humans deserve human rights in the first place, and internal reasons inferred from how the practice and culture of human rights has evolved so far.

4. The Forgotten Alternative

Why do all accounts of human rights so far considered turn out to be, in the end, unsatisfactory? Is there a common misperception they all share, no matter how different their starting points are? Or does the problem perhaps lie with the very request for a foundation? In what follows we defend the hypothesis that a common failure has led all current approaches to unsatisfactory results. What is missing, we submit, is the simple intuition, latent in all major documents of human rights, that human beings are *worthy* creatures, despite the atrocities for which they have been responsible. Within 'humanity', by virtue of which, the documents say, we have human rights, there is supposed to be something extraordinarily valuable and awe-inspiring that serves as an insuperable barrier against certain forms of degradation. This kernel of value, which we will specify along Kantian lines in the next chapter, serves as protection not only against the violations of our dignity that others cause to us, but also against the degradation we can bring upon ourselves.

When contemporary philosophers, even those of orthodox orientation, attempt to spell out this crucial 'something', things like reason, intelligence, language or the like are often cited. This cannot be the right path, for the simple reason that by themselves these features, even if considered as peculiar to us, can be the source of exceptional evil. It is hard to believe why we should respect a species that puts its higher power at the service of cruelty and exploitation. Hence, intelligence and might, important and impressive as they are, are unlikely candidates to spell out human worthiness. What we need is a trait capable of satisfying three main conditions: (a) humans need to have this trait exclusively or developed at a level considerably higher than other animal species; this is important for justifying the privileged treatment of humans compared to other species implicit in the culture of human rights; (b) this trait must be good in itself, not merely in the sense in which intelligence is always good or happiness is good in itself, but in the sense that having it bestows an intrinsic dignity on the subject; (c) this dignity must be strong enough to rule out certain forms of abuse and stable enough to protect the subject independently from the evil for which she may be responsible. In short, humans need to be truly special beings if human rights are to be justified, a lesson that in our view even the orthodox school has largely forgotten or consciously abandoned.

This esteem/dignity perspective, so clearly embedded in human rights culture, seems to be largely ignored or carefully avoided by contemporary approaches. Why is that? Two reasons, not mutually exclusive, seem to be relevant. On the one hand, genocides, mass killings and ethnic cleansings, while not a peculiarity of the past century, were carried out in a systematic and 'scientific' manner perhaps unmatched by other historical periods. Grounding human rights on the dignity of our species after such a spectacular proof of its capacity for evil and cruelty may well appear foolish. Alan Dershowitz (2005) thinks that rights in general, and human rights in particular, should be grounded as institutional barriers to evil. They arise from the perception of the wrongs humans are capable of, rather than from their alleged dignity. On the other hand, the idea of human dignity, specified as a consequence of some characteristic of human nature, seems problematic. If dignity is expressed in theological language – humans have dignity because they are the offspring of God – then the foundation clearly becomes divisive. Some people do not believe in God, and most believe in different gods. But even if dignity is spelt out in secular terms, as something grounded in a feature of our 'nature', the very notion of human nature is not significantly less divisive than that of God, and an outdated and perhaps parochial recourse to metaphysical reasoning seems to be implied. One could still avoid the dilemma by adopting Jacques Maritain's famous remark that we agree to have dignity as long as we do not ask ourselves why, but this would obviously amount to giving up the foundational exercise altogether.

Despite these difficulties, the next chapter will attempt to show that human dignity can be defended, and its ground made visible, without denying the atrocities humans are capable of or offending the major ethical and religious sensitivities of the contemporary world by adopting parochial and divisive worldviews. What we will be offering is thus a defence of the traditional understanding of human rights, as entitlements arising from one or more dignity-conferring properties humans have. Such a defence, however, will take very seriously the risk, intrinsic to this approach, of falling into old-fashioned metaphysics or simple-minded humanism. And considerable intellectual labour will be necessary to avoid that outcome.

3 • The Foundation of Human Rights: The Dignity Approach

In the preceding chapters we have offered our interpretation of what a truly Kantian theory of human rights should look like, and the major lines of thought in the contemporary debate. In particular, we have focused on the question of the justification of human rights, that is, the ground of their normativity. In the present chapter, we submit the sketch of an alternative foundation, and one, it is hoped, more promising than those we have already encountered. Our proposal is inspired by Kant and exploits some of the points made in the first chapter. In a nutshell, this is the argument. We start from the premise that we are autonomous beings, a view that is not only at the centre of Kant's philosophy but also – as we will show – of (a) common sense and (b) all major cultural traditions and revealed religions, at least when reasonably interpreted. Autonomy is not to be understood merely as the ability to choose one's path in life, or as the ability to be rational in the sense of purposive agents. With Kant, we refer to a capacity distinct from and 'higher' than practical freedom. We have in mind the ability to act under self-imposed moral constraints. This capacity – it will be argued – shows us as *worthy* creatures, and reveals the deepest and most stable layer of human value. Reflecting on our autonomy, we turn out to be beings with this fascinating feature: being able to silence all natural impulses, even the strongest instincts of survival, and act from our conception of duty.

After a more detailed account of the argument (section 1), where the Kantian roots of our approach will be further explained and acknowledged, we will focus on two points (section 2) that mark our distance from Kant. On the one hand, on the basis of contemporary science, we reject Kant's assumption that the capacity for moral agency is a peculiarity of humans. As a consequence, it will be crucial for our approach to show how this does not commit us to extending human rights to all primates, if not to all mammals. On the other hand, we hold that humans act autonomously not only when they follow the Categorical Imperative, but also when they adopt different moral formulas – like the Golden Rule – or act virtuously in an Aristotelian sense. In other words, we want to sever Kant's account of autonomy and dignity from his analysis of morality as necessarily grounded on the Categorical Imperative. Although at some cost, this will give our approach the latitude necessary to consider actions performed under a variety of moral rules as instances of authentic moral behaviour. This is crucial in constructing a notion of human dignity that can be accepted outside the small circle of Kantians. We then turn to the comparison with the three major philosophical accounts of human rights as reconstructed in chapter 2. Since we have already signalled their main weaknesses, the crucial task now will be to show that our approach fares better, a task particularly urgent in relation to those approaches that appear to be similar to ours. We will first show that Griffin, despite his appeal to the supreme value of purposive agency or personhood, the closest thing we have to autonomy in the contemporary debate, should not be conflated with our approach. Moreover, since our foundation clearly belongs to the orthodox camp, we shall have to show that it can contribute to cure weaknesses, or better omissions, typical of the current orthodoxy (section 3). We will then turn to accounts of human dignity recently introduced into the debate that constitute powerful competitors to our own approach. The accounts by Jeremy Waldron, George Kateb and Michael Rosen will be analysed and criticized.

The first four parts jointly serve the purpose of introducing our proposal (sections 1–2) and clarifying it indirectly, that is, *par différence* with alternative accounts (sections 3–4). The rest of the chapter is devoted to some of the major objections that – it is easy to predict – will be levelled against our foundation. First and foremost, one can be sceptical that we are autonomous in the sense indicated by Kant. After all, his arguments for that conclusion are hardly non-problematic, as decades of fierce debate among Kant scholars show. A closely related worry is to say, with Gewirth, that, even if real, autonomy in Kant is not an empirical characteristic 'since it applies only to rational beings as things-in-themselves' (Gewirth 1984: 10). Hence 'the Kantian derivation of rights from inherent dignity does not satisfy *the condition of empirical reference* as regards the characteristics of humans to which one appeals' (Gewirth 1984: 10). Section 5 will be devoted to these kinds of internal criticisms. A different worry, dealt with in section 6, echoes the argument Raz mounts against Griffin. If we are to be treated in a manner adequate to our status as autonomous beings, what exactly do we need to include in the goods protected, besides security from the injection of chemicals that impair our ability to be self-masters? Where do we stop in the list of goods adequate to our autonomous status? Finally (section 7), we shall show, albeit very sketchily, why an appeal to autonomy is not a parochial move and even less a simple-minded and misplaced appeal to the Enlightenment. As a matter of fact, we will argue that the value of autonomy plays a key role in the manner in which major religious traditions conceive of the world of human affairs and of its relation to God.

1. The Dignity Approach

In the 'Oration on the Dignity of Man', the manifesto of the Italian Renaissance, and one of the most fundamental texts ever written on the worth of our species, Pico della Mirandola famously makes the point that God, having decided to create man to have someone who could contemplate the splendour of his creation, faces a shortage of material (quite surprising for the Almighty). God, says Pico, 'had no Archetype from which to fashion some new child, nor could he find in his vast treasures-house anything He could give to His new son'. And yet this little difficulty did not stop God, and he turned an obstacle into an opportunity. The shapelessness of the new creature would become the centre of its worth. God chose to give humans the very power to determine themselves whatever they would decide to be. And so God spoke:

> Adam, we give you no fixed place to live, no form that is peculiar to you, nor any function that is yours alone. According to your desires and judgement, you will have and possess whatever place to live, whatever form, and whatever functions you yourself choose. All other things have a limited and fixed nature prescribed and bounded by our laws. You, with no limit or bound, may choose for yourself the limits and bounds of your nature. We have placed you at the world's centre so that you may survey everything else in the world. We have made you neither of heavenly nor of earthly stuff, neither mortal nor immortal, so that

with free choice and dignity, you may fashion yourself into whatever form you choose. To you is granted the power of degrading yourself into the lower forms of life, the beasts, and to you is granted the power, contained in your intellect and judgement, to be reborn into the higher forms, the divine. (Pico 1948: 224–5)

Notice that Pico does not say that we have dignity when we turn ourselves into the higher forms. He clearly says that the source of our worth lies in our capacity to turn ourselves into *whatever* we decide to become. The radical freedom to become beasts or quasi-divine entities, our place half-way between earth and heaven, *this* is the ground of our dignity and of the superiority of our species over the rest of the universe. For Pico our dignity is no longer, as in St Thomas, a reflection of the place that God selected for us in the scheme of things. It rather lies in the inexistence of such pre-fixed place.

Thus Pico insists more on our radical freedom to go in any direction in the process of self-constitution than on a moral conception of autonomy. Pico does not say, as we do, that our worth lies in the permanent, incorruptible ability to choose the moral law, in our 'autonomy' understood in the sense we have been explaining. Pico seems to praise more our ability to constitute ourselves in *whatever form of being we choose*. And this suggests that our dignity is grounded in our capacity to do wrong as well as to do right.[1] Still, Pico comes close enough to our understanding. On the one hand, he opens the path for a foundation that no longer rests on the ontological place occupied by humans in the pre-given, fixed structure of the universe, but on a capacity that grants us the freedom to pick that place. On the other hand, no matter how much he insists on our amoral freedom, it is evident that he himself believes that our value ultimately rests on our ability to choose the 'divine' in us. If our 'dignity' rested on the possibility to choose which specific 'beasts' we want to become, his argument that we occupy a special place in the universe would hardly be convincing.

The capacity to stretch towards the 'divine' – to use Pico's emphatic expression – is the ground of human dignity, and human dignity is the foundation of human rights. This could be the slogan of the approach we defend. A slightly more expanded way of making the same point would be to say that the capacity to act on self-imposed moral constraints, possibly to the detriment of our strongest inclinations, is the source of the value and respect we owe to all human beings. Autonomy is thus the foundation of human rights via the notion of human dignity. The individuals that belong to the human species, including those that have that capacity impaired temporarily or permanently by fortuitous circumstances, have the peculiarity to being able to put aside self-serving interests in the name of what they consider obligatory.[2] This captures one of the senses in which dignity has been traditionally used, namely the ability to endure circumstances that challenge our sensuous nature. This is also why Kant describes humans' worth in terms of dignity, as opposed to other praise-attributing terms such as excellence, skill, goodness, and why he thinks that we owe reverence or respect (*Achtung*) to humans, as opposed to deference, awe, sympathy and the like.

As announced, the notion of autonomy we operate with is quite specific and should not be conflated with the 'simple' capacity to set freely one's ends and pursue one's goals, or with the capacity to act 'rationally', if by that is meant the ability to choose effective means for one's ends. The distinction between the common-sense notion of autonomy (self-determination) and the one at work here (capacity for moral agency) is important in understanding the way in which our approach links the possession of a faculty to the intrinsic worth that entitles humans to the protections of human rights. In fact, why should the sheer possession of a capacity ground any worth? The fact that humans have a peculiar capacity hardly grounds any special protection. We have already noticed that ours is probably the only species that kills for sheer amusement (cats may be another example) or for cold, long-term calculation of interest. It may also be the only one capable of lying with a high level of sophistication. Now, these peculiarities obviously do not ground any merit and therefore entitle us to no special protection. Things, however, are different with autonomy. This feature is not only peculiar to, or most developed in, the human species. It also has an intrinsic value, as it shows humans as capable of behaviour that – we assume – exacts respect. We are not merely self-masters, but also, and most significantly, potentially righteous ones. We are not merely free; we are free to choose a path of integrity and mutual respect. And precisely because we have this capacity, precisely because morality is within our reach, we are entitled to an amount of respect unfettered by contingent circumstances.

Our approach is thus a direct answer to the question 'why do humans possess dignity?' We assume that one of the major tasks of philosophy, applied to the tricky field of human rights, is the attempt to spell out what lies behind the intuition – taken for granted in all major human rights treaties – that humans have dignity. From the 1948 UDHR to the two International Covenants, including all conventions that have been piling up in the various generations of human rights, no document fails to make a direct or indirect reference to human dignity. And yet the documents consciously avoided explaining why we have dignity. As is well known, the fear was that any rich philosophical account of dignity could appeal to comprehensive doctrines, to use Rawls's notion, and therefore be potentially divisive. There are however two main reasons why we should not consider this an insurmountable obstacle. Silence on the reasons we have to believe that human beings have dignity will not convince those who think that it is permissible to treat some of them below certain standards of respect. If we do not know why we have dignity, it is very likely that we will not know what this entails, and we will have a difficult time clarifying why and when human rights trump strong normative considerations, in the form of maximization of general utility, the furthering of certain ideologies, or the protection of traditional practices. Moreover, failing to unpack the notion of human dignity gives no direction regarding related crucial questions for the theory of human rights. As we have already said, and just to give an example, it is unlikely that we will know what rights should count as human rights unless we know why human rights should exist in the first place. It may not be impossible to come up with an answer to this and other similar questions before we clarify what dignity is and entails. But few would deny that some progress on the foundational question will help greatly.

2. A Kantian Foundation, not Kant's

Since we ground human dignity (and as a consequence human rights) in the Kantian notion of autonomy, it is natural to grow the impression that what we are doing here is simply a rehearsal of Kant's doctrine. At best, we would be applying Kant's explanation of human dignity to the contemporary debate. But we promised an approach inspired by Kant, not cut and copied from him. Where then is the difference? Two main points mark our distance from Kant. On the one hand, we assume that authentic moral behaviour does not occur only when the agent acts under the constraints of one of the formulas of the Categorical Imperative, but also when agency is inspired by other moral principles, as long as they conform to broadly accepted constraints of the kind implicit in the Golden Rule. On the other hand, we deny that moral behaviour is a prerogative of human beings. We hold that bits of behaviour that fit most of the features we usually attribute to human moral agency (e.g. consideration for the well-being of other members of the species, readiness to sacrifice and so on) take place among primates and other mammals.

Let us start with the first point of departure. We have been saying that our peculiar ability to act on moral imperatives grounds human worth and dignity. We also specified that these moral imperatives have to be categorical in kind. Only if humans are seen as capable of overcoming all natural impulses, thereby making no concession to their sensuous nature, can we reasonably speak of a peculiar worth that entitles them to special protection compared to the rest of the animal world. This does not that mean that we hold that moral agency needs to take place through a conscious adoption of one of the formulas of the Categorical Imperative. We rather assume that humans are conscious of moral constraints, with *some version* of the moral law serving as the guiding rule for practical deliberation. Finally, we assume that this moral law is close enough to the Golden Rule, which in turn bears some resemblance with the Universal Formula of the Categorical Imperative.[3] What matters is that humans are capable of authentically disinterested, impartial and *in this sense* moral agency, and that they all face some version of the moral law in the process of practical deliberation. Obviously, humans are capable of highly immoral behaviour. But this is no obstacle for our approach. It is the human capacity to act on duty, no matter what its specific form, that is at the centre of our approach, not the actualization of that capacity. We argue that this is the most fundamental layer of our worth, it is what our dignity consists of. And we assume that recognizing this feature in us generates respect for human beings.[4]

Kant thought that the only non-heteronomous moral theory was his own. He also believed that the moral law (in one or another formulation of the Categorical Imperative) is universally valid and evident to any natural human understanding. It is natural to infer from that that he would not be ready to attribute any moral value to behaviour that is inspired by principles other than the Categorical Imperative. More importantly, he would reject the idea that humans express their capacity for moral agency even when they act on principles other than the Categorical Imperative (at least in one of the Kantian formulations). I do not think that we need to follow this path. People may act on an authentic conception of duty even when they endorse a principle like the Golden Rule. And I would submit that even clear cases of heteronomous moral theories can express the same central capacity for moral agency we are appealing to. For example, one may believe that morality's source is in God and still adhere to divine commands not out of fear of divine punishment or similarly heteronomous motives, but because one endorses those commands and makes them truly one's own. If this process of endorsement is carried out, one no longer obeys an external command, but acts from a self-imposed moral constraint. And this bit of 'agency from duty' should in our opinion count as a legitimate expression of the autonomous faculty on which our worth rests.

There are of course limits to the freedom we are given to pick a specific formulation of the moral law. It would be absurd to construe as instances of autonomous agency Nazi officials' steady commitment to die in the Berlin bunker with Hitler. But *alas*, the moment we affirm that not all formulations of the moral law reveal our autonomy, we need to draw some lines. Fortunately, we do not start from zero in this enterprise. It is common knowledge that the Golden Rule 'Do unto others as you would wish them to do unto you' is echoed in all major religious traditions of the world. Not accidentally its iconic representation in the mosaic by Norman Rockwell has become one of the symbols of the United Nations. Its cross-cultural validity makes it fit for the task. Albeit imperfect, open to considerable variance in dependence of the normative context in which it is inserted, and vulnerable to distortions (think of its compatibility with an ethics based on the reciprocal permissibility of violence), this common basis is good enough for our purposes. It captures the dimension of impartiality and fairness that constitutes the gist of duty.[5] In asking us to act on principles which we would like others apply to us, the Golden Rule rests on our ability to act independently of contingent sensuous motives or just for the sake of conformity to principles; that is, it rests on our autonomy.

This departure from Kantian orthodoxy may still appear insufficient to many contemporary theoreticians of human rights. If we let human dignity depend on a capacity of detachment from our sensuous inclinations, that is, if we remain within a deontological approach, no matter how liberalized in its overarching formula, the impression is that there is no hope that our foundation could be favourably received by approaches to morality traditionally opposed to deontology such as utilitarianism, virtue ethics and moral sentimentalism. And if there is no possible overlap at least with the major Western schools of ethical thought, what concrete chance do we have to 'buy in' non-Western approaches? While we deal with the second part of the problem at the end of this chapter, we can say the following, albeit as usual in a cursory way, about the first.

Regarding utilitarianism, let us keep in mind that the greatest happiness for the greatest number of people is a principle as impartial and disinterested as the categorical imperative or the Golden Rule (perhaps even more than the latter). For an agent to act on the utility principle, the adoption of the rule requires pretty much the same ability to take distance from one's own interests and inclinations, because what promotes the greatest happiness for most people may very well contrast with the interests of the individual. Moreover, a utilitarian needs to explain why pleasures and displeasures of human beings count for anything unless some reasons to care for such beings are given or taken for granted. Of course the utilitarian sees in the capacity of suffering, not in that of acting morally, the main ground to identify entities that deserve to be protected by morality and rights. But since this capacity is clearly not a prerogative of humans, a moderate utilitarian, that is one who acknowledges some difference in worth between humans and animals, still needs a reason to ground humans' special treatment and still needs to find a criterion to explain why humans are entitled to a special protection compared to other animals. And our suggestion that a comparatively superior capacity to chose our sacrifices, so to speak, could be an answer to this question. Obviously, there is no guarantee that moderate utilitarians would look at that specific capacity. But the fact that they could, without prejudice to their general commitments, at least shows that there is no incompatibility between a broadly construed utilitarian approach and our foundation.

Things are more complicated with utilitarian approaches à la Peter Singer that advocate an equal consideration for all animals. For Singer (1979) and others, who follows closely Bentham here, what counts for defining those entitled to an equal consideration of interests is explicitly not the capacity for reason (no matter whether understood in the sense of autonomy or in competing manners) but *merely* the capacity of suffering. Not accidentally, often for these philosophers the very talk of *human* rights amounts to non-sense. Two considerations are relevant here. To begin with, the sceptic a foundation of human rights is addressed to is usually someone who does not deny that humans are entitled to more consideration than animals. He is rather someone who sees no wrong in discriminating *among humans*. Secondly, even if our foundation won't convince extreme defenders of animal rights (probably an ambition too high for *any* foundation), our recognizing bits of moral life in the animal world (our second point of departure from Kant) goes precisely in the direction Singer at times alludes to. For example, Singer concedes that in many circumstances, mainly in virtue of the capacity for self-awareness, human beings can suffer more than animals and this entitles them to a protection different than that deserved by mice or other mammals. Granted, we do not claim that it is the superior ability to suffer, but our superior ability to dignify ourselves with moral choices, that makes us more worthy than animals. But the structure of the argument is similar. In both cases, prerogatives, rights and entitlement to moral concern are seen as proportional to the possession of different capacities or of the same capacity at different degrees. In the end, all utilitarians à la Singer need to accept of our foundation is the idea that our peculiar capacity for moral behaviour, our autonomy (whose reality a utilitarian is not committed to reject in light of his other beliefs), makes *some* difference in the diversified application of the equal consideration principle, in addition to (not instead of) the other capacities utilitarians usually appeal to.

Utilitarianism however may seem an easy case. After all, its major point of friction with deontology is not the view of human nature and its worth, but the aggregate nature of the theory (the lack of consideration for the separateness of persons, as Rawls put it). And nothing in our foundation is incompatible with the intuition that *all things being equal* it may be permissible to sacrifice the human rights of few for protecting the human rights of many, if necessary.[6] More difficult cases seem to be virtue ethics and sentimentalism because the rejection of autonomy, understood in the way here suggested, seems to be required by the idea – common and central to both approaches – that emotions and feelings are a constitutive or at least significant part of the motivational background of any moral action. While moral sentimentalism (at least with Hume) is committed to the idea of the inertia of reason (feelings are the sole forces that moves people to act), virtue ethics insists that morality or better virtue is not about doing what is required independently of feeling, but about having or training ourselves to have feelings that harmoniously incline us towards what is right.

Let us start with virtue ethics. One may think that a virtuous person that has trained her passions so that no conflict arises between what she ought to do and what she wants to do – a sort of Aristotelian hero – shows no less worth than the moral person that is able to overcome her passions to follow the moral law – the Kantian hero at the centre of our approach. Why should human worth lie in our ability to be master of our passions and not in our ability to train them in such a way that they are allies, not obstacles, in our moral life? This is a classical issue in moral philosophy and there is no space to deal with it adequately here. Two points however are relevant and can be made in the limited space we have. To begin with, it seems that the Aristotelian hero just described must have decided autonomously at one point in her life to train her passions in the right manner. An autonomous act in the Kantian sense thus seems to be at the origin of the process. Moreover, and more importantly, insisting on the categorical nature of morality is fully compatible with thinking that we should train our passions so that they do not stand in the way of duty. Kant himself makes this point repeatedly. In the *Metaphysics of Morals* for example he talks of a 'duty to sympathize actively' with the ones who suffer and of an 'indirect duty to cultivate the compassionate natural (aesthetic) feeling in us' (*MS* 6: 457). And as a way to cultivate this sympathy Kant mentions a 'duty not to avoid places where the poor who lack the most basic necessities are to be found' and 'not to shun sickrooms or debtors' prisons' (*MS* 6: 457).

What about moral sentimentalism, and Hume in particular? Kant's acknowledging the importance of passions in the execution of duties takes us close to the spirit of moral sentimentalism, but only to a point. To show that Humeans need not be opposed to our foundation is more important to recall how Hume himself recognizes that morality cannot be reduced to a natural, mechanical, emotional subjective reaction to what causes sympathetic pleasure or displeasure. When Hume talks about the necessity to correct the bias of our emotional reaction in favour of the near and dear or when he deals with the 'virtue in rags' problem, he recognizes that morality is about impartiality and the ability to take distance from personal inclinations. Ultimately, in deciding what is virtuous and what is vicious Hume thinks we rely on our ability to discern what personality traits are beneficial or harmful *in general,* i.e. in relation to all people potentially affected by those traits. And at times he talks of a 'common point of view' from which these traits are to be judged. Both this 'taking distance' and the appeal to the ability to reach a common perspective are consonant with, if not enabled by, the ability to master our immediate passions for the sake of morality, that is the capacity we claimed is at the centre of human dignity. They are reminiscent of the features of impartiality and rule over unchecked inclinations we kept in our otherwise liberalized deontology.

This concludes the discussion of our first point of departure from Kant. The second breach of Kantian orthodoxy, perhaps not disconnected from the one just explained, is the following. While we believe that, of all the animal world, the capacity to act from duty is most developed in the human species, we also believe that humans do not possess it exclusively. Since the pioneering work by Rosemary Rodd, *Biology, Ethics, and Animals* (1990), followed by the philosophically more sophisticated *Taking Animals Seriously* (1996) by David DeGrazia, we know that animals have a rich mental life that includes self-awareness and moral dilemmas. More recently, Frans De Waal has argued that if we define normativity as adherence to an ideal or standard, then 'there is ample evidence that animals treat their social relationships in this manner' (De Waal 2014). In particular, he points out that most animals show acts that are costly to the performer but benefit the recipient. Moreover, animals show empathic responses to the distress of their fellows. Finally, some large-brained animals (primates) show a form of helping that entails awareness of how the other will benefit from being helped (De Waal 2006). The same point is reinforced by Bekoff and Peirce (2009) who find unmistakable traces of 'moral' behaviour not only in higher mammals but even in rodents, with rats that refuse to accept a reward because this would cause other rats a shock. Similar conclusions are reached by Bartal, Decety and Mason (2011), who observe how rats free caged mates even when this entails the necessity to share with them a reward. Even outside academia, common sense knows quite well that 'moral' prescriptions may lead animals to sacrifice their life for the sake of their offspring, and, at times, even for the sake of humans, as the numerous examples of heroic behaviour by dogs prove beyond doubt. Thus morality, defined loosely as adherence to some impartial norm or ideal to the possible detriment of one's selfish interests, does not seem to be a prerogative of humans, even when the 'ideal' requires the highest sacrifice.

This conclusion is hardly surprising. In our scientific paradigm, still dominated by evolutionary theory, and rightly so given the absence of credible alternatives, it is to be expected that morality is not considered as emerging out of nowhere but following the development of the species, with 'higher' ones simply taking a trait – in this case pro-social behaviour – to a higher level of completion, as opposed to creating one afresh. Within the Darwinian scientific paradigm, one should expect that there is no gap between humans and other species: morality, like other bits of behaviour, is an evolved trait that we unquestionably share with other social mammals. Yet another of the traits we thought uniquely ours turns out to be robustly present in other sufficiently close animal species.

Obviously, in observing animal moral behaviour scientists operate with a definition of morality that is loose enough to allow cross-species generalizations. This is significantly distant from the definition of morality we attribute to humans, central to which is an *impartial* commitment to abstract principles of fairness, such as the Golden Rule or the Categorical Imperative, where feelings of solidarity or empathy are not necessarily part of the picture. Nobody argues that animals undergo a process of moral deliberation in which different alternatives are scrutinized for consonance with abstract moral rules. The same evidence that suggests forcefully the presence of a broadly defined moral life in animals also suggests how this is governed by feelings of empathy for other subjects (not necessarily fellow members of the same species). This sort of morality, however, is not different in kind from the morality our approach attributes to humans, and on which their value supposedly rests. In fact, what is common is the readiness to sacrifice one's interests for the sake of a social, or at any rate non-selfish end. Both in the case of human and in that of non-human mammals, what grounds the worth of the species is the ability to follow a rule that transcends the satisfaction of individual needs or desires.

Should we then concede human rights to animals, perhaps to higher mammals? If human value is tied so closely to morality and morality is not a prerogative of our species, are we committed to the immensely counterintuitive conclusion that dogs and cats should have exactly the same amount of protection human rights promise to offer to our species? Maybe, but more likely no. We can concede that behaviour inspired by a duty-based morality is not a prerogative of humans without denying the huge differences in the degree to which different mammals display an ability to detach themselves from selfish drives. The freedom from natural drives humans have gained through their evolution is vastly superior to the distance even the most sophisticated primates display. If we identify, as we do, the worth of a species with the ability of its individual members to sacrifice for a moral cause (where 'moral' is broadly and loosely understood as non-selfish behaviour for the sake of some ideal), we can say that humans reach peaks of moral behaviour (and of course of degradation) unknown to other species. In a sense, evolution has generated so great a difference between humans and non-human mammals in this regard that what used to be a difference in degree has now come to *appear* as a difference in kind. While animal moral behaviour suggests a general reconsideration of the way in which our relation to animals is usually conceptualized, nothing in the argument suggests that any worth one attributes to humans must be the same as what one should attribute to other mammals.

I doubt Kant would be happy with a foundation of basic rights that concedes so much latitude both in the identification of what counts as moral behaviour and in the determination of the set of potential moral actors. I therefore suspect that my fellow Kant scholars will not be happy with my use of Kant's notion of autonomy and dignity. Still, I believe that we can profit from Kant's intuition of a profound link between autonomy, morality and dignity without embracing aspects of his thought that, quite independently of their intrinsic merits, are either likely to produce cultural resistance or appear as too influenced by a worldview whose anthropocentrism had just adjusted to Galileo but had not been hit by Darwin. I am ready to buy my foundation a chance of compatibility with most contemporary worldviews and a better fit with contemporary science at the cost of some uneasiness of my orthodox colleagues.

3. False Friends: Dignity vs Personhood and the Silence of the Orthodox

Probably the best way to understand the essence of the dignity approach is to contrast it with the apparently similar personhood approach proposed by Griffin. It will be recalled that Griffin indicates normative agency or personhood as the conceptual point where the best moral theory at our disposal and contemporary human rights practice stand in reflective equilibrium. The main difference between our position and Griffin's is that we avoid his version of coherentism, resting as it does on the harmony between two contingent facts: the moral theory considered here and now as the best, and the current practice of human rights. Our argument does not require that the practice of human rights agree with whatever protections we hold as due to humans by virtue of their dignity. Obviously, as a matter of fact, there is agreement. We have already noted how prominently dignity figures in all major human rights documents. At the same time, however, there is no perfect overlap, because one can easily argue that the existing lists of human rights do not adequately capture the specific kind of respect humans have by virtue of their autonomy. There is at the same time too much and too little. For example, a prohibition on offering a job that does not guarantee paid holidays may not be required by a respectful attitude towards human autonomy; while not only the death penalty but also life imprisonment could be a punishment incompatible with recognizing the possibility of moral redemption on the part of the culprit. The fact that our approach is neither too distant nor too close to current practice and existing lists of human rights is encouraging, because we do not want to 'philosophize from nowhere', so to speak, but at the same time we want to keep some critical distance from how human rights are practised and conceived of today.

Moreover, and this is the central point, our reference to the autonomous status of persons, with the ensuing obligations ultimately generating human rights, is different from Griffin's appeal to self-determination as the defining and value-rich feature of personhood. In fact, Griffin construes self-determination as a mere capacity to choose our own path in life. He says: 'we value our status as human beings especially highly, often more highly even than our happiness. This status centers on our being agents – deliberating, assessing, choosing and acting to make what we see as a good life for ourselves' (Griffin, 2010: 8–9). And from this the conclusion, 'Human rights can then be seen as protections of our human standing or, as I shall put it, our personhood' (Griffin, 2010: 8–9). In the language we introduced in the first chapter, Griffin's self-determination is best understood as practical freedom. In contrast, we appeal to the specific Kantian notion of autonomy as superior to mere practical freedom. And we say that autonomy commands respect for human beings quite independently of the fact that humans care about the capacity to choose their path in life. The crucial feature is that humans have the capacity to follow the moral law. *This* generates respect.

Notice a further difference. We make no mention of the notion of interest in a feature we have. We speak of a respect generated by the discovery that we have a certain faculty, quite independently of the interest we may take in what this faculty can do for our lives. We *admire* something in us that dictates a certain way of treating ourselves and other humans. In Griffin, this dimension of admiring is completely absent. The crucial feature of our approach is that autonomy is not construed as a peculiar and exceptional feature of human beings, which carries the weight of grounding the dignity of each human being *by virtue of its peculiarity and exceptionality*. There are many things peculiar to our species that are unable to ground any respect or dignity. What is important about autonomy is not that it is a feature peculiar to human beings (in a certain sense, it is not, as we saw above). What matters is that it is a worth-conferring feature, something that forces us to see each and every human being as endowed with a potentiality for goodness.

The same considerations are relevant to seeing why current orthodox thinkers like Tasioulas and Schaber fail to exploit the full potential intrinsic in an appeal to dignity. While Schaber thinks we can start our foundation from dignity because authoritative documents indicate dignity as the basis of human rights, thereby refusing to justify or at least explain why we have dignity, Tasioulas

FOUNDATION: THE DIGNITY APPROACH 73

offers as tentative ontological basis for human dignity features distinctive of human beings such as language, reason, judgement and the like. Unlike autonomy, however, they are hardly intrinsically good, because they can be and have been put at the service of horrifying goals. If we want to give support to this omnipresent notion of human dignity, so evidently crucial for the practice and culture, if not for the philosophy, of human rights, then we need something more than features we exclusively possess or that make our 'price' higher than that of any other species, to use Kant's language in the crucial passage quoted in chapter 1. We need both a feature that we possess exclusively or at the highest degree of development *and* a reason to believe that that feature is intrinsically good. And of all the distinctive features of humans, only autonomy seems to be able to meet this second requirement.

4. Alternative Accounts of Dignity: Waldron, Kateb, Rosen

The notion of dignity has never attracted the attention of philosophers the way it seems to have done more recently. In the last five years, a voluminous collective work (McCrudden 2013) has explored this notion from different perspectives, and influential philosophers such as Jeremy Waldron, George Kateb and Michael Rosen have published three monographs that attempt to unpack its normative content. Since we have discussed some of the views of dignity collected in the McCrudden volume, in particular Tasioulas's, we focus here on the analyses by Waldron, Kateb and Rosen. Their accounts provide an opportunity to clarify further, *par différence*, the view of human dignity we defend.

4.1 *Waldron's Political View*

Jeremy Waldron offers what could be considered a political view of human dignity. Central to his analysis is the distinction between two fundamental ways in which the concept of dignity could be approached, either from philosophy to law or the other way around. In the first approach, one offers first a metaphysical foundation of human dignity and then inquiries whether existing bodies of laws (often constitutions or other fundamental documents) have adequately rendered the content and normative force highlighted by metaphysics. The other approach proceeds from the way in which the law has defined dignity in particularly important documents, treaties and constitutions, and then moves to philosophy to compare and possibly correct metaphysical doctrines of human dignity. Waldron endorses the second approach because he believes, inspired by a conversation with Joseph Raz, that 'the natural habit' of the notion of dignity is the law. Dignity, he claims, is not a term we encounter in ordinary moral discourse, but rather in particularly significant juridical documents. Philosophy has borrowed this notion from law to make sense of ideas present in ordinary moral discourse such as respect and value. But, Waldron concludes, '[i]f it has been imported from law to perform this constructive and explicative function, then we had better turn first to jurisprudence to find out something about the distinctive *legal* ideas that the moral philosophers have appropriated' (Waldron 2012: 14).

Two ideas in this reconstruction are quite problematic: (a) dignity does not appear so much in ordinary moral discourse, and (b) its 'natural habit' is the law rather than philosophy (or morality). In response to the first point, we can use Michael Rosen's example (Waldron 2012: 83) of a real-life circumstance that he witnessed personally. One of his friends appealed loudly to dignity ('Give her some dignity') to defend the privacy of a tabloid celebrity who was assailed by photographers at the hospital where she was being treated for cancer. This is just one example, but everybody can come up with plenty of real-life cases where ordinary people do appeal to 'dignity'. In my own experience, a few days ago the coach of the soccer team for which I play (do my best to play, I should say) motivated us before a match that followed an unbroken series of defeats by saying, 'We need to win. And we need to do it for ourselves. It is a matter of dignity.' Now, if my coach – an almost illiterate man – used the concept of dignity, this is rather strong evidence that the concept is open to everybody, truly everybody, not just philosophers.

Arguing against the second part is even easier. In *De Officis* Cicero talks of the 'dignity of the human race' in a way quite similar to what both we – ordinary people – and the law understand by that expression, namely that mankind has a specific worth superior to that of animals. In the Middle Ages we might refer to Aquinas, for whom the dignity of something is understood as its proper place in the order and hierarchy of the universe. At the beginning of the modern era (1465) we saw how Pico dwells on the special nature of man and comes to a conclusion very close to our understanding of human dignity. Shortly after Pico's lifetime, his oration was given the title of *De Dignitate Hominis Oratio*, which proves that the concept had travelled safely from the ancient world to the fifteenth-century humanists who rediscovered it. Also, implicit in Locke's defence of natural rights is a recognition of humans' dignity, which the English philosopher sometimes mentions to mark humans as particularly worthy creatures. For example, in section 15 of *The Second Treatise of Government*, where he defends natural rights as inherent to human beings as such, he speaks of 'a life fit for the dignity of man', which could not be attained if those rights were not recognized. Needless to say, the most obvious example of a philosopher who made dignity a central notion of his thought is Immanuel Kant. The *Groundwork of the Metaphysics of Morals* contains thirty-three occurrences of the word 'dignity' and dates from 1785, four years before the French Declaration of the Rights of Man and Citizen (1789) and six before the US Bill of Rights (1791), where arguably one finds the first significant appearances of the *concept* of human dignity in the law, though not the word 'dignity' itself. Given all this, one can hardly believe that the 'natural habit' of the notion of dignity is the law and deny that philosophy did not precede, prepare and shape the legal reference to human dignity. Historically, the direction of the evolution is precisely the opposite of what Raz and Waldron suggest.

Waldron's proposal to reduce the degree of obscurity that surrounds the philosophical notion of dignity by looking at the way in which this concept is used in major legal documents is problematic for two additional reasons. To begin with, in most documents (e.g. the Italian and German constitutions, human rights declarations and treaties, and so on), the dignity of human beings is simply treated as a given and not explained. What guidance would those documents provide? Secondly, history provides abundant examples of what we now consider bad understandings of the notion of dignity or related notions entrenched in the law. As Waldron knows well, the privileges reserved to a group of people were justified in terms of a higher value of that class compared to the lower ones. In other words, the law has often misunderstood the notion, scope and meaning of dignity, and if contemporary legal documents have finally corrected these mistakes, it is because the equal worth of humans was first introduced and defended by philosophers (e.g. Kant) and then approved by public opinion. Why should we today proceed otherwise? Why not continue to defend a philosophical account of human dignity and see whether it throws some light on contemporary disputes regarding what human dignity entails and how it should be further protected through legal documents?

Finally, central to Waldron's account is the idea that if we want to understand dignity we need to think in terms of an extension to all human beings of privileges connected with rank that were formerly attributed to a restricted group. The high rank and consequent rights once attributed only to those who – not accidentally – were called *dignitaries* has been democratized to the point of becoming universal. Waldron here makes an important point. In fact he captures the 'esteem' element that we indicated as the hallmark of our approach. But our story of how this element of admiration has been established differs from the story told by Waldron. While he holds that the evolution in question happened primarily within the boundaries of the law, we hold, less originally, that it was the philosophical contribution coming from the natural law tradition and from the Enlightenment that shaped a public consensus regarding the dignity of *all* men which *then* translated into legal documents. Moreover, the enlargement of scope (the extension to all human beings) produced or perhaps came with a transformation of the feature that supposedly bestows dignity on the beneficiaries. If in the pre-modern world, the feature had by necessity to be something capable of marking the difference between individuals – birth, race, presumed moral virtues, education and so on – with the Enlightenment it had to become something that we all share. This feature was identified with the human capacity for reason, understood both as the capacity to think for oneself, as well as in terms of practical autonomy, the capacity for autonomous actions.[7]

4.2 Kateb's Existential Approach

George Kateb's account of dignity is, like ours, inspired by Kant. Moreover, his analysis leads to many conclusions that we are ready to endorse: (a) humanity has dignity by virtue of a common *specific* feature; (b) since all individuals belonging to that species share that property, then all individuals have dignity; (c) our dignity is based on a feature that our species possesses, uniquely or to a degree substantially higher than any other. Finally, Kateb lists a series of very reasonable conditions that any defence of the idea of human dignity must meet:

1. We must show that the very idea of human dignity adds something to a theory of human rights. In other words, it must be shown that whatever normative force we think human rights have, something of that force would be lost if we did not appeal to dignity.
2. History shows so many and such serious examples of human cruelty towards other human beings that insisting on the dignity of human beings is almost an offence to those who have suffered the consequences of those evil actions, besides being unsupported by evidence. Hence human dignity seems to be false.
3. In light of the same cruelty, we need to explain why we hold that human dignity applies to all human beings and not only to those who have acted righteously or at least refrained from major acts of cruelty.
4. We must show why affirming human dignity does not lead to 'monstrous human pride', to use Kateb's fortunate expression. It is a pride that in turn can easily lead to a view of animals, and of nature as a whole, as merely at our service. Hence human dignity may be not only false but also extremely dangerous (Kateb 2011: 4–5).

The bulk of Kateb's strategy for dealing with these points is to say that humans are only partially natural creatures. We constitute a break in the order of nature. In a Kantian vein, Kateb identifies this partial discontinuity with our freedom. The human species, 'is the only animal species that is not only animal, the only species that is partly not natural, and that is therefore unpredictable in its conduct despite its genetic sameness from one generation to the next' (Kateb 2011: 11). But Kateb is ready to follow Kant up to a point because the German philosopher leads us astray when he 'holds that human dignity or worth lies in the uniquely human capacity on earth [...] to act morally' (Kateb 2001: 13). This is wrong because 'free agency is a broader concept than moral agency' (Kateb 2011: 14). The ground of our dignity is our unique capacity to act free from natural determinations, quite independently of whether our conduct is moral or mainly free. Kant is wrong in linking dignity and moral agency 'into an unbreakable knot'. We are aware of our uniqueness as a species any time we act freely, because this agency is incompatible with any naturalistic reduction of the human experience.

The main problem with this idea, as we have already mentioned, is that, even if we grant that we are special creatures, partially disconnected from nature and able to exercise the 'stewardship of nature' (as Kateb at times puts it), still this is insufficient to prove that humans are worthy of anything. As we said repeatedly, the sheer fact that we have a unique characteristic (radical freedom) hardly proves anything about our worth. Unlike other species, we kill for futile motives, we endanger the continuation of life on planet earth, we make other fellow human beings suffer for fun, we have an unmatched record of tragedies inflicted on our fellow humans and so on. What we need is: (a) a feature that we possess uniquely or better to the highest degree; (b) a feature that by itself proves that we possess intrinsic value; and (c) that this feature gives us a worth that cannot be wiped out by the evil we or other fellow human beings have done or may do. We proposed our capacity – in all circumstances and independently of our past history – to act not only undetermined by nature, but also *justly*. We still have not said enough to prove this point. But it is already clear that the feature we are looking for is not the amoral, practical freedom Kateb appeals to.

4.3 Rosen: A Quasi-Kantian, Secular View of Dignity

Michael Rosen distinguishes two moral perspectives that have a direct bearing on the way one conceives of dignity. The first perspective, that Rosen labels after Raz 'humanism', turns on a fundamental and prima facie self-evident principle that everything is good or bad depending on its contribution, actual or possible, to human life and its quality. The other perspective is a duty-based morality. It holds that there are at least some authentic and legitimate duties that do not benefit anyone. The realm of obligation is detached from the good. At least not all moral obligations can be explained in terms of the benefit (actual or possible) that they promise.

Rosen prefers the second approach. The attitude of respect that most cultures have towards corpses or fetuses would be hard to explain by adopting the humanist principle. Using G. E. Moore's famous thought experiment, if we were asked to choose between bringing into existence an extremely beautiful world or an extremely ugly one, knowing none will ever be inhabited, it seems that we would choose the former and that it would be rational to do so *even if we knew for certain that our choice will have no practical consequence for ourselves or others.*

Like Kant, Rosen thinks that our duties have little to do with the benefits that could be generated by compliance with them. Kant, however, is not right on all counts. To start with, in doing her duty, an agent does not necessarily need to relate (with an attitude of respect) to something whose existence is intrinsically valuable and that human beings embody. We do not need to pinpoint the characteristic that generates our reverence towards humanity. It is sufficient to realize that these duties are so profound that they inevitably generate that reverence. In Rosen's words, 'our duties are so deep a part of us that we could not be the people that we are without having them. In failing to respect the humanity of others, we actually undermine humanity in ourselves' (Rosen 2012: 157). Moreover, Kant's argument rests on a dubious reference to a noumenal world, which should be avoided if possible. And it is possible. If we sever duty from the existence of a transcendental kernel of value (our capacity for moral agency), human dignity will no longer be dependent on the existence and knowability of a something that allegedly belongs to the noumenal realm. Finally, if human dignity is about respecting a specific objective feature humans embody, then human rights end up sanctioning only actions that show *contempt* towards human beings. But, Rosen argues, important as dignitary harm may be, human rights are primarily about protecting people from more serious forms of harm, such as extreme pain, starvation, violence. Human rights should protect Jews, to cite Rosen's own example, not only from the degradation of being transported in a manner traditionally reserved for cattle, but from murder.

Let us start from the first point. Rosen thinks that a satisfactory account of human dignity may stop with the recognition of the brute fact that we do pay homage to the value of humanity, as indicated by the respect we pay to 'things' – like corpses

– that 'symbolize' human beings although they are not fully identifiable as such. Is it really so? Does this phenomenology of duty (or of duty towards humanity in particular) take us further than the sheer affirmation that there is such a thing as human dignity? Imagine a sceptic who questions either that humanity has intrinsic value or the normativity of human rights based on that value (or both). Regarding corpses, the sceptic may affirm that the respect we pay to them, even if real, could have its origins in religious sources that have eventually become a habit even for non-religious people. It seems that all Rosen could do to counter this interpretation is to invite the sceptic to look within her heart to discover the true source of the duty in question as well as the significance of that duty for our identity as human beings. Is that enough? We all know that people who committed the most egregious violations of human rights (including the cruellest disregard for their victims' corpses) proved to be able to live quite comfortably with their identity. Even to die for that identity, if one remembers that most Nazi top officials decided not to surrender in Berlin. The point of giving a philosophical account of human dignity – it seems to me – is that of having a rational basis from which one can show potential violators that mistreating humans is, quite independently of their feelings or perceived identities, wrong.[8]

What about the charge that Kant's (and our) approach makes dignity depend on the existence and knowability of a noumenal realm?[9] This is a serious charge that deserves careful scrutiny and we defer the discussion to the next section. Regarding Rosen's final point, it is dubious that our approach or Kant's reduces human rights to protection against dignitary harm. Being respected by virtue of one's humanity does not include only protection from things such as being transported in cattle trucks. Is not inflicting undeserved pain a violation of the status of an individual as a free moral agent? Seen from the opposite angle, is there a consistent way to say that we are respecting the humanity of persons if we transport them in a comfortable means of travel – say first-class seats of an aeroplane – just to throw them in the ocean, as the Argentinian generals gave orders to do during the *guerra sucia*? Quite simply, on any reasonable interpretation, respecting people's humanity includes both avoiding dignitary harms and (at least) avoiding the most serious offences to their freedom, security and physical integrity.

5. Are We Really Autonomous?

So far we have criticized recent accounts for their failure to capture what seems to be the most fundamental layer of human dignity. But what about the weaknesses of our own account, with its idea of anchoring human dignity to autonomy, understood in the sense close to the one Kant had in mind? Among the various objections that could be mounted, perhaps the most fundamental is the thought that after all we could not be as autonomous as we like to think. On the one hand, those who doubt, for religious, philosophical, sociological or psychological reasons, that we are as free as is commonly assumed might find it counterproductive to link our dignity so rigidly to our autonomy. We might be non-free, determined beings but we would be still capable of suffering. So why not anchor our dignity to our vulnerability, as opposed to some abstract, less evident property? On the other hand, since we are linking human dignity not to a generic, relatively non-problematic notion of freedom, but to something specific and demanding, that is, to our autonomy understood as a capacity to act in full independence of any sensible motive, it appears that we are setting the bar for ourselves even higher than it is for those like Griffin who appeal to personhood. Finally, Kantian autonomy is a faculty of which by definition we can have no experience. By assuming its reality, we are presupposing a sort of fracture in the chain of causal events through which we usually read our world. Given all this, is an appeal to autonomy really a good idea?

In order to answer this objection, it is crucial to understand what needs to be proved about our autonomy in the context of a foundation of human rights. Although here we enter the terrain of metaphysics, this does not mean that our ambition needs to be that of solving once and for all the never-ending disputes among philosophers about the 'reality of freedom', the existence of truly moral behaviour or the like. What we need is an account of human autonomy that (a) rests on good, albeit non-conclusive philosophical reasons, and that (b) is consonant with the way in which humans – across cultures – look at themselves. To construct such an account we can start (but only start) from the way in which Kant thought that the 'reality of freedom' could be proved. What follows is of necessity a brief and simplified account of a complex and difficult story that Kant develops over the years, with substantial changes and even with what most interpreters see as a reversal in the general direction of the main argument.

After an attempt in the *Groundwork*, the *Critique of Practical Reason* grounds the thesis that we are autonomous (albeit only from a practical point of view – a phrase that will be explained in due course), on an appeal to the so-called 'fact of reason'. On the most reasonable reading, this 'fact' or 'fact as it were', as Kant sometimes puts it, is the immediate consciousness that each of us has of the inescapable authority of the moral law. To understand this idea of the immediate 'facticity' through which we become conscious of moral constraints, it is perhaps best to use Kant's own example. Kant invites us to imagine whether, threatened with death by a prince who wants us to give false testimony against an innocent man, we could resist the threat and face the consequences. None of us, Kant suggests, knows whether he or she would resist. But it is quite clear that each of us knows (a) what ought to be done and (b) that he or she *could* do it, regardless of the consequences (*KpV*, 5:30). In other words, faced with a moral issue of this kind, everybody's reaction will infallibly combine certainty about what ought to be done, uncertainty, perhaps scepticism, that we would be courageous enough to do the right thing, and yet undiminished certainty that we *could* do it. The encounter between our consciousness and the dictates of morality, the Kantian 'fact of reason', proves that our freedom or capacity for self-determination extends further than the capacity to respond intelligently to needs or desires. Negatively, we can act even if no empirical drive motivates us. Positively, we can find a pure interest in the rightness of the action that morality demands. These are in fact the two sides contained in the thought of autonomous agency: independence of external factors (including our sensuous drives), and yet ability to find a motive to act 'within ourselves', that is, in our own reason.

Of course, as Kant knew very well, there is always the possibility that when I think I am acting from duty, I am instead motivated by sensuous drives, as in the familiar case of moral acts performed, more or less consciously, to win social admiration or some form of personal satisfaction (I do it to feel well with myself). These exceptional cases, however, cannot shake our immediate consciousness that we can always do what morality commands. This point seems to be so entrenched in our self-knowledge that denying this capacity would entail a substantial restructuring of the way in which we usually look at our agency. Ultimately we would have to abandon the thought that the ultimate decision-making authority regarding our lives lies within ourselves. The very idea that we are agents in control of our lives, as opposed to mere states of affairs in causal chains that we can neither initiate nor stop, would be at risk, if not removed altogether.

This very sketchy account of the way in which Kant proves 'from the practical point of view' that we are autonomous, or, to use his terminology, that pure reason is practical, is to be complemented by a reflection on whether the Kantian notion of autonomy is close enough to cross-cultural common sense. This is important because we do not want to ground human rights on a notion, no matter how solid after philosophical scrutiny, that does not appeal to the ordinary understanding of people across cultures and traditions, with legitimately no interest in the subtleties of Kantian scholarship. To approach this question it is best to ask what would happen to the picture we have of ourselves if we were to think that we are not autonomous in the sense specified. Common sense concedes all sorts of mitigating circumstances for immoral actions that were strongly motivated, *almost* necessitated, by our sensuous interests. Again, to take an extreme example, quite invariably across cultures, one resists passing too harsh a judgement on, say, a mother who lies (or even offers false testimony in a tribunal) to save her son's life (you can fill in the details of how that could happen). Nonetheless, some blame remains. At times – imagine a false testimony that ruins someone else's life – the consequences of a lie, no matter how understandable, can be serious. Implicit in common sense is the idea that humans could do what morality requires even in the most adverse circumstances. Otherwise, blame (some or much) would make no sense. This shows how the negative side of autonomy, independence of sensuous necessitation in all circumstances, is quite solid in common sense. What about the positive side of autonomy, that is, the ability to find a reason to act – a pure interest – in the sheer fact that the action is required by morality? While it may be difficult to find narratives of behaviour explicitly inspired by the Categorical Imperatives, examples of agency generically inspired by duty abound in world literature and in the sacred texts of major religions. Think of Abraham in Christianity and Judaism, Asiya in Islam or Arjuna in Hinduism, just to give the best-known examples. As we have said before, what duty requires may vary (within limits) across traditions. What is quite constant is that examples of moral heroism always imply some form of self-sacrifice, control over one's passions, and the ability to be motivated strongly enough by the thought that 'that is what ought to be done'.

Thus the Kantian notion of autonomy, even if it appears as loaded with thick metaphysical assumptions, comes very close to a rather uncontroversial (and transcultural) notion of agency. According to common sense, you are an agent, as opposed to something that is operated or 'acted' on by someone or something else, if and only if you have the ability to decide – pretty much in any circumstances, even the most difficult – the course of your action. This property, as we showed in chapter 1, is not simply the ability to decide what are the most efficient means for an end someone else (or something else) has set for you. This is a form of freedom that is quite widespread in the animal world. Agency in the specified sense requires a full control over one's choices. If someone were to justify a theft with the excuse that she could not master her passions, only two possibilities would be before us. We can either believe the story, but then we would assign to the person some sort of sickness (kleptomania in this case) and consider her less than an agent. Or we could refuse to believe the story, still consider the person an agent, and at most concede some mitigating circumstances (e.g. she was particularly in need of the stolen item) without removing blame altogether. This shows that autonomy (not mere practical freedom) is an essential component of the way in which common sense, not only Kant, considers human nature.

Ultimately, as we said, we will never have a scientific proof of our autonomy, because the possibility always remains that our most fundamental form of freedom is – perhaps from the point of view of an omniscient observer – just an illusion. Perhaps all our allegedly moral actions are nothing but bits of unrecognized egoism or even worse effects of forces unknown and unknowable to us. Yet, this is simply not the way we conceive of ourselves. More precisely, it is not the way we are constrained to conceive of ourselves if we assume we are rational agents, as opposed to anonymous evolving states of affairs. This is the sense of Kant's famous qualification that his proof of the reality of freedom holds 'only from the practical point of view'.[10] As the example above shows, when we are to decide what to do, that is, when we assume a practical perspective, we know 'as a fact', as a 'fact of reason', that the ultimate deciding authority of our actions lies within ourselves. We are in a certain sense condemned to consider ourselves as autonomous as long as the fact of reason presents itself with the inescapability each of us experiences *in foro interno*. Moreover, and quite independently of any reference to Kant's doctrine of the fact of reason, humans do conceive of themselves across cultures (and more will be said on this in section 8) as autonomous entities, at the same time never determined by antecedent circumstances and further able to find a reason to act on the thought that something simply is the right thing to do.

6. The Value/Right Conflation and the Threshold Objection

In a famous essay Joseph Raz provided a powerful objection to all accounts of human rights that move, like ours, from the identification of some valuable features of human beings to the claim that we have a set of rights to the conditions that make the enjoyment and/or the expression of those features possible (Raz 2010). Taking Gewirth and Griffin as his main targets, Raz argues that the basic misconception that infects any traditional account is that it misconceives the relation between values and rights. The simple fact that certain conditions are necessary for our life or for a worthy life does not prove that we have a right to them. Even if we agree with Griffin that personhood is the most important feature shared by all human beings and that we all recognize this importance, we have still to prove that we have a *right* to the conditions of personhood, whatever it may be. By the same token, Raz argues, if being loved is the most important thing to me (and objectively the most important thing for a human being) then I would have a right to being loved.

In addition to the value/right conflation, Raz notices another major flaw in the traditional account. Even if we grant that human rights guarantee the exercise of people's 'most important property', it is difficult to set a limit to the things people need to exercise successfully that property. If we understand personhood as the capacity to decide one's plan of life and pursue it free of obstacles, then it is difficult to spell out exactly what one needs to be a person. Griffin talks of 'minimum education and information' as well as of 'minimum provisions of resources and capabilities' as the threshold below which one is no longer a person. But this is evidently problematic. To begin with, as Danto (1984) noticed in his critique of Gewirth, slaves obviously have both basic education and capabilities, otherwise they would be worthless for a master. If we mean more than the minimum education and resources slaves have, then setting in a non-arbitrary way the amount of goods necessary to fulfil the requirements of personhood becomes difficult. Intuitively, human rights are not rights to a good life, but to a decent one. But who is to say what decency for an entity endowed with personhood requires?

To what extent do these two critiques affect our approach? Starting from the first objection, the question becomes whether the specific orthodox approach we defend is guilty of the value/right conflation Raz imputes to Griffin. Remember that what distinguishes our approach from Griffin's is that we do not start from the premise that we are interested in a capacity of ours (autonomy) and for that very fact we are logically bound to take the conditions of autonomy seriously (up to the point of protecting them through a set of rights). We are saying that human beings are inherently worthy creatures and *for that reason* they ought to be treated in a certain way. Autonomy is not for us 'the most important thing' and we are not entitled to human rights because of the importance we attach to it. We *are* worthy creatures that deserve respect regardless of whether we recognize the value of that feature. Moreover, unlike Griffin, for our approach autonomy is not objectively valuable in the same way in which love or being loved is. It is not a commodity of some sort. It is a status. It means occupying a place in the universe that rules out certain forms of treatment as incompatible with that status. In the same way in which only certain forms of addressing judges or high public officials are consonant with their role and function, so one cannot sincerely esteem the human status attached to our autonomy and at the same time engage in the sorts of abuses, discriminations and offences we usually understand as human rights violations.

If we have a relatively easy way out from Raz's first critique, are we not as vulnerable as all other traditionalists to the second? The question, for our approach, can be reformulated as follows: what actions or omissions are required to esteem human beings in the proper manner? What do we have to do to ensure that we are taking seriously enough humans' autonomy (in the Kantian sense)? Or, more directly, what rights are to be considered human rights in order to make them adequate protections of such autonomous status, and not of everything that is valuable in life?

There is no easy answer to this question and we admit that finding a threshold is a problem for us as much as it is for other orthodox approaches. There is however a key advantage we can exploit. And this has to do – again – with the inherently deontological, as opposed to interest-based, nature of our approach. We do not need to ask what we need to do to ensure that human beings keep their status as autonomous, let alone 'realize' it or the like. In our approach, this status is never lost, no matter how degraded and base the condition humans find or put themselves in. Our question is rather: 'what posture do we (individuals and institutions) need to adopt to respect the status humans are entitled to by the fact that they are the sole fully autonomous beings on earth?' This question does not ask what factual conditions need to be realized for ensuring that human beings keep their autonomy, or have a reasonable chance of success in doing so. This question asks how individuals and institutions have to treat people if they want to be respectful of their dignity. Is there a clear-cut answer to this question? Obviously not. To be sure, our moral sense tells us with a good degree of approximation that all the times we use humans merely for ends they have not freely chosen, we are acting in a way inconsistent with that status. The same moral sense also tells us that political decisions that make utterly impossible or extremely difficult the survival of those beings when alternative institutional settings are available, are also incompatible with that rank. Analogously, any form of arbitrary discrimination is ruled out by anyone who takes that status seriously. Conversely, letting people suffer the consequences of bad choices they have made is compatible with their autonomy. Also, respecting people as autonomous is fully compatible with the fact that we do not love them. Thus we can easily avoid the case Raz uses to ridicule the orthodox view in its general form.

To be sure, this is still insufficient to set a clear threshold. In fact, even lying to people may be considered as incompatible with taking their autonomy seriously, and yet nobody would say that there is a human right to trustworthy private relations. It is no accident, however, that Kant himself construed lying as a violation of a moral duty, not of a juridical one. Those we lie to, argues Kant, remain free to believe us or not (*MS*, 6:238). Hence their sphere of external freedom is not diminished by our lies. Now human rights, even if grounded on a moral property, remain juridical or proto-juridical constraints. There is and there should be no human right to sincere private relations because being told a story we can freely believe or not is fully consistent with our status of autonomous beings. A completely different case would be one in which the institutions and social structures in which one lives did not provide the necessary means (mainly education) to be able to resist manipulation by one's fellow citizens.

Beyond the specific case of lying, a promising way to answer the threshold objection is to say that the specific ways in which societies decide what it takes to respect people in a way consistent with their autonomous status legitimately vary, depending on socio-economic and cultural contexts. Each society is expected to spell out in its own way what respecting human beings requires, and there is nothing incompatible with our approach in acknowledging that the threshold will vary with time even within the same society. Obviously the latitude of the possible reinterpretation of this standard has limits, because taking people as the only autonomous beings on earth is not compatible with everything. For example, discrimination according to sex, race or religious belief is ruled out, no matter how discriminatory practices are embedded in a given society. And this immediately makes it evident that acknowledging some variance in the threshold does not mean betraying the universality of human rights, let alone giving in to relativism. As we already said, there are things that institutions and individuals around the world do to humans that are utterly and irremediably incompatible with their status as autonomous beings. The culture and practice of human rights has already determined these things with a certain degree of precision. The fact that no infallible and uncontested threshold has been set is a fact that not only our approach but the whole culture of human rights may be charged with.

Obviously the political view Raz admires has no difficulties in setting the threshold, but this comes at a very high price. The threshold for the political view is simply what the practice of human rights has determined. Whatever the international community considers enough to constitute a breach of national sovereignty, that is the threshold. For example, if we consider *The Responsibility to Protect* as the accepted set of rules for the international community, anything that the document considers a good ground for imposing political, economic or military sanctions is the required threshold. The problem with this procedure is evident and takes us back to the general problem with the political view we have already encountered. The philosophical talk of setting a threshold for human rights becomes a fully political compromise, reduced to the de facto consensus reached in the international community. No critical space is left, and future possible shifts of the threshold will be determined merely by the striking of a new political balance.

The difference with our approach is that while the political view simply mirrors what international practice decides or, as we shall see in the next section, appeals to the problematic notion of global public reason, we see the philosophy of human rights as best carried out through a methodology that recalls Rawls's reflective equilibrium. On the one hand, in a traditional manner we start from the recognition of humans' autonomy to determine what, given certain historical circumstances (what Griffin calls practicalities), treating autonomous people requires. On the other hand, we check the tentative threshold determined by moral reasoning with the practice of human rights to correct and adjust our hypotheses. And we continue by correcting one source or the other, or better one source *through* the other, until we reach reflective equilibrium.

Two examples may illustrate the point. Imagine we wonder whether the practice of paying male employees in private enterprises slightly more than equally qualified female employees violates the human rights of the latter.[11] Let us assume that both male and female employees are paid very well, so that there is no doubt that all have their 'basic needs' fulfilled. Let us further assume that men are better paid than women *on average* and that firms have no explicit policies leading to that result (something which would obviously violate not only human rights by the constitutional principles of most liberal countries). It is safe to assume that the practice and even the jurisprudence of human rights (as emanating for example from the European Court of Human Rights) would find it hard to spot a human rights violation here, but the question as to the possible violation of the human rights of female workers remains legitimate. Starting from the premise, suggested by our approach, that human rights emanate from the *equal* respect we owe to humans by virtue of their autonomy, the conclusion we are led to is that there is a violation for which firms are collectively responsible, and which calls for some reparatory action by institutions and private individuals in a position to influence retributive policies. This conclusion would hardly be available if we adhered to the political view, because the only source of normativity would be – by definition – the practice of human rights so far experienced. In this case, however, the practice is not giving us any guidance. Even worse, if we had to take the silence of the practice as a permission, given the fundamental juridical principle that everything not explicitly forbidden is allowed, we would have a conclusion drawn from the practice that conflicts with our intuitions. Only if we start from a theory not fully modelled on the practice can we keep the critical distance required to assess cases like the one just considered.

Conversely, imagine that our moral reasoning leads us to believe that, given people's autonomy, lies commonly told by politicians to electors (ranging from populist exploitation of fear among the electorate to false promises) count as violation of the electors' human rights. Such a conclusion would be blocked by the distance between these moral wrongs and the offences human rights traditionally try to avoid. No activist has ever attempted to introduce a human right to non-manipulative political communication. A fortiori, there cannot be a human right to sincere private relations. In this case, it is the practice of human rights that corrects the theory and establishes limits to the scope of the protection that follows from the recognition of humans' worth.

The moral of the story is that although autonomy is the ultimate ground of the respect we owe to people, serving not only as the basis for human rights but for the whole of morality, the specific respect that is articulated by human rights will be determined by a number of considerations that heavily depend on how we understand what it means to offer basic protections to human beings. This threshold will be influenced by a number of unpredictable factors: how the culture and practice of human rights will evolve, the resources available at a given historical point, new possibilities offered by the progress of science and technology, and a better philosophical understanding of what our autonomy entails in terms of what is owed to us simply by virtue of that faculty.

Finally, notice that the practice and culture of human rights to which Raz appeals already operates with a distinction between violations of different importance. The widely influential *Responsibility to Protect* sees genocide and ethnic cleansing as the sole cases in which a military intervention by the international community is justified, while less serious offences justify less dramatic responses (e.g. economic sanctions, public condemnation and so on). This suggests that rights place themselves on a scale of increasing distance from the centre (protection from genocide and ethnic cleansing) down to the famous case of Article 24 of the UDHR, which establishes a human right to 'periodic holidays with pay'. A precise and detailed 'hierarchy' of human rights is still to be written, and much clarity in the human rights discourse would come from a chart of this sort. Raz's implicit solution of slavishly following whatever the international practice of the moment says impoverishes a process that is best seen as two-tiered, in which critical reflection and practice both play an irreducible role. It would already be a great improvement for philosophy if we were to agree that what the practice does is to help articulate a normative core that – we propose – rests on the idea of individual autonomy. While it would be foolish to think it possible to produce a list of human rights simply by unpacking the content of people's capacity for moral behaviour, we also think that no reference to the contemporary practice or culture of human rights blind to its normative heart will ever suffice to produce a proper list.

7. Reflective Equilibrium Vs Global Public Reason

A major objection against our approach, arising from scholars broadly belonging to the political view, focuses precisely on our preference for a methodology that resembles Rawls's reflective equilibrium. The problem is that we look for a foundation of human rights not only within the practice or the predominant culture of human rights, but also through an appeal to philosophical reflection. Many find this appeal misplaced because we would be grounding political obligations, often backed by sanctions and at times leading to military intervention, on the ideas of philosophers.

No matter how convincing, this way of proceeding appears unfit to justify the use of force against potential HR violators. Shall we tell them that they haven't done their philosophy homework well enough to unpack the content and implications of individual autonomy? Even if reflective equilibrium is not limited to philosophy, but presupposes a mutual process of correction between practice and philosophy, the amount of philosophy it includes is sufficient to disqualify it as method for justifying political obligation. Following Rawls's methodology in *Political Liberalism*, scholars like Cohen (2006), Beitz (2009) and Ferrara (2014) tend to prefer public reason over reflective equilibrium as the instrument through which human rights can and should be identified and justified. Appealing to a reflective authority that does not simply mirror a *modus vivendi*, but promises to yield an agreement for the right reasons among world major comprehensive doctrines, these scholars avoid the weakness typical of the political view, namely an a-critical acceptance of whatever the practice has established. At the same time, however, since the appeal is to *shared* normative principles, they manage to justify coercion by presenting human rights as norms one cannot reasonably reject, pretty much like domestic public reason establishes constitutional essentials by appealing to shared political values.

Is global public reason really a promising tool for human rights? We think it is not for four main reasons. To begin with, let us keep in mind that the perspective of public reason presupposes a willingness, and, I would say, a habituation to establish a degree of detachment from our deepest comprehensive convictions in favour of a negotiation with other individuals who adhere to reasonable comprehensive doctrines radically different from the one we uphold. Not accidentally, Rawls confines the idea of public reason 'to a conception of a well-ordered constitutional *democratic* society' and clarifies that '[t]he form and content of this reason are part of the idea of democracy itself' (Rawls 1999: 131). In other words, public reason presupposes a *liberal* attitude toward difference shared by all reasonable citizens, liberal and non-liberal. Non-liberal citizens living in a liberal democratic society are expected to share an ability to adopt, when discussing public and political issues, a viewpoint that is detached from their comprehensive doctrines. This expectation is well-grounded because they are socialized within a society whose institutions are mainly based on liberal values and on neutrality toward comprehensive doctrines.

One cannot expect the same, though, of non-liberal citizens socialized within non-liberal institutions. Why should they discuss about justice (national or global) by adopting a detached viewpoint? Public reason can hardly be generalized to non-liberal peoples in such a way as to become a *global* public reason. Obviously, non-liberal peoples may arrive to the same normative conclusions concerning human rights dictated by global public reason. In all likelihood, however, they will do so not because they use this instrument, but because of some overlapping with parts of their comprehensive doctrines. Representatives of the dominant religious group in a hierarchical society, for example, may be ready to concede to non-believers something consonant with human rights (say the right to protest against the government). But they will concede it not because they adopt the point of view of global public reason, but simply because the value of tolerance is part of their comprehensive doctrine, or, more precisely, of a progressive interpretation thereof (think of an updated implementation of the tolerance practiced within the Ottoman empire). When representatives of the religious majority concede that minorities will be no longer merely 'consulted' in the process of law making, but actually given a weight through the right to active electorate, most likely they will do so thanks to an innovative interpretation of their comprehensive doctrine, not through an appeal to global public reason. If the detachment from one's own deepest convictions is, as it seems, a typically liberal attitude, why should we rely on global public reason in the process of definition of HR?

Secondly, while public reason is a promising tool to become 'as tolerant as we can' inside a liberal-democratic state, namely to respect the fact of pluralism of our societies, one should never forget that the main reason why we can afford to be tolerant towards illiberal forms of life is that citizens preserve the 'right to exit' any illiberal context in which either they simply find themselves or that they have previously chosen, but no longer endorse. This right to exit, however, is not guaranteed in illiberal polities, simply because it is the basic structure itself that promotes discrimination. For an adult woman living in a liberal society, to forfeit freely her right to vote as long as she decides to do so in virtue of her, say, religious beliefs, is one thing. To live in a country in which there is no way out from this condition of discrimination is quite another. Global public reason cannot capture this crucial difference because it has an intrinsic tendency to identify as legitimate representatives of a people only the voice of the cultural or religious majority.[12]

Thirdly, a global public reason constituted by representatives of 'peoples' runs contrary to the reiterated point made by Amartya Sen (See 2006) regarding the dangers – intellectual and political – of grouping human beings according to one criterion of classification. The selection of representatives of different 'civilizations' or even of smaller entities (peoples) that collectively constitute global public reason is ultimately the outcome of a previous, morally far from neutral, grouping of human beings according to *one* preferred criterion. If rights in general and human rights in particular are intrinsically and appropriately biased in favour of individuals over groups, why should we abandon this perspective when such bias would be most beneficial, namely when the need of defending individuals from all possible forms of a majority's oppression, is particularly urgent?

Fourthly, even if one concedes that global public reason does *not* over-represent the views of the majority, one still has to check how *informed* and free is the consent individuals give to practices that undermine their equal dignity and rights. Sometimes ethicists highlight this point by talking about adaptive preferences. It may be instructive here to recall Xiaorong Li's interesting position on female genital mutilation. She argues (Li 2001) that this practice should be allowed in a liberal-democratic country and banned in non-democratic countries, even if arguably the practice is rooted in the traditions of the latter and nearly absent in the former. This paradoxical 'double standard', that turns upside down the commonsensical idea that a morally dubious practice is to be allowed where it is culturally rooted, and banned where it is not, rests on the powerful consideration that only in a free country can one be relatively confident that the practice is authentically chosen by the individual, namely it is not an adaptive preference. To the contrary, the suspicion that the alienation of one's rights is not freely chosen or informed enough is unavoidable in authoritarian societies. The case of female genital mutilation shows that a preference is authentic not merely when alternative models are available, but when one is free to abandon the practices imposed by the tradition to endorse alternative identities. Of course, if there are reasons to believe that some of the preferences that influence global public reason are merely adaptive, it follows that this methodological instrument is hardly reliable for identifying and grounding human rights.

8. The Parochial Objection

Perhaps the most fundamental objection to our approach points out its allegedly limited reach. How parochial is a foundation based on autonomy? Are we not simply generalizing the Western, formerly Protestant, then Enlightened, now secular fixation on individualism and self-mastery? What about other cultures in which human worth does not depend on individual autonomy? What about non-Western traditions, like Confucianism, Buddhism and Hinduism, in which the very idea that the individual is the centre of all value is downplayed, if not explicitly rejected, in favour of other values? Human rights have often been accused of being wonderful Trojan horses of Western colonialism: you first introduce human rights in a non-Western cultural and social context, then sooner or later individualism, capitalism, secularism, sexual licence, disruption of old *mores* and the whole Western package will infallibly follow. This accusation has been launched even independently of a foundation like ours that is explicitly based on individuals' ability to be moral agents. Hence it looks as if we are making an old problem worse. No doubt, this is what scholars like Dershowitz (2005) and Ignatieff (2001) would say against our attempt. While for them any foundational exercise is ultimately counterproductive, *this* exercise would certainly be judged as particularly damaging because *most* divisive.

Do things really look so bad for our foundation? Clearly, there is only one way to know whether our foundation runs into such serious difficulties. We need to make a journey – of necessity a cursory one – into the essence of the major non-Western cultural 'constellations'[13] to see whether the idea of individual autonomy is for them as alien as commonly assumed. It is inaccurate, and perhaps offensive, to talk about 'non-Western' cultures and traditions, as if they could be placed in one or a few categories. And even within the same constellation the process of internal self-differentiation is at times so refined that to speak, say, of 'Islam' or 'Hinduism' is as reasonable as it is to speak of Christianity with no regard for the divide between Catholics and Protestants. It is possible, nonetheless, to distinguish some common themes in those traditions in pretty much the same way as it is possible to speak of an undifferentiated Christian perspective on the world.

A good starting point in this difficult journey is the recent work by Alessandro Ferrara on multiple democracies. In *The Democratic Horizon: Hyperpluralism and the Renewal of Political Liberalism* (2014) Ferrara explores the consonances and dissonances between what he calls 'the spirit of democracy' – a general disposition favourable to the common good, equality, individuality and openness to diversity – and the cultural traditions present in various non-Western contexts. Although he focuses on democracy and not on human rights, his definition of democracy makes his analysis by and large applicable to our present problem. In fact, Ferrara defines democracy as a system that presupposes the commitment (by rulers and citizens) mainly to individuality, equality and openness to diversity, and then shows that these values are well represented in non-Western traditions. On the one hand, a system committed to these values is *ipso facto* committed to respecting people as entities equipped with an intrinsic worth that forbids using them for ends they have not freely endorsed. Hence the spirit of democracy rests on the recognition of individual autonomy as a sovereign value. On the other hand, Ferrara's three values are well represented in the normative gist of human rights. In fact, very few would deny that the values of equality and openness to diversity are at the centre of the official documents of human rights as well as the informal 'practice' of them. The human rights to freedom of thought, conscience and religion (UDHR, Article 18), to freedom of opinion and expression (Article 19) and to peaceful assembly and association (Article 20) all point to a strong commitment to openness towards diversity. Individuality is protected by the very language of rights, most of the time claimed by individuals against more or less institutionalized groups. Moreover, all rights protecting a fair trial can be read as provisions for the protection of individuals and affirmations of the essence of individuality, that is, personal responsibility. Finally, even when the UDHR affirms the responsibility of individuals towards the community ('Everyone has duties to the community in which alone the free and full development of his personality is possible', Article 29), it immediately affirms the essence of all individualism, that is, that my freedom can be restricted only to ensure that other individuals enjoy the same amount of the same good ('In the exercise of his rights and freedoms, everyone shall be subject only to such limitations as are determined by law *solely for the purpose of securing due recognition and respect for the rights and freedoms of others* and of meeting the just requirements of morality, public order and the general welfare in a democratic society', Article 29; my emphasis).

What about equality? Although human rights do not explicitly include 'a right to democratic government', and a fierce debate among scholars focuses on the question whether there should be one (Rawls 1999; Cohen 2006; Caranti 2011a; Cristiano 2011, 2015; Peter 2015), the UDHR does grant to all humans the right to *perfect* formal equality ('All human beings are equal in dignity and rights', Article 1). *Pace* Rawls, the same document protects against all forms of discrimination ('All are equal before the law and are entitled without any discrimination to equal protection of the law. All are entitled to equal protection against any discrimination in violation of this Declaration and against any incitement to such discrimination', Article 7). It further grants a right to elections with universal suffrage ('The will of the people shall be the basis of the authority of government; this will shall be expressed in periodic and genuine elections which shall be by universal and equal suffrage and shall be held by secret vote or by equivalent free voting procedures', Article 21), and envisages that the goods protected by human rights are enjoyed 'in a democratic society' (Article 29).

Ferrara's notion of 'the spirit of democracy' is thus close enough to (a) the value of individual autonomy on which our foundation rests, and (b) what we may call 'the spirit of human rights'. It follows that the consonances he notices between world cultural and religious traditions and the spirit of democracy are also legitimate points of agreement between the same traditions and the values underpinning human rights. We can thus proceed by saying something about how each major cultural and religious tradition – Islam, Confucianism, Hinduisim, Judaism – relates to the values – pluralism/openness to diversity, equality among individuals, individualism – which jointly express a recognition of the fundamental value of individual autonomy. A caveat is necessary, however, in the preliminary. As argued with particular clarity by Abdullahi Ahmed An-Na'im in the case of Islam, often there is no sense in attempting to reconstruct a compatibility between the fundamentals of a faith *in its traditional or most conservative form* and human rights as we understand them today. For example, Islam in its received form includes a submission of the individual to Allah, a surrender of individual freedom to the divine will, God as the exclusive owner of rights, major inequalities between Muslim and non-Muslims as well as between men and women. To ignore these points and to insist on a quick and easy compatibility of Islam and human rights is both inaccurate and counterproductive. What we can do, instead, is (a) notice that similarly controversial principles were present in coeval self-interpretations of most religions (including Christianity); (b) stress that none of all these principles were unusual for the seventh century AD, independently of religion; (c) insist on the fact that the self-understanding of religions and the interpretations of sacred texts vary significantly in time, often conforming to the *Zeitgeist* of specific historical moments. It follows that what we look for are ideas present in the various religions that can serve as the basis for *developing* reconciliation, as opposed to easily given agreements. With this caveat in mind, let us start our journey.

Pluralism/Openness to Diversity. Sources for accommodating the value of pluralism in Islam are not difficult to find. Ali Ihsan Yitik (2004) reminds us that Islam has always had room for salvation outside its borders. Nothing like the motto *extra ecclesiam nulla salus* is present in the Qur'an. Nasr Abû Zayd adds that 'there is no one single verse in the Qur'an stipulating world punishment, or legal penalty, for apostasy; freedom of religion in the form of "no coercion" is widely quoted even by the traditional *ulamâ*' (Zayd 2004: 27). Sadik Al-Azm (Al-Azm 1970), Abdullahi Ahmed An-Na'im (An-Na'im 2001), Mohammed Talbi (Talbi 1998) – just to name other scholars coming from different regions of the 'Islamic world' – argue that one can reinterpret the Muslim tradition and make it coherent with the tolerance inherent in human rights culture by discarding Shari'a as a late and unnecessary addition to the core of the Islamic faith.[14] More directly, as pointed out by El Fadl (2003), diversity and differences among human beings are claimed in the Qur'anic discourse as divine gifts to humankind (11:119). Moreover, El Fadl continues, this idea is also exemplified in a tradition attributed to the Prophet asserting that disagreement and diversity of opinion in the *umma* (Muslim nation) is a source of divine mercy for Muslims.

Regarding the Confucian tradition, which is becoming the new official ideology of post-Marxist China, most scholars, both Asian and Western, emphasize that a marriage between Confucianism and human rights/democracy is possible, and nobody mentions in this context the desirability of watering down human rights' commitment to pluralism and individuality.[15] As reminded by Ferrara, in the Confucian tradition, a fundamental difference separates 'agreeing' and 'harmonizing', as illustrated by two examples from the Commentaries to the *Analects*. Master Yan explains that

> There is a difference. Harmonizing is like cooking soup. You have water, fire, vinegar, pickle, salt, and plums with which to cook fish and meat. You heat it by means of firewood, and the cooking harmonizes the ingredients, balancing the various flavours, strengthening the taste of whatever is lacking, and moderating the taste of whatever is excessive.

Harmonizing presupposes a plurality of voices that coexist 'peacefully' (Confucius 2003: 150). This is contrasted with the attitude of the 'yes-man' Ran Qiu:

> What his lord declares acceptable he also declares acceptable; what his lord declares wrong, he also declares wrong. This is like trying to season water with more water. Who would be willing to eat it? It is like playing nothing but a single note on your zither. Who would want to listen? (Confucius 2003: 150)[16]

To be sure, the *Analects* and its commentaries offer resources for drawing a distinction between harmonizing and agreeing, between *he* and *tong*, but also for blurring that distinction. It is mostly up to the members of a religious community to decide in which direction to go. The only thing we need to prove, however, is that pluralism is not incompatible with any reasonable interpretation of the texts.

What about the oldest of the major religions practised in the world, Hinduism? The recognition of the intrinsic difficulty for human beings to identify the right course of action and, as a consequence, the necessity of tolerating a plurality of 'ways' towards the truth, is at the centre of the most important text of the Hindu tradition, the Bhagavad Gita. It will be recalled how that sacred text starts with the inner conflict felt by the hero Arjuna, who is expected to fight and kill his own relatives in the Kurukshetra War. Most commentators interpret the location of the text – a battlefield – as a metaphor for the 'war within' in which Arjuna is caught. Krishna ultimately convinces Arjuna that he ought to fight (and kill), thereby overcoming his doubts. This could be taken as a sign of religious fanaticism, but Arjuna's very humane 'war within' remains an essential part of the story. Also, we should notice that Krishna helps Arjuna out of his doubts through the 'eightfold path'. Krishna asserts that all paths lead to God 'leaving then room for the notion of other religions embedding specific aspects of the truth' (Ferrara 2014: 128).

As in the case of Confucianism and Hinduism, Buddhism presents contradictory elements that can be geared either to the conclusion that Buddhism is tolerant and accepts pluralism or to its opposite. Haynes (1991) argues that Buddhism's reputation as the religion most hospitable to other paths to the truth is largely undeserved, while Murti (1980) – to which Haynes is reacting – stresses that Buddhism combines the belief in the unity of Ultimate Being with the freedom of different paths for realizing it. Moreover, as stressed by Jayatillake (1991), where one is reborn depends on one's behaviour, not on the orthodoxy of one's beliefs. Hence Buddhism is able to acknowledge and appreciate the good in other religions.

Let us finally mention the Jewish tradition, even if the rather limited number of adherents (0.2 per cent of the world population in most estimates) hardly makes it a 'major' religion of our times in quantitative terms. Still, as anticipator and 'older brother' of Christianity, and given its reputation of being more hostile to pluralism than Christianity itself, its treatment is in order. As argued by Michael Walzer in his 'Two Kinds of Universalism', Judaism has often been criticized as a tribal religion, the very emblem of a creed immune to tolerance towards the non-elected, who at best are supposed to be enlightened by the Jews' example and privileged relation to God. Walzer shows that although this interpretation is hardly inconsistent with the Bible (think of Isaiah's description of Israel as 'a light unto the nations'),[17] the line of prophecy originating with Amos goes in quite the opposite direction. Amos has God ask: 'Are ye not as children of the Ethiopians unto me, O children of Israel? [...] Have I not brought Israel out of the land of Egypt,

And the Philistines from Caphtor, And the Syrians from Kir?' The passage suggests: (1) that the Jews are no more elected than other peoples; (2) that there are many paths to liberation; (3) that peoples can be equally enlightened/liberated by the same supreme authority (God) in different ways; (4) that the plurality of paths is compatible with a residual and welcome quota of universalism, namely the idea that oppression is always bad.

Individuality. A tradition may display care for the value of individuality in different ways. If for example a plurality of voices over strict observance is seen positively, this proves that individualism is not alien to a culture. In this sense, all we said before about plurality counts to a certain extent as evidence of a commitment to giving some consideration to the value of individuality. But care for individualism could also be discovered by looking at the way in which political power is legitimized within a tradition. If the consent of individual citizens is required, then *ipso facto* individual voices are valued. And, from this perspective, evidence in favour of a commitment to individualism is abundant in each of the major traditions under consideration.

The authority of the leaders (*Imam*) of the Muslim community comes from the consensus of individual members and depends on the individual Iman's merits. Similarly in the Buddhist tradition kings derive their legitimacy from the general consent of individuals. As Ferrara notices, 'Several of the Jakata stories in the *Pali Canon* implicitly suggest that people had a right to overthrow a king who was cruel, unjust or incompetent' (Ferrara 2014: 129). Regarding Judaism, Robert Bellah has noticed how prophets like Amos contested theologians' authority to side with the idea that God relates directly to people. The king possesses no monopoly when it comes to interpreting the divine will, which evidently opens up a space for a quasi-Protestant individual responsibility for the relation with God. Moreover, in the Bible it is often suggested that the same God who gave humans guidelines also created them as individuals. Indeed, the Mishne Torah, by Moses Maimonides, one of the most authoritative rabbis, asks: 'Why was the human created as an individual? To teach us [our great individual responsibility] that each person must say "the entire universe was created for me".' Finally, and in contrast with the popular notion of a Confucian tradition fond of authoritarianism and conformity, and as such insensitive to the value of individuality, scholars such as Tan (2004) and Herr (2010) have noticed that underlying Confucian politics is the idea that each person has an equal capacity to reach moral perfection and that societal structures are to be criticized, changed and even overthrown if they stand in the way of the individual journey towards personal improvement. Interesting also is the passage from the *Analects* in which it is said that 'Men are close to one another by nature; they diverge as a result of repeated practice' (17.2), which emphasizes a fundamental equality among individuals by nature.

Equality. If we are to prove that the notion of individual autonomy is not alien to non-Western traditions, then showing that the equality of all human beings is germane to those cultural contexts is a central component of the overall argument. To be sure, one could attribute autonomy and responsibility even to individuals who belong to different castes – even a slave can be considered as autonomous under a certain description – and this would entail that the two values do not necessarily go hand in hand. However, this line of reasoning assumes a sense of individual autonomy quite different from the one we are using. It should be recalled that for Kant autonomy is the *overarching* value individuals possess, the *sole* ground of human dignity. All other features (intelligence, education, not to mention birth or lineage) merely attribute a price, not a dignity, to humans. At the most fundamental level, then, autonomous individuals are all equal. It follows that no cultural or religious system can be said to harmonize with the central value of autonomy unless it includes a strong commitment to the equality of all human beings.

The case of Confucianism is relatively easy. In the *Analects* we read a passage that resonates the Sophists' 'democratic' commitment to oppose the traditional prejudice of differences 'by nature' among men. Confucius says that 'men are close to one another by nature; they diverge as a result of repeated practice' (Confucius 2003: 17.2). If Confucius has in mind, as it seems, the idea that for humans the solidification of traditional exclusionary practices, not nature, is the source of any notable differences among human beings, then he is intriguingly similar to Antiphon the Sophist, rightly considered a precursor of the natural rights doctrine. In a famous passage from *On Truth* we read:

Those born of illustrious fathers we respect and honour, whereas those who come from an undistinguished house we neither respect nor honour. In this we behave like barbarians towards one another. For by nature we all equally, both barbarians and Greeks, have an entirely similar origin: [...] for we all breathe into the air with mouth and nostrils and we all eat with the hands. (Pendrick 2002; quoted in Untersteiner 1954: 252)

In the *Bhagavad Gita* Krishna says, 'I am equally disposed to all loving entities; there is neither friend nor foe to me' (9, 29). This rules out any interpretation of the hero Arjuna's war, that we have already mentioned, as a conflict between two sets of individuals differentiated by nature in their worth. Moreover, many commentators insist that the caste system is a medieval addition to the body of laws inspired by Hinduism with no roots in the sacred texts. Mitra (1982: 82), for example, argues that 'Theistic Hinduism upholds human equality on the basis that all are God's creatures. Nontheistic Hinduism emphasizes the identity of the essence of all humans.' In his interpretation of *Dharma*, Gandhi linked the 'right to have rights' to the performance of our duties, not to the belonging to a caste (*Young India*, 8 January 1925).

This quick journey round the major religious traditions of the world has done little more than suggest the resources at our disposal to avoid a facile dismissal of a foundational argument that sees individual autonomy as the pivotal value on which human rights rest. The idea that autonomy is a fixation of the West, or perhaps of the Protestant West, is too simplistic even to be given serious consideration. To the consonances between the individualistic spirit of human rights and the 'spirit' of major religions we could add a consideration that perhaps is more important than all the specific points listed above. No religion, or at least no serious interpretation of a religious tradition, has room today for a forced adherence to the professed faith by potential believers. It is recognized without exception that only a free and autonomous endorsement makes the individual merging into a community of believers worthy. This means that independently of the extent in which the principle is spelt out in clear terms, individual autonomy is recognized as an essential ingredient – actually a precondition – of any authentic religious experience. This is obviously compatible with the possibility that the amount of freedom left to individuals *after* their choice to adhere may vary substantially depending on the specific faiths and their dominant interpretations. Still, *pace* Giansenists and radical Lutherans, religion and individual autonomy cannot be at odds with each other. A strong notion of autonomy, with the individual assumed as free to remain deaf even to God's law, is part and parcel of the religious mentality *in general*. And a moment of freedom grounds *all* duty to which an individual can be bound after she chooses to adhere to a faith. For our purposes, we simply need to notice how similar, if not identical, is this notion to the Kantian notion of autonomy with which we have been operating. In both cases, the individual is an earthly king with the power to receive or reject the law (whether moral or divine makes no difference here). Obviously, our specificity is that we say that this power entitles humans to an unconditional degree of respect while a religious mind may assume that if the individual makes the wrong choice, his or her value is lost. Yet the recognition of this supreme power by human beings cannot be denied even by the most conservative religious mind, which is more than sufficient for removing the spectre of a strict incommensurability between human rights (as reconstructed within this interpretation) and all religious traditions reasonably interpreted.

Part II:
Peace

4 • The Kantian Model

The first part of this book has offered our reading of Kant's theory of innate rights and of its repercussions on the contemporary debate. This was a quasi-Kantian new foundation of human rights normativity, or better the very first elements of an argument still to be developed and defended against foreseeable attacks. We now move to the second part of Kant's political legacy. The question is no longer how Kant *could* be used for some pressing issues of our time, but rather how he *has been* used. In fact our present goal is to assess critically how the normative indications Kant offers to reach a durable and lasting peace, interpreted in one of the major research programmes of our times as the theory of the democratic peace (DPT). On specific points other scholars have already done work in this direction. Lars-Erik Cederman (2001) insisted on people's gradual and slow moral learning as an irreducible component of Kant's thought that scholars of DPT, including those sympathetic to the theory, tend to underestimate. Georg Cavallar (2001) proposed Kantian interpretations of the democratic peace alternative to Doyle's. Michael Williams (2001) argued that processes of mutual liberal recognition, based on the Kantian notion of respect for decent individuals and peoples, are crucial in explaining the fact of democratic peace (as well as the aggressive posture of democracies towards illiberal states). McLaughlin Mitchell (2002) interestingly rephrased Kant's evolutionary argument of spontaneous evolution to perpetual peace by focusing on how democratic norms of third-party dispute management become international norms as the number of democracies increases. Our natural starting point will be a close analysis of Kant's original model. The present chapter offers a reading of the development of Kant's theory of peace. While the analysis follows the chronological order of Kant's political writings, starting from the intellectual and political background that led the shaping of Kant's ideas, now and then we will have to make short incursions into Kant's thought as a whole to clarify some of the most complex and debated interpretative puzzles. The chapter is by no means an exhaustive account of all hermeneutical issues relating to Kant's theory of peace that would deserve to be analysed. Our goal is more modestly that of discussing the interpretative points that have had an impact on contemporary DPT, and perhaps that of proving to readers why we think that DPT scholars have at times learned from Kant a lesson quite different from the one he meant to offer.

1. The Intellectual and Political Background of Kant's Project

Kant's 'philosophical project' does not arise from a void. Although profoundly innovative and in many regards revolutionary, it was heavily influenced by identifiable intellectual sources and specific political events: on the one hand, the work of the many authors who reflected on the problem of war before Kant; on the other, the rapidly unfolding course of late eighteenth-century European politics to which Kant reacts. Conceptually, two intellectual traditions influenced Kant's reflection on war: (a) the natural law tradition, which includes the ancient *ius gentium*, and (b) preceding peace projects crafted and forcefully proposed by authors with whom Kant was certainly familiar. Politically, the situation in Europe shortly after the French Revolution (*To Perpetual Peace* was written in 1795) called for a general reconsideration of international affairs in light of the presence of a completely new political actor, the French Republic. The revolution had set in turmoil the already unstable balance of power in Europe. France was perceived by the European autocracies not 'merely' as a dangerous model for domestic rebels but also as a new power ready to export its principles through some sort of republican crusade. No matter whether inspired by an authentic desire to 'help other oppressed peoples for the cause of freedom' – as emphatically proclaimed in a decision of the French National Assembly – or by more worldly considerations of self-defence (could the Revolution survive surrounded by unfriendly reactionary powers?), France was signalling to the world a significant temptation to wage war on the *ancien régime*. Being a very interested (almost enthusiastic) spectator of events in France, Kant was of course aware of all this, and *To Perpetual Peace* must be seen, besides its intrinsic intellectual value, as an effort to cope with this turbulent political reality. Both the intellectual and political background of Kant's peace project had been reconstructed by scholars such as Archibugi (1995), Burgio (1991) and Mori (2008), even before Reidar Malik devoted an entire monograph to this theme (Malik 2014). In what follows we will do little more than select from the work of these scholars the aspects we deem particularly relevant for our purposes, in particular for the confrontation between Kant's model and DPT.

Starting with the intellectual background, we know that Kant had a thorough knowledge of the natural law school and of the treatises on *ius gentium* still being written in his time.[1] This school notoriously attempted to introduce, following different routes and methodologies, norms of conduct in contexts – that of the relation between states and of the relation between states and foreign citizens or stateless groups – traditionally considered outside the scope of the law. The tradition as a whole had no ambition to identify the causes of war or to propose reforms aimed at establishing perpetual peace. Its more moderate goal was to show that even actions not regulated by social contracts between individuals and sovereigns were under some moral and proto-legal constraints. This perspective is what leads Kant to be bitterly critical of some of its foremost exponents. Famous is the trenchant comment in *To Perpetual Peace* Kant reserves for Grotius, Pufendorf and Vattel, who are dismissed as 'sorry conforters' (ZeF, 8:355).[2] They are 'comforters' precisely because they attempt to mitigate the damage brought about by wars, as opposed to indicating a way to solve the problem once and for all.

Despite this critical attitude, Kant was clearly influenced by the natural law tradition. As Archibugi (1995) notices, the clearest influence is perhaps that of Christian Wolff, who in 1749 wrote a treatise with the title *The Law of Nations according to a Scientific Method*. For Wolff the *natural law* of nations (*ius gentium*) binds each nation to respect other nations' rights. These rights are established by an impersonal (hence universal) moral law. In addition, there is a *voluntary law*, based on tacit or potential consent, that binds each nation to respect certain moral rules in its treatment of foreigners.[3] The right to asylum, basic individual rights and the duty to respect obligations between nationals and citizens of other countries fall in this category. Interestingly enough, because it precedes Kant's appeal to universal reason as the ultimate source of normativity in international affairs, Wolff thought that the existence of such a consent can be safely assumed because nature itself sets these rules. Nature binds states to those principles even if no formal act or contract is actually signed. As Wolff put it against Grotius, this law 'is not left to their [the states'] caprice as to whether they should prefer to agree or not' (Wolff 1934: 16). Finally Wolff believed that the law of nations is not complete unless the voluntary law is complemented by a 'kind of democratic form of government' ruling in each individual state. Single states are thus thought of as subordinated to a supreme state that Wolff at times calls *civitas maxima*, or even 'international society'. Single states' sovereignty is limited. Wolff explicitly speaks of a right to intervention by international society in case of violations of natural, voluntary and stipulative law by a single nation. This intervention should be carried out by a *rector*, a sort of executive power of the *civitas maxima*.

Although Wolff tends to undermine the revolutionary potential of his proposal by insisting that the *civitas* is a merely fictional entity, the innovation over the tradition of the *ius gentium* is enormous and destined to create a flow of theoretical consequences. To begin with, in Wolff's system, the *civitas* was necessary to establish for each nation the obligation to abide by the norms of the natural law. For Wolff, each national player is supposed to act *as if* the *civitas* existed. Secondly, Wolff understood the necessity to limit national sovereignty for the sake of peace at a time in which the power of the state was usually considered unlimited.[4] Thirdly, he paved the way for others (including Kant) to bring this theoretical development to its natural end, that is, the stipulation of a *non*-fictional supranational entity capable of regulating relations between national players.

The natural law tradition, however, did not merely suggest to Kant the idea of a supranational federation. Another issue, widely debated within that school, became particularly important for the development of Kant's thought, namely the determination of the circumstances in which the use of force between states was to be considered as legitimate. We should bear in mind that the *ius gentium* was mainly an attempt to identify precisely the conditions that make war between states just, thus taking it for granted that some wars were legitimate. In fact, on the legitimacy of certain wars the tradition spoke with a unique voice. Interestingly, Kant goes in the opposite direction by explicitly criticizing the *ius gentium*. He simply declares all interstate wars as illegitimate, not because there is something inherently wrong in the idea of using force (Kant was not that kind of pacifist), but because without a supranational federation that acts as independent authority, parties would be the judge of the legitimacy of their own actions. As Kant says about the sorry comforters Grotius, Pufendorf, and Vattel: 'Their philosophically and diplomatically formulated codes do not and cannot have the slightest *legal* force, since states as such are not subject to a common external constraint' (*ZeF*, 8:355). Hence a legalistic point leads Kant to depart from one fundamental assumption behind the very idea of *ius gentium*, the possibility of determining on merely moral grounds the legitimacy of a war. Properly understood, Kant uses precisely the same argument against the right to rebellion. But while on the first issue he is praised for being a warm-hearted and coherent pacifist, on the second issue he is usually criticized as a conservative attached to the status quo, no matter how indefensibly despotic.

As I have said, the authors of the natural law tradition were not the only source of inspiration for Kant. A different and yet equally important tradition, that of the peace projects, constituted a crucial point of reference for the German thinker. It is very likely that Kant, like most learned German readers of that time, ignored the peace projects of the early modern period: *Querela pacis* (1517) by Erasmus, *Krieg Büchlin des Friedes* (1539) by Sebastian Frank, *Nouveau Cynée* (1633) by Éméric Crucé, *Gran Dessein* (1635) by the Duc de Sully, *Angelus Pacis* (1667) by Comenius, *Essay towards the Present and Future Peace of Europe* (1693) by William Penn. He did know, however, the *Projet pour rendre la paix perpétuelle en Europe* (1713–17) by the Abbé de Saint-Pierre, at least at second hand, given the popularity of the essay, or through the *Extrait* written by Rousseau in 1761. It is not clear whether Kant also knew the *Jugement* that Rousseau wrote, no longer to summarize sympathetically the view of the abbé but to criticize him bitterly.

Unlike the *ius gentium*, perpetual peace projects did not aim to introduce some elements of law into the lawless human activity *par excellence* – war – but to identify the institutional mechanism through which war could be abolished (at least in Europe) forever. Starting from a conservative standpoint, Saint-Pierre proposed the creation of a council of the European sovereigns, a union in which each state was given one vote and any power could take part independently of its internal constitutional form (regardless of whether republican or despotic, to use Kant's language). The union was supposed to apply sanctions, even through military action, to violations perpetrated by a single member against the rules set by the union. In addition, and here is the most conservative aspect of Saint-Pierre project, the union was to intervene anywhere that an insurrection of subjects threatened the legitimate authority of one member. This was the only kind of interference in the internal affairs of a state to be allowed. The union had no say on the way in which the sovereign treated subjects.

The conservative nature of Saint-Pierre did not pass unnoticed among the progressive minds of the French Enlightment. In his *Jugement*, Rousseau comments that Saint-Pierre's project fails to grasp how the hidden cause of wars in Europe was that very *ancien régime* that the union was in fact intended to strengthen. Similarly Voltaire considered the union a mere pact among despots to maintain their power, and therefore incapable of tackling the real cause of war. For Voltaire absolute sovereigns waged war with the same light-heartedness through which they decided about a hunt, knowing that no serious consequence would accrue to them. Needless to say, the very same example, almost word for word, is used by Kant in the first definitive article.

Despite these evident shortcomings, from which Kant also distanced himself, Saint-Pierre's project had the great merit of insisting on the necessity of creating a real supranational institution. As we saw, in the Wolffian interpretation of the *ius gentium*, that remained at best as a fictional entity. In contrast, Saint-Pierre devoted his entire life to establishing the union that he considered a necessary premise for a durable peace. Thanks to Saint-Pierre the tradition of perpetual peace projects stopped being a mere moral peroration and became a real political option. The Congress of Utrecht, in which many saw the first serious attempt to create a European league for the purpose of security, was held in the same year as the first version of Saint-Pierre's project was published (1712). This temporal coincidence shows that his ideas were far from being detached from his time or merely chimerical.

Quite independently of the question of its possible realization, Saint-Pierre's focus on the institutional mechanisms puts his project on a level of complexity and thoroughness incomparably superior to earlier intellectual efforts to cope with the problem of war. As

Alberto Burgio has well reconstructed it, the history of European reflection on the problem of war can be seen as a gradual progress from the idea that war is mainly due to individuals' immoral dispositions (aggressiveness, greed, desire for aggrandizement and so on) to the insight that war is primarily caused by certain war-prone *institutional* features (the absence of international organization, the despotic nature of domestic regimes, restriction on international trade, tendency to autarky and so on). This evolution, leading to what I have elsewhere called Kant's 'Copernican revolution in peace theory' (Caranti 2006a), shows how much Kant owes to preceding authors. Despite the radical originality of his theory, Kant brought to completion a long progress ultimately culminating with the full realization that progress towards peace had to start with reforming institutions instead of trying to change individuals' hearts and souls. From the Middle Age up to Saint-Pierre, one can see how philosophers of war and peace gradually shift their attention from allegedly sinful predispositions of humans to the principles of justice on which national institutions are founded.[5] Saint-Pierre greatly contributes to this long evolution, and Kant and Rousseau can be seen as those who introduce the last, albeit admittedly radical, refinement.

The reconstruction of the conceptual background from which Kant's model for peace arises needs to be complemented through a consideration of the political situation that precedes the essay. Again Archibugi (1995) constitutes here a valuable source of information. In France the political debate in the years between 1789 and 1795 turned around the opportunity to 'export' the revolution to other European states. Two sets of considerations were used in favour of an expansion. On the one hand, a moral argument mainly turning on the duty to assist other peoples who were striving for their own freedom. On the other hand, a prudential consideration that insisted on the need to eliminate some European despots for the sake of national security. How can France be secure – it was often argued – if surrounded by despots who are only waiting for the occasion to launch the Restoration? How could France remain inert while a league led by Britain had been established with the explicit aim of crushing the Republic? Half-way between the crusading party and those who considered any initiative inopportune and counterproductive was the position expressed in the pamphlet *Épitre du vieux cosmopolite Syrach à la Convention Nationale de*

France, published anonymously a few months before *To Perpetual Peace*. Syrach, whom many identify as the Polish publicist Kronowsky, warned against the risks of adopting an aggressive attitude to expand the ideals of the Revolution abroad. The European 'Cosmofederation' had to be achieved not through force but through 'enlightenment, culture and universal maturity'.

Syrach's pamphlet is telling because it contains at least three main features of the essay by Kant: (1) the denial of a right of interference, even for the most noble ends (corresponding to the fifth preliminary article); (2) the rejection of Rousseau's idea that, like individual states, the world republic also had to be established by force (it was assumed that no other means could overcome the states' interest in maintaining their unlimited sovereignty); and (3) the reiteration of the idea that the world federation is attainable and therefore a legitimate political end towards which one is bound to strive. Quite independently of the agreement between Kant and Syrach on these specific points, it is striking to see how precisely the same problems of the pamphlet are also debated in *To Perpetual Peace*. This shows that Kant's essay appears as the answer by a world famous philosopher (in the 1790s Kant was widely known and respected) to the hottest political issues debated in the European context. And it is interesting to see how Kant's project is struggling to find a compromise between many different, not always reconcilable, positions: the universal validity of the Enlightenment principles and respect for the autonomy and sovereignty of each people; the awareness of the difficulty of implementing perpetual peace projects and yet the moral obligation to strive towards it; the awareness that violence can produce considerable progress in domestic and international institutions combined with the denial of the right to rebellion; the utility both of provisional rules of international 'good practice' (the preliminary articles mainly echoing the *ius gentium*) and of permanent dispositions (the definitive articles mainly derivative from the perpetual peace tradition); the purely moral nature of the obligation to strive for perpetual peace combined with the necessity of showing that a durable peace is attainable, perhaps even *guaranteed*, to avoid contradicting the *ultra posse nemo obligatur* principle. In particular, the problem of a guarantee of perpetual peace is a point of constant worry for Kant. Not only was it incumbent on Kant to show that his project was more than a mere chimera (a preoccupation common to all authors of the perpetual peace tradition). For him there was the additional difficulty of showing that a prediction as to the necessary end of history (perpetual peace) was not incompatible with the epistemological principles he had defended in the critique of reason. A prediction regarding an alleged 'Cosmopolitan Purpose' of the political world had to be shown to be compatible with the limits imposed on reason by Kant's tribunal. His two first important political writings, *Idea for a Universal History with a Cosmopolitan Purpose* (1784) and *Theory and Practice* (1793), to which we now turn, are in fact mainly devoted to this issue.

2. *Idea* (1784): The Cosmopolitan Constitution is Written in Our Destiny

Three years after the publication of the first edition of the *Critique of Pure Reason*, at a time when Kant's interests seemed to be quite distant from politics and mainly devoted to the extension of the critical method to the realm of morality, the German thinker came out with a bold, provocative essay half-way between politics and the philosophy of history. As the title indicates (*Idea for a Universal History with a Cosmopolitan Purpose*), its main thesis (or better 'idea', in a technical sense in need of explanation[6]) is that history tends towards a pre-established end, namely the creation of a civil society at the domestic level and the establishment of a 'constitution' at the international level. By cosmopolitan constitution Kant means generically a federation of states capable of regulating their relations in such a way as to avoid all wars. Through nine theses that constitute a uniquely complex argument, Kant attempts to demonstrate that nature leads humanity towards this double institutional achievement.

The essay as a whole is Kant's first attempt to come to terms with one of the key problems of his entire political thought, that is, history. Kant's normative theses in politics, not only at the level of international relations but also concerning domestic institutions, largely depend on the truth of the thesis that humanity, despite its many shortcomings, is destined (almost forced) to proceed towards a future characterized by representative government, the rule of law, and permanently peaceful international relations. Some philosophers today consider this perspective a dubious if not dangerous legacy of the Enlightenment. Viewing history as a progress towards a pre-established end – the critics argue – is the first step towards the assessment of individuals and cultures according to the degree of closeness to that end. It means – they continue – to rank societies by their level of development, and presumably to assign the highest mark to the Western world. In other words, this metaphysics of history is inherently parochial, West-centred and potentially dangerous in that it justifies intervention to raise underdeveloped societies to the allegedly cosmopolitan, but in reality capitalistic and individualistic stage. If non-Western cultures are simply 'late' in the glorious walk towards the ultimate end, as opposed to interested in following other equally legitimate paths, this perspective tends to provide a justification to liberal crusades for the global extension of Western ideals.

In contrast, others philosophers and political theoreticians see the three waves of democratization, the birth of global and regional supranational institutions (the UN and the EU to cite the most important ones), and the global acceptance of the human rights culture (at least at the level of official declarations), as unmistakable confirmations of Kant's teleology. They argue that this view of history is not only empirically confirmed, but also ethically opportune, especially if separated from any crusading, aggressive inclination, and combined with the thought that the universal principles to which Kant refers can be interpreted as moderately soft limits to reasonable moral pluralism. Properly interpreted, they say, history shows that Kant was right in predicting a natural development of our species towards juster and freer institutions, domestically and internationally. And he was equally right in considering all this 'a good thing' according to the universal standards set by pure practical reason.

Fortunately we do not need to take sides in this debate. While one can hardly doubt that Kant's political philosophy, and in particular the meaningfulness of a perpetual peace project, rests on a teleological view of history, it is crucial to determine how much teleology Kant needs, or, in simpler terms, to what precise teleological proposition he is committed. Hence, we need first to understand his theses about historical progress. Secondly, we have to assess whether such theses are a reasonable basis for believing in progress. While the second question is the object of chapter 7, we can start here with the first.

THE KANTIAN MODEL 117

Reduced to the bare essentials, Kant's theses are as follows: (1) The natural dispositions of all natural creatures are destined for a full and complete development. (2 and 3) In human beings, the chief natural feature, that to which all other human dispositions are subordinate, namely reason, is best developed only in society. (4) The means by which nature attends reason's development is human beings' antagonism (unsocial sociability). Human beings have a tendency to associate, but at the same time to compete with one another. To regulate conflict, they are forced to create a state. After some time, the laws protecting individual rights are interiorized and the people enter the moral stage. Society, from a pathological forced union, becomes a moral whole. (5) Only a society in which the maximum of freedom of each is rendered compatible with the freedom of all other members guarantees the full development of reason. Hence the first goal that nature sets for human beings is that of achieving a civil constitution.[7] (6) This goal is extremely difficult to attain and takes a long time. Human nature is in fact a 'warped wood' and those who rule will tend to abuse their power. Since any state needs rulers (one or many makes no difference), and since rulers are human, a state in which no one is violated in his sphere of freedom and rights presupposes not only the right conception of a just constitution, but also long experience and people's good will to accept and defend the constitution. (7) A *perfect* republican constitution, moreover, is possible only if the relation between the republic and other states is regulated by laws, i.e. if all states abandon the lawless condition of the international arena and enter a federation in which each state, even the smallest, can use the force of the law and not that of violence to defend its security and rights. (8) The history of the human species can be viewed as the realization of nature's hidden plan for human beings, namely the establishment of a perfect constitution (domestically and internationally) that alone guarantees the full development of the natural dispositions of humanity (reason). Experience gives us the first few signs of the existence of such a plan for humanity. The egoistic pursuit of states' interests unintentionally leads each state to create the conditions (such as the development of education and culture of the citizens for the sake of state's prestige, or respect for citizens' freedom for the sake of commercial strength) that will inevitably lead to the just domestic and international constitution. (9) It follows that a view of history that attributes to it a pre-established end is possible and serves the purpose of fastening the achievement of that very end.

There is of course a lot to quarrel with in Kant's argument as it is presented. Chapter 7 of this book is devoted to the discussion of the weaknesses and strengths of Kant's argument in *Idea*. For the moment, it suffices to notice that one need not abandon Kant's view of progress because of the now superseded framework of 'natural dispositions' in which it is inserted. We will see that the mechanism of unsocial sociability introduced in proposition 4 is an empirical claim that can be questioned, but that is clearly separable from any reference to natural dispositions. It is no more metaphysical than a prediction of global demographic growth based on empirical knowledge of today's trends. In addition, one should notice that Kant offers some extra empirical considerations in support of his teleology. In commenting on the eighth proposition, he says that 'the mutual relationships between states are already so sophisticated that none of them can neglect its internal culture without losing power and influence in relation to the others' (*IaG*, 8:27). Today, when the prosperity of a country largely depends on the level of education of its citizens, his remark sounds even truer than it could at the end of the eighteenth century. Since a general level of education among citizens is incompatible with dictatorial rule, and promotes economic initiative and freedom in general, we again face a mechanism that leads states (willingly or unwillingly) towards republican institutions. In addition, Kant continues, 'civil freedom can no longer be so easily infringed without disadvantage to all trades and industries, and especially in commerce, in the event of which the state's power in its external relations will also decline' (*IaG*, 8:27–8). Again, in our globalized times, is there a state that can severely limit the liberties of its citizens without diminishing its economic force (Sen 1999) and power in relation to other competitors?[8]

Obviously, even these additional considerations can be questioned. Our point, however, is not that the evidence cited by Kant in support of nature's 'hidden plan' for humankind is beyond dispute. It is rather that Kant appeals to facts and real mechanisms, not merely to dogmatic teleological premises generating a circular argument. Instead of lamenting the dogmatic/metaphysical bases on which Kant's project rests, we should rather devote our intellectual energies to understanding whether the unsocial sociability argument and the other elements of Kant's teleology harmonize with the evolution of international relations from Kant's time to our days. There are at least three more or less uncontested 'signs' that confirm Kant's vision. To begin with, the spectacular diffusion of democratic institutions through different stages from 1945 on. Secondly, the increase of economic freedom even in politically autocratic countries (China is only the most evident example) that is making the whole world economically interdependent (hence potentially more pacific, given Kant's logic). Thirdly, the institution and general success story of regional organizations (EU, AU, ASEAN and so on) that have at least decreased the level of anarchy and unaccountability at the international level. All these are 'signs', inconclusive and insufficient as they are, that confirm Kant's expectations. If someone in Kant's time had been informed of these achievements, he would have had a hard time being a sceptic.

There is another important aspect we need to address before leaving this early work: the role of morality in Kant's teleology. The mechanism of unsocial sociability seems to yield the expected results independently of any moral improvement of citizens. All that is required is that humans are given an understanding that allows them to learn from their mistakes. Many contemporary scholars indeed read Kant's entire theory of peace in this de-moralized fashion. Parallel to a tendency to read Kant's political thought as independent of the truth of his ethical system,[9] an amoral view of the evolution of international relations seems to be particularly attractive because it does without any commitment to the hope of the moral improvement of humanity and the universal validity of moral principles. If humans are supposed to establish peace by following merely their self-interest, there is hope that they will converge towards that goal. If they are supposed to follow moral rules – inherently less attractive than self-interest and subject to profound disagreement among individuals and peoples, then the whole project seems to be utopian.

To endorse such a 'sterilized' view of *Idea* in particular, and of Kant's political thought in general, however, would be a mistake with serious consequences. If we look carefully at the mechanism presented in *Idea*, the juridical condition (domestically and internationally) is to be achieved through an evolution in three steps: from the lawless antagonism of the state of nature (first step), the civil condition arises thanks to individuals' ability to use prudential reason and therefore see their best interest (second step). But once just domestic institutions are in place, the development of true moral dispositions among citizens is expected and, to use Kant's words 'a *pathologically* enforced union is transformed into a *moral* whole' (*IaG*, 8:21). Kant insists on this point when he says that before we can consider ourselves morally mature, 'a long internal process of careful work on the part of each commonwealth is necessary for the education of its citizens' (*IaG*, 8:26). Kant thus assumes that in the civil condition individuals gradually come to a point of refinement of their inclinations. Respect for the sphere of freedom of my neighbours will no longer rest on fear of sanctions, but spontaneously fall from a free endorsement of the demands of pure practical reason. In other words, moral maturity is realized when the rightness of the institutions is internalized and made citizens' second nature.[10]

Although the process is not complete unless a lawful condition is also established at the international level (the main thrust of the seventh thesis), an improvement of individuals is nonetheless crucial for curbing possible aggressive plans by democratic *demoi* against neighbouring countries, especially if sufficiently weak. People's moral progress is thus necessary, among other things, to block a nation's recourse to violence when the cost-benefit calculation would *favour* a bellicose course of action. To leave everything to the general unwillingness of people to bear the costs of war, which amounts to a reduction of Kant's model to the indication of the first definitive article of *To Perpetual Peace*, or to institutional mechanisms in general, makes Kant's project vulnerable to rather obvious historical counter-examples: colonialism, nationalism and the inherent aggressiveness of new states (including new democracies).

It remains to clarify the role of international institutions for moral progress. The gist of the seventh proposition is that without the establishment of a 'law-governed *external relationship*' between states, no domestic 'perfect civil condition' can be achieved. Although Kant does not explain what a *perfect* civil condition is, the most likely candidate is a republic that rules over citizens who have internalized the rightness of the principles on which it rests. Now, as stressed by Bobbio (2005), it is difficult for a state (and for a people) to be fully loyal to its liberal democratic or republican principles if surrounded by neighbours whose foreign policy is unrestrained by common membership of intergovernmental organizations (IGOs). The unlawful condition caused by the absence of international institutions, in other words, would have negative effects even for the morality of peoples. As Kant puts it,

> But as long as states apply their resources to their vain and violent schemes of expansion, thus incessantly obstructing the slow and laborious efforts of their citizens to cultivate their minds, and even depriving them of all support in these efforts, no progress in this direction [moral maturity] can be expected. (*IaG*, 8:26)

To sum up: the rightness of domestic and international institutions and the morality of individuals are mutually reinforcing factors. If the process starts with the reform of institutions (sheer self-interest leads to the creation of the national commonwealth, which in turn fosters people's morality), the moral refinement of peoples seems to be necessary for fully just behaviour on the part of states in the international arena. Conversely, while the rightness of international institutions is a necessary ingredient of individuals' morality (the *perfect* civil constitution), the increased morality of citizens is necessary to enable the spontaneous limitation of domestic sovereignty in favour of the federation. Morality is what renders the deal acceptable even if on some specific occasions the rules of membership run contrary to domestic interests.

We are now in a position to grasp Kant's view of the whole process leading to perpetual peace and to break it down in successive steps. For clarity we can summarize it in six stages of historical development:

1. Worldwide state of nature.
2. Despotic civil condition at the domestic level (no republic, only despotic regimes) and no international institutions. For Kant a despotic regime, in which the rule of law is enforced, is better than the state of nature.
3. Mixed domestic condition, i.e. some republics, some despotic regimes, and no international institutions. The move from a despotic regime to a republic is either achieved through revolution (illegal but irreversible) or through the sovereign's free adoption of a liberal constitution. Institutional improvement is encouraged by philosophers who can counsel rulers if they

remain free to express their view (the 'freedom of the pen'). Once a republic is established, the process of moral improvement of its citizens begins. Republican citizens internalize the rightness of their institutions and, possibly, citizens of neighbouring countries living under despotic regimes will admire republican achievements, thus exercising pressure on their own rulers to concede a republican constitution. This is more or less the stage of the world in Kant's time.

4. Mixed domestic condition and some international institutions.[11] International institutions are created out of states' perception of their best interest. After repeated experiences of war atrocities, states learn that war is rarely beneficial and thus renounce some of their sovereignty to enter international institutions. Moreover, the moral improvement of citizens, begun in the preceding step, encourages the establishment of international governmental organizations. By curbing excessive nationalism and aggressive ideologies, it favours a reasoned extension at the international level of the principles of non-aggression and arbitration that citizens have experienced in their interpersonal relations. The process of moral improvement of republican citizens is in turn reinforced by the presence of international institutions. Republics tend towards the *perfect* civil constitution. I believe that Kant would consider the world in which we currently live as having achieved this stage of evolution.

5. All republics and international institutions. Thanks to the combined influence of the republics' example, the approval of domestic intellectuals, the moral improvements of citizens and the security offered by international institutions, despotism is globally overcome.

6. Once the institutional and moral improvement of citizens and institutions is completed, the cosmopolitan constitution is finally achieved.

3. *On the Common Saying* (1793): The Role of Moral Progress

Almost ten years after his first attempt, Kant returned to the same problem that motivated *Idea*: how can one prove that perpetual peace is not merely a dream? This time the question is framed in a larger project aiming to show how the unconditional demands of morality are compatible with the reality and concreteness of human affairs in three main areas: the common life of individuals, the domestic policy of a state, and international relations. Obviously, it is the last case that mainly interests us. There Kant reiterates his thesis that a 'juridification' of international relations, far from being the hope of well-meaning minds, is something that can and ought to be pursued. While Garve and Hobbes were the main targets of the first two parts of the essay, this time Kant's opponent is Moses Mendelssohn, a philosopher widely admired in Germany and well respected by Kant himself. Mendelssohn believed, like many postmodern thinkers today, that the human race has never made any *moral* progress. While it temporarily takes a few steps forward, it soon reverts to its initial degree of brutality. Hence the morality of the human race as a whole, quite apart from individual achievements, constantly 'fluctuates between fixed limits'. No stable and real progress is ever made. Interestingly, Mendelssohn does not merely express a pessimistic attitude. His critique of the Enlightenment strikes an epistemological chord when he charges with intellectual arrogance those who 'presume to guess the plan of providence for mankind'. This is more or less what Kant had tried to do in *Idea*.[12]

Kant's reply is articulated in a long and complex argument that culminates with the reiteration of the tenet, already present in the 1784 essay, that 'the distress produced by the constant wars in which the states try to subjugate or engulf each other must finally lead them, even against their will, to enter into a *cosmopolitan* constitution' (*TP*, 8:310). The first thing to notice is that the argument of *Idea* based on nature's interest in the development of our 'natural dispositions' is completely abandoned. This does not mean that Kant's view of history is now free from any appeal to old-fashioned metaphysics. For example, Kant criticizes Mendelssohn because his view of history 'cannot be reconciled with the morality of a wise creator' (*TP*, 8:308). This appeal to God, however, is just a quick reference, probably meant to spot a possible contradiction in Mendelssohn's thought rather than a considered judgement.[13] In fact Kant soon afterwards lists more serious reasons for assuming, as he does, that humanity is progressing not only culturally but also morally.

To begin with, he makes his usual point that a denial of moral progress amounts to a violation of our 'inborn duty of influencing posterity in such a way that it will make constant progress (and I must assume that progress is possible)'. Unfortunately, although better than a dogmatic appeal to God's morality, the 'ought implies is' argument here hardly improves the situation. In fact, Kant is addressing those who are sceptical regarding the meaningfulness of obeying such a duty. If one doubts that peace is ever attainable, it will not help to reiterate the idea that 'thinking positively' is a moral duty. Similarly, scepticism about humanity's moral progress will not be lessened by an appeal to our inborn duty to influence posterity towards that progress.

At last, Kant bites the bullet and makes four interesting points that should be seen as a single, complex argument: (a) the failure of previous attempts to establish perpetual peace does not prove that the purpose is inherently unattainable any more than unsuccessful attempts to fly by means of lighter-than-air balloons proved that these devices were ill conceived; (b) the human race in our age has made considerable moral progress compared to previous ages[14]; (c) the continuous outcry against human cruelty just proves that our moral sensibility has refined, not that the amount of evil perpetrated has increased, in the same way in which the higher number of family abuse reports today proves that women's trust in the public authority has increased, not that abuse is more frequent; (d) most importantly, the approach of the desired end (perpetual peace) does not depend on what we, as individuals, do; rather, it depends on a larger natural mechanism that forces individuals, independently of their disposition, towards that end; humans are forced to learn from the past atrocities of wars. In the same way in which nature led even a group of devils (provided they have understanding) from the state of nature to the civil condition, so will nature also lead a group of ill-motivated states to the cosmopolitan constitution.[15]

Kant reiterates the first and the last point at the end of the essay. To begin with, he introduces the famous metaphor of humans as 'earthly gods' to stress that our transcendental freedom renders any event compatible with natural laws possible for us, and therefore also the attainment of perpetual peace. Furthermore, as a 'subsidiary' argument, he relies on the 'very nature of things' that will force humans to do what practical reason commands. Hence if they are not able to follow the moral law, nature will step in to provide that 'push' lacking in their will (*fata volentem ducunt, nolentem trahunt*).

Evidently, the bulk of the argument steers away from any commitment to a thick metaphysics of history and boils down to the consideration that enlightened self-interest will prevail as a determining factor in international relations and lead states (especially republics) to abandon the lawless condition of their mutual relations. The argument is very abstract, but certainly radically different from an appeal to what agrees with the grace of a creator. As a matter of fact, Kant is offering a prediction based on factual truths (impossibility for each commonwealth to impose its rule on all others, humans' ability to see, sooner or later, what is in their best interest, cautiousness of common people in deciding to enter a war) that are neither metaphysical nor dogmatic. The whole argument is evidently *fallible*, to use Popper's mark of non-metaphysical theories. In fact it is highly contested. Realists have often stressed that enlightened self-interest leads states (especially those particularly strong), not to enter a paralysing federation, but to become hegemonic global forces. For a realist, states' best policy remains that of increasing their power vis-à-vis other countries, and possibly to establish global leadership.

An adequate answer to this realist objection is in this context impossible. In any case, we are not obliged to venture one. For our purposes, it is sufficient to highlight how the Kantian teleology rests on a controversial, yet perfectly legitimate (by our and Kant's own epistemological standards) assessment of the conditions necessary for the flourishing of each country, combined with a belief in people's ability to realize what those conditions are and act accordingly.[16] The plausibility of the duty to strive for the establishment of perpetual peace requires nothing more than that. A proof that perpetual peace is not incompatible with what we know about human affairs – a proof that it is a 'real possibility', to use Kant's technical language – is enough to create for us an obligation to do everything in our power to establish such a condition. This is what interests Kant most. His target, here as well as in *To Perpetual Peace*, is mainly those sceptics who deny the very meaningfulness of any effort to establish a lawful international order, either because they are authentically pessimistic, or – more often – because they have an interest in the persistence of the status quo.

The Kantian story of how humanity will reach the juridical condition, however, does not stop here. At the very end of the essay, Kant makes a passing reference to the significance of human moral progress. We saw that, already in *Idea*, Kant mentions the 'moral progress of our age' as one of the reasons that makes the project of perpetual peace at the same time concrete and worth pursuing. With a certain emphasis, Kant now comes back to the same problem by saying that the mechanism that forces us to do what practical reason commands 'involves human nature, which is still animated by respect for right and duty'. And he adds: 'I therefore cannot and will not see it [human nature] as so deeply immersed in evil that practical moral reason will not triumph in the end.' Kant relies again on something more that an impersonal natural mechanism based on humans' prudential reasoning and ability to learn from the past. Quite evidently, he relies also on humans' *moral* progress. An international community made of true devils, to return to Kant's famous metaphor, will hardly yield the desired result because, unlike individuals, states are not characterized by roughly the same power and strength. Hence, it is very possible that self-interest will prompt powerful states to keep their full sovereignty and ignore the obligation to enter the federation. Morality is supposed to provide the reasons in favour of the federation that some national players will not find in enlightened self-interest. Moreover, as we have already noticed in *Idea*, morality has a role to play even for those states that would be favoured by the existence of the federation. It removes any obstacle that may come from excessive national pride or attachment to the autonomy of a national community. In this case, it forces into appropriate limits the otherwise legitimate aspiration of states to self-determination. From this perspective, the idea of an impersonal historical development, where radically bad humans are forced to abandon immoral tendencies because they recognize their best interest, amounts to a gross oversimplification of Kant's vision. As we said in commenting on *Idea*, what captures Kant's intuitions better is a two-level form of progress, or if you prefer, the model of a virtuous circle between institutional and personal (moral) improvement. The justice of institutions gradually permeates individuals' souls, and they in turn adhere more authentically and steadily to the principles on which their government is based, thereby generating further institutional progress.

A final point is in order. Already in *Idea* Kant was very keen to emphasize that the process ultimately leading to perpetual peace was extremely slow. He reiterates this thesis in this essay by talking about an 'immeasurably long undertaking' (*TP*, 8:310). This emphasis on the remote distance of the cosmopolitan condition may appear as Kant's way to make his theory immune to criticism. If the end point of progress is to be reached in a non-linear way and at an indefinitely remote point in the future, then no empirical event that runs contrary to the theory's prediction (e.g. increase of international insecurity, in military expenditure, collapse of IGOs will ever be sufficient as a refutation. Hence, the hope of reaching perpetual peace, so the criticism continues, is no different from hope in the afterlife.

While this risk is inevitable in any non-linear progressive teleology, we have already seen that Kant's emphasis on how slow and gradual the process is should be understood as a provision of prudence and as a discouragement to moral fanatics, rather than as a preventive move against possible counter-examples. Moreover, few would deny that since Kant's time we have made any progress towards the cosmopolitan condition. The 'signs' needed to believe that history is evolving in the direction foreseen by Kant are evident enough. Massive democratization, unprecedented expansion of zones of security, diffusion of the culture of human rights, creation of regional international institutions with a success story in increasing security – not only the EU, but also largely non-democratic and mixed federations such as the League of Arab States (Hossouna 1975) and ASEAN (Pennisi 2012), just to give two examples. Even if the past century has brought an increase of violence through the two world wars, and the recent phenomenon of terrorism produces a general feeling of uncertainty, one can hardly deny that citizens who live in liberal democracies are now more secure than the citizens of European states in Kant's time. Finally, recent misappropriations of Kant's ideal, like the infamous slogan 'Fight them, beat them and make them democratic' advocated by neoconservatives, suggest the care with which one should handle the model. Kant's insistence on the slowness of the progress was meant to stop similar degenerations that, as we saw, had started already in the aftermath the French Revolution and of which Kant was well aware.

4. *To Perpetual Peace* (1795): the Completion of Kant's Project

Only a few months after the peace treaty between France and Prussia in April 1795, Kant has a manuscript called *Zum Ewigen*

Frieden. Ein Philosophischen Entwurf ready to offer to the publisher Nicolovius. The publication of the essay was probably the greatest literary success Kant had in his life. One year after the publication, there were already three translations into French.[17] Shortly thereafter an English translation appeared, and around the end of the century the essay was at the centre of the intellectual debate, at least in France and in Germany. By the time Kant died (nine years after the book's appearance), his 'philosophical project' had reached its tenth edition. After that, its popularity started to decline. The cosmopolitan orientation of the essay meant as an antidote to the excesses of nationalism, its progressive view of history, as well as its a-historical, abstract, universal definition of the just state, would displease the taste of a increasingly Romantic intellectual milieu.[18] After various ups and downs of fortune, with 'returns to Kant' especially in the aftermath of the two world wars, the birth of democratic peace theory in the early 1980s, the fall of the Berlin Wall, with the subsequent third wave of democratization, and the occasion of the 200th anniversary of its publication gave Kant's essay a new *élan*. Today, one can hardly dispute that Kant's project (or better a mainstream interpretation of it that we are about to challenge) is part of the background knowledge not only of philosophers, but also of international relations scholars, historians, political scientists and, most importantly, political leaders of contemporary liberal democracies.

Kant articulates his project according to the structure typical of the international treaties of his time. We thus have six preliminary articles, three definitive articles, two supplements, two appendices. The definitive articles are the centre of the entire work. Here Kant provides his 'philosophical project' in favour of peace. Albeit peripheral, the other parts are nonetheless crucial for a proper understanding of the definitive articles themselves. It is therefore necessary to offer a detailed analysis of these parts, starting with the preliminary articles.

The preliminary articles are guidelines for good conduct that rulers should follow before the conditions spelled out in the definitive articles are fully realized. They are *preliminary* in this sense: their role is to make the transition to the world envisaged by the three definitive articles as easy as possible, or perhaps, more modestly, to guarantee that, while waiting for the realization of the three definitive articles, the situation does not reach a point of no return. As such, they recall the tradition of natural law, strongly interested in introducing some elements of lawfulness into the otherwise lawless context *par excellence*, i.e. war (*inter arma enim silent leges*). As we saw, Kant considered these attempts to make war less atrocious the work of 'sorry comforters'. In fact, one may legitimately wonder whether the preliminary articles are meant to do anything different from what Kant had bitterly stigmatized about the work of Grotius, Pufendorf and Vattel. After all, they are nothing but counsels, left to the good will of rulers, aimed at making war less likely or burdensome. However, while for these authors the mild regulation of an otherwise lawless reality was the end point of the project, for Kant it is nothing but a preparatory stage, very much as an anaesthesic is merely the preparation for surgery aiming at the eradication of an illness. To continue with the metaphor, there is nothing wrong in relieving a patient from immediate, acute suffering by using painkillers, thereby making her better able to endure the necessary treatment. But limiting one's therapeutical strategy to palliatives is at best ineffective and at worst counterproductive in that it delays the identification – let alone the solution – of the problem.

Against this background, we are in a position to analyse the six preliminary articles. They read:

1. No conclusion of peace shall be considered valid as such if it was made with a secret reservation of the material for a future war (*ZeF*, 8:343).
2. No independent existing state, whether it be large or small, may be acquired by another state by inheritance, exchange, purchase or gift (*ZeF*, 8:344).
3. Standing armies (*miles perpetuus*) will gradually be abolished altogether (*ZeF*, 8:345).
4. No national debts shall be contracted in connection with the external affairs of the state (*ZeF*, 8:345).
5. No state shall forcibly interfere in the constitution and government of another state (*ZeF*, 8:346).
6. No state at war with another shall permit such acts of hostility as would make mutual confidence impossible during a future time of peace. Such acts would include the employment of *assassins* (*percussores*) *or poisoners* (*venifici*), *breach of agreements, the instigation of treason* (*perduellio*) within the enemy state, etc. (*ZeF*, 8:346).

Particularly intriguing among these normative suggestions is the prohibition of standing armies. By that Kant means professional forces (either composed of citizens or foreign mercenaries), contrasting them with a system of conscription by which all citizens are trained to be capable of defending their country. Kant's preoccupation is that the existence of professional forces tends to generate a race among states to have the strongest army, which could have the perverse effect of making a 'short war' aimed at reducing the military strength of a competing state or preventing its increase less costly than a proportional enlargement of one's own army. Today we know that professional armies have a further complication in the creation and expansion of a war economy that risks defusing the peace potential of the first definitive article. Republican citizens may find a war advantageous if they have hired professionals to do the fighting. In the presence of professional armies, much of the interest-based aversion to war democratic citizens are expected to have necessarily vanishes and all hopes have to be placed in a sufficiently strong deontological repugnance on the part of citizens and leaders. Moreover, the powerful lobbies interested in the material advantages of war have already shown that they can defuse the logic of the first definitive article by exploiting citizens' confidence that the fighting will not touch them or their nearest and dearest. The case of the 2003 Iraq war is most instructive in this perspective.

Let us also pause on the fifth preliminary article, because it helps to complete the picture of Kant's 'recipe' that one could hardly obtain by looking merely at the definitive articles. Given two states, A and B, the fifth article forbids A's interference in B's internal affairs, even if B looks 'scandalous' to A, i.e. if the injustice perpetrated in B by the rulers arouses feelings of solidarity for the victims among the citizens of A. Kant here condemns any sort of crusade led by 'virtuous' states (the 'republican' or 'liberal-democratic' ones) against despotic regimes. To be sure, Kant expresses appreciation of the violent overthrow of despotic regimes (like the one carried out by revolutionary France). The fifth article, however, clarifies that such a transformation must not be planned or considered as a point in the political agenda of powerful republican states. Only from the perspective of impersonal spectators can we rejoice in the removal of a dictatorship and the rising of a new 'republic', which is, in fact, precisely what Kant does and what we do when we see dictators on the run around the world. This sympathetic reaction, however, must never be turned into an authorization *ex ante* for a military campaign to bring the world closer to republican standards. This would turn Kant's project into the crusade model that certain realist authors (and self-interested politicians) have construed and attempted to pass as inspired by Kant (Caranti 2006b).

The accusation of encouraging a 'perpetual war for perpetual peace' was famously raised by Kenneth Waltz (Waltz 1959). For Waltz the imposition of a universal model of justice (the republican model) creates the basis for a dangerous mentality in democratic leaders. In their relations with autocracies they do not see merely a *different* entity but an *evil* one. This very assumption transforms any possible dispute – often a mere conflict of interests – into a fight between Good and Evil, usually crueller and more difficult to stop than a 'normal' war. Moreover Kant's theory can even become the *cause* of the dispute if the democratic leader finds in the alleged propensity to peace of democracy a justification for waging war against autocracies. Outside the realist camp, Archibugi (Archibugi and Beetham, 1998) raises two similar points when he argues that from Kant's theory it is tempting to infer two dangerous corollaries. One is the democratic pre-emptive temptation just mentioned. The other is the idea that there is only one just constitutional pattern, and only one way of transforming that ideal into concrete institutions. Experience teaches us, however, that democracy comes in many different forms, some possibly somewhat distant from the way in which the 'republican' ideal has been realized in North America or Europe.

In response to these criticisms, one should first concede that Kant *does* hold fast to only one model of justice. In his mind, there is no cultural difference that can justify discrimination between citizens before the law or, to use our terminology, gross and systematic violations of human rights. It is thus true that Kant shows a very low degree of flexibility about that. It is also true, however, that, save for some republican essentials, many different constitutional models seem to satisfy Kant's definition of the juridical condition. As we shall see later, an oligarchy or a monarchy may be acceptable provided that the way in which power is administered (*forma regiminis*) is republican, namely that powers are separated and that those in power rule by making a serious effort to interpret the 'general will'. Clearly, many different sorts of traditions, cultures and political commitments are compatible with Kant's constitutional essentials (although, obviously, not all). While Kant's rigidity on these minimal requirements appears to many as a virtue of his theory – a sort of bastion against the distortion of relativism – Archibugi and Waltz see it as his original sin. Their defence of cultural differences and traditions, however, risks becoming a fashionable yet ultimately empty position, dangerously similar to the 'anything goes' option.

Turning to the 'crusade' charge, the fifth preliminary article of *To Perpetual Peace* explicitly condemns these enterprises. Kant there says that, as a general rule, the 'lawlessness' of a state does not justify any interference from other states. One could still criticize Kant on the basis that an endorsement of a democratic crusade is demanded by the *logic* of his theory, regardless of his actual intent. But even this modified criticism is not well grounded. As we shall see in detail in our discussion of the 'guarantee' of perpetual peace, the progress envisaged by Kant is more similar to some sort of impersonal unfolding than to a well-planned extirpation of autocracies by virtuous states. From this perspective, it is quite clear how Kant can consistently hold that the republican form is unconditionally the *sole* just *forma regiminis* while at the same time condemning any form of imposition of it, either by internal rebellion or, even worse, by intervention of external forces. Also – even if this is more difficult to accept – he can consistently condemn violence (internal or external) for the sake of justice *ex ante* but rejoice *post facto* when a dictator is removed violently, i.e. after violence has actually occurred.

Finally, one should keep in mind that Kant assigns to individuals as well as to peoples a worth ultimately coming from their ability for self-determination. This explains why he thinks that a people must be the author of the transition towards a juridical condition. Leaving aside the by now largely proved impracticability of forced processes of democratization (Russett 2005), a crusade would undermine the autonomy of the people and would be inspired (in the most optimistic scenario) by paternalism – a moral stance that Kant notoriously looked on unfavourably. Even noble interests, such as a commitment to the removal of injustice caused by detestable rulers, could not be tolerated within the broadly antiutilitarian approach to ethics and politics Kant held. For him, the violation of the autonomy of a people could never be compensated for by an increase in the overall justice of the world system.[19]

Let us move now to the definitive articles where interpretative problems are far more challenging than what is required to dispose of the caricatured interpretations of Kant's project we encountered so far.

4.1 The First Definitive Article

The first definitive article contains the prescription for each and every state to become 'republican'. It reads: 'The Civil Constitution of Every State shall be Republican.' Three main features characterize a republican constitution: *freedom* of each member of the society; *dependence* of everyone upon a single and unified legislation; and legal *equality* for everyone, that is, non-discrimination before the law. Two additional requirements are: (a) rulers must legislate by interpreting the general will; (b) there must be a sharp distinction of powers; in particular, the legislative is to be well separated from the executive (*ZeF*, 8:352). These constitutional features are thought to be relevant to the cause of peace because only in a republic can people influence the decision on whether the state should enter a war. Since citizens would suffer from the atrocities of a violent conflict, there is reason to believe that they 'will have great hesitation in embarking on so dangerous an enterprise' (*ZeF*, 8:351). The opposite is the case for a despotic regime. The despot here is not a fellow citizen, but the owner of the state. As such, he can wage war with great ease, because 'a war will not force him to make the slightest sacrifice so far as his banquets, hunts, pleasure palaces, and court festivals are concerned' (*ZeF*, 8:351).[20] The despot, Kant goes on, can thus 'decide on war, without any significant reason, as a kind of amusement, and unconcernedly leave it to the diplomatic corps (who are always ready for such purposes) to justify the war for the sake of propriety' (*ZeF*, 8:351).

Some points in this apparently linear argument need to be clarified. First of all, Kant does not say that it is *impossible* that citizens will choose to embark on a bellicose adventure. He merely says that it is *unlikely*.[21] The first article leaves open the possibility that democratic citizens, after due reflection, find the costs of war worthwhile. Security, greed, national pride or some combination of these factors can outweigh the cost a people is expected to pay.

This leads to the second point: the logic Kant is using in this context is merely utilitarian. As far as the first article is concerned, the republican people can be as attracted by violence (and by the gains one can attain through it) as any other kind of people (or despot). At this stage of the argument Kant has still attributed to democratic peoples no deontological opposition to war. Kant's point can thus be reduced to this: as long as there is an owner of the state, there will not be a careful cost-benefit calculus that at least forestalls 'inefficient' wars. But the first article leaves room for wars in the interest of republican peoples. After all, as history has abundantly shown, and supporters of DPT have finally come to admit, sometimes a republican or democratic people (or a large majority thereof) strongly desire war.[22]

A closely related point completes what we said about the second preliminary article. If the army of a republic is professional, let alone mainly made of private contractors, the cost/benefit calculation will more easily favour war than in the case in which the army is based on conscription. Instead of considering whether I or my nearest and dearest will risk their lives on the battlefield, we, as republican citizens, are asked to make a considerably easier calculation of whether the costs of this semi- or fully private army is a good investment, all things considered.

The points we have made all lead to the conclusion that a republican government is by itself no assurance of peace. Since Kant meant to provide a recipe that would guarantee the elimination of war (not just its becoming less likely), it follows that he did not intend his first article to be sufficient. In other words, contrary to what one often reads in contemporary international relations theory, Kant did *not* believe that the problem of war could be reduced to a question of the right domestic institutions.[23] In fact, the first definitive article, without the other two, does not guarantee *anything*, not even the elimination of conflicts between republics. That Kant's project presupposes the convergence of many peace-inducing factors, of which only one is the internal republican constitution, is a point as trivial as it is forgotten.[24]

One less trivial point also usually overlooked is that Kant's confidence in the pacific tendency of republics is to be read without passing in silence over his general distrust of democracy, a distrust that should make readers a bit more careful than they usually are in identifying the Kantian republic and what we now call a liberal democracy. Immediately after expounding the general thesis of the first article Kant adds few remarks 'to prevent the republican constitution from being confused with the democratic one, as commonly happens' (*ZeF*, 8:351–2). Following Aristotle, Kant claims that the various forms of state can be classified by using two very different criteria: either by taking into account how many rule (the *forma imperii*), which gives us the usual tripartition in monarchy (that Kant calls here 'autarchy'), oligarchy, and democracy; or they can be classified by considering the way in which the sovereign power is exercised (the *forma regiminis*), independently of how many exercise it.[25] The last criterion is the more important, but unfortunately, also the more difficult to interpret. Kant says that the *forma regiminis* 'relates to the way – as defined by the constitution (that is, an act of the general will whereby the mass becomes a people) – in which the state makes use of its plenary power' (*ZeF*, 8:352). And there are only two ways in which a state can make use of its power, the republican and the despotic. A state is republican if, as we saw, the executive power is separated from the legislative. It is despotic if this separation does not occur and 'the laws are made and arbitrarily executed by one and the same power' (*ZeF*, 8:352).

Kant here emphasizes the necessity of a separation between two powers, the legislative and the executive, and does not mention the judicial power. This has, however, little significance because in the *Metaphysics of Morals* he follows Montesquieu more closely in distinguishing between the '*ruling power* (or sovereignty) in the person of the legislator, the *executive power* (in the person of the individual who governs in accordance with the law), and the *judicial power* (which allots to everyone what is his by law) in the person of the judge (*potestas legislatoria, rectoria et judiciaria*)' (*MS*, 6:313). More interestingly, for Kant 'the legislative power can belong only to the united will of the people' and 'the laws it gives must absolutely incapable of doing anyone injustice' (*MS*, 6:313). This repetition, almost word for word, of Rousseau's notion of *volonté générale* suggests that by legislative power Kant means first and foremost the constitution which binds us together and that is in principle unanimously accepted by all citizens. Derivatively, however, the legislative power also encompasses all laws that should reflect what the general will would say in specific circumstances. A republic is thus a system in which no parliamentary majority, merely by virtue of being a majority, can enact partisan laws that are discriminatory against some citizens. If that happens, there is no guarantee that the laws are 'absolutely *incapable* of doing anyone injustice' and the pre-political entitlements of human beings (their external freedom) are in danger. Some citizens (those who rule or those represented by the rulers) may be doing an injustice to those who are not in power and the supreme power no longer mirrors the general will.

The requirement that legislative power is to represent the general will is crucial to understanding why, for Kant, democracy, at least 'in the truest form of the word', is necessarily a despotism, why the notion of a republican monarchy (or oligarchy) is not a contradiction, and why Kant can keep his faith in the peace potential of representative government, that is, the empowered people, while distrusting democracy. The key point is that any executive power must remember, when it makes decisions necessarily affecting the citizens, that it is obliged to interpret the general will as best as it can. This 'burden of representation', we might call it, weighs in the same way on one, some or all who are called to exercise power. A king can act 'in the spirit of a representative system' doing its best to interpret the general law in its rule. Kant makes this point clearly in the *Contest of the Faculties* when he claims that there could be monarchies in which the king is 'acting by analogy with the laws which a people would give itself in conformity with universal principles of right' (*CF*:184). Of course, this would still be a 'defective system' because, unlike the case of an elected president, it is left to the good will of the king to be sincere and effective in this interpretation. *Mutadis mutandis*, the same can be said of an oligarchy.

But why does Kant say that the same does not apply to democracy, at least to democracy 'in the truest sense of the word'? Kant's explanation is that democracy

> establishes an executive power through which all the citizens may make decisions about (and indeed against) the single individual without his consent, so that decisions are made by all the people and yet not by all the people: and this means that the general will is in contradiction with itself, and thus also with freedom. (*ZeF*, 8:352)

A few lines later Kant adds that a democratic system makes impossible the proclaimed attitude of Frederick II, who claimed to be the 'servant of the state' – an emphatic way of saying that the executive power represents the general will. This is so 'because everyone under it wants to be a ruler'. Democracy in the truest sense of the word is for Kant a system in which everyone is asked to represent his or her own interests only. This creates an attitude incompatible with the feature that should characterize the act of ruling, namely representing. While in a democracy I represent my will or that of my group, or even that of all citizens, if they happen to agree (*la volonté de tous*), the only thing that a republican ruler should try to represent is the general will.[26]

We are now in a position to see the reason for Kant's distrust. While in the case of a monarchy or an oligarchy one can at least hope that the legislative power in its decrees is led by a sincere attempt to interpret the general will, in the case of a democracy, so understood at least, such hope would be impossible. Citizens are *expected* to represent themselves only. Moreover, they do not even need to justify their decisions as arising from attention to the common good, in the way a king or an oligarchy must do, because citizens are the ultimate source of power. By mistaking the will of all for the general will, or even more grossly the will of the majority of them as the general will, they think that anything they choose is right and respectful of the rights of each individual. The unchecked power of a self-determining multitude opens up the possibility that the inborn and natural rights of some citizens will be compressed, if not denied altogether. The more people are in power, the less likely it is they will remember the burden of representation – a burden that no political power, not even that 'of the people by the people' can escape.

Notice how this democratic 'perversion' – by the light of Kant's argument – is inevitable in the case of a direct democracy. In a direct democracy each citizen is literally speaking for herself alone. This is where Kant departs from Rousseau most clearly. But although Kant is not explicit about it, one can reasonably infer that the same attitude can very well infect citizens who are called to elect their representatives. This is certainly the case if the power of the majority is not checked by a constitutional law that secures everyone's freedom over and above decisions of the majority. If this were the case, then again 'all decide for or even against one who does not agree; that is, "all", who are not quite all, decide, and this is a contradiction of the general will with itself and with freedom.' But, less obviously, the same holds also in the case in which a majority acts within constitutional limits but in a strongly partisan way. A constitutionally scrupulous legislative power may very well enact laws that protect the interests of some instead of all. Hence there are reasons to believe that the sheer presence of constitutional limits would not be sufficient to satisfy the high standards Kant imposes on his republic. A polity in which everyone elects representatives having only his own interest in mind seems to be as perverted and despotic as a direct democracy. The voter in this system is not called to represent anyone or anything but herself and her interest. It does not matter if she recognizes the fundamental rights of other people. It still is the case that in this regime the legislative is not thought of as bound to 'represent' the general good but only the good of a faction.

This should help us to see why Kant is so suspicious of democracy, but it should also help us to conceive a form of democratic regime that does not run the risks Kant foresees. If the supreme law and the spirit of republicanism have shaped the minds of the citizens in such a way that they elect representatives with a clear mandate to issue laws not only formally consistent with the constitution but also capable of furthering the principles there expressed; if, in other words, the 'burden of representation' is accepted by electors and elected, then there is no reason why a democracy could not be republican. Actually, if care for the general good is embedded in the polity, democracy has a clear advantage over the other two *formae imperii*. As Kant says, they 'are always defective' because the executive power is exercised by one or few who by definition cannot represent all. Especially if they are not elected, let alone if unchecked by constitutional limits, one can at most hope that they freely choose to exercise their power in the right way. By contrast, in a republican democracy citizens vote and influence the political power and make sure that rulers further the general good and accept the burden of representation.

Of course even in a monarchy it is possible that the monarch truly 'represents' the people. This is why we can have, without contradiction, a republican monarchy. A king or an elected president, as well as a republican oligarchy, can exercise power by making his best effort to interpret the general will. In the end, it does not matter how many people are in power. What matters is (1) that they are clearly distinguished from those who interpret the constitutional laws and check the conformity of general laws to them (the judiciary); (2) that they exercise power and issue ordinary laws or governmental decrees in the right manner, that is, by having constantly in mind that the art of good ruling presupposes the subordination of special interests to the dictates of the general will. Only on this condition will the Rousseauian/Kantian criterion of legitimacy be satisfied and no one will be in a position to say that political power is exercised against his will.

What we have said should suffice to convince readers that the Kantian republic is an ideal-type that cannot be satisfied by the mere presence of elections and constitutional guarantees. The Kantian republic is an ideal that each concrete republic should always strive towards. If a polity is so divided that the promises of its republican constitution are constantly betrayed by the spirit (if not by the letter) of ordinary laws, or if a polity is so divided that the general good is rarely taken as the supreme guidance of legislators, then ballots and supreme courts will not suffice. And what looks like a republic is actually a despotic regime or will be rapidly deteriorate into one. This opens up a series of considerations to keep in mind for the comparison – offered in chapter 6 – between Kant's model and DPT. Let us list them in descending order of importance.

1. Liberalism and republicanism are not the same thing; elections and constitutional limits are not enough for the standards of a republic. A republic, over and above being a liberal democracy, includes at least: (a) active participation of the citizens; (b) a legislative power that acts in the spirit (not just by the letter) of the constitution; (c) an informed electorate that does not merely select leaders having in mind their private interest; (d) citizens socialized within just institution long enough to have internalized the republican ethos and capable of reacting to any infringement of their fundamental freedoms.[27]
2. A republic is not merely a set of institutions. It includes a shared public ethos to be reached through a long process of education of citizens.[28] This shared public ethos determines internal political preferences, but also, and most relevantly, choices in foreign policy, by rejecting war even to the possible detriment of national interest, and independently of whether the state faces other democracies or autocracies. No perfect republic is

possible if relations with other states are not brought under common laws.[29]
3. The republican state is an ideal that is to be continuously striven towards. No existing state can be said to have reached the ideal, nor is a state secured once and for all in the progress made towards that ideal.
4. A republican government does not merely respond to the majority of the electors, but is judged by the conformity of its decisions to the best interpretation of constitutional values.
5. The notion of representative government includes more than a mechanism that ensures the transmission of preferences from citizens to rulers. It presupposes an authentic interpretative effort to apply republican principles to all particular circumstances.

An obvious retort to this rich interpretation of the Kantian republic would point to Kant's famous disenfranchisement of various sectors of the population, in particular dependent workers and women. Kant notoriously claims that these citizens should not be given the right to vote (let alone be elected). If a substantial part of the population is excluded from the right to contribute to form (or interpret) the general will, are we not really in the condition Kant feared about democracy, where some citizens 'decide for or even against one who does not agree'? If what we called the burden of representation is not equally shared by all citizens, what guarantee do we have that the legislative power mirrors the *volonté générale*, as opposed to the will of some faction in society?

The key point against this too obvious retort is again the notion of representation. On our reading, being a citizen in a Kantian republic entails the ability to distance oneself from one's own interests and, a fortiori, presupposes a considerable amount of freedom from direct or indirect pressures and conditionings coming from other individuals. The Kantian citizen is a free, deliberative, autonomous citizen who accepts the burden of representation and upholds policies that are genuinely in the interest of the general good or, which is the same, that have a real chance of expressing the 'general will'. From this perspective, if some citizens are de facto dependent on others for their subsistence and thus do not enjoy that required amount of autonomy, they are not given the right to vote, not because they are less worthy than 'active citizens', but simply because their condition of dependence makes them vulnerable to conditionings and influences by those from whom they 'receive orders or protection' (*MS*, 6:313). In a state in which votes can be 'controlled' or 'exchanged' in such a manner, and the powerful can dispose of a number of votes proportional to the number of dependants, laws can hardly be said to reflect the general will.

After all, Kant is quite explicit as to the reason for excluding 'apprentices', 'servants', 'minors (*naturaliter vel civiliter*)', and 'women' from the right to vote (*MS*, 6:314). What makes them 'passive citizens' is that they all 'are obliged to depend for their living (that is, food and protection) on the offices of others (excluding the state)' (*MS*, 6:314). In such conditions of dependence, there is no hope that they can live up to the high standards of deliberating capacity that Kant requires of republican citizens. As Kant puts it succinctly, 'they have to receive orders or protection from other individuals, so that they do not possess civil independence' (*MS*, 6:315). Kant's exclusion thus appears as motivated by something nobler than chauvinism, namely the concern that powerful citizens do not increase their influence through the exercise of their power of blackmailing dependants. Anyone who has some experience of the phenomenon of the 'exchange vote' – typical of some political realities (e.g. southern Italy) where local bosses literally exchange political consensus for some material benefits – knows that Kant foresaw with full clarity a degeneration of democracy and universal suffrage. Needless to say, Kant's exclusion of all women as such, as opposed to all *dependent* women, is problematic. At best, this reflects the de facto almost universal condition of dependence of women in Kant's times (but with considerable exceptions even then!) and at worst a patriarchal residuum. The point remains, though, that if one looks at the logic of Kant's exclusions what makes women unfit to vote is not their gender but their (contingent) socio-economic condition. If the latter changes for the better, there is truly no Kantian reason that could justify any discrimination.

One last point: Kant could be wrong in the belief that dependants are really incapable of an autonomous formation of political will. He could also miss the point that attributing to them the right to vote is a way (perhaps the most effective way) to empower and thus emancipate them. After all, they would have at least something to exchange with the powerful. But even if true, this is clearly irrelevant to the question we are discussing, which is whether Kant has a consistent theory of the republic and whether the rich interpretation we have proposed is compatible with Kant's distinction between passive and active citizens. If Kant makes a mistake in political science (failure to recognize the empowering, emancipating potential of the right to vote) this does not necessarily translate into a mistake in political philosophy. Kant does have a coherent vision of the republic, and the ideal elements we highlighted – mainly, the burden of representation that (active) citizens are expected to accept and the autonomous condition that it presupposes – constitute a crucial yet often overlooked element of this vision.

4.2 The Second Definitive Article

The second definitive article contains the following prescription: 'The Rights of Nations shall be based on a Federation of Free States.' Here Kant envisages a form of international organization that enables the diverse nations to leave the state of nature, which today, by and large, still characterizes the international scene. The move to a civil condition closely resembles the passage imagined for the individuals before the creation of the national state, but the analogy has its limits. For Kant, an established state, unlike an individual in the state of nature, is already a rightful entity whose autonomy is to be respected. In fact, it can never vanish into a universal state and cannot be forced to give up its sovereignty. As he puts it, 'states [...] already have a lawful internal constitution, and have thus outgrown the coercive right of others to subject them to a wider legal constitution' (*ZeF*, 8:356). But since reason dictates the duty to achieve peace, and peace requires 'a general agreement between the nations', it follows that 'a particular kind of league, which we might call a *pacific federation (foedus pacificum)*' (*ZeF*, 8:356) is required.

Among the many interpretative challenges posed by the second definitive article, two strongly interrelated questions are particularly relevant for the contemporary debate. The first relates to Kant's rationale for preferring a federation over a world republic, which includes the question concerning the powers of this supranational institution. The second concerns the criteria by which states qualify to enter the Federation. Let us start from this second question.

4.2.1 The Federation: Club of Democracies or Mixed International Organization?

What states can enter the federation? Are only republics allowed to enter or is any kind of state eligible? Unfortunately Kant does not provide a clear answer to this crucial point. His preferred membership criteria remain obscure and we are left with the task of reconstructing his view from bits of textual evidence and systematic considerations that measure how each of the two hypotheses squares with the general picture offered by the whole of Kant's thought. Depending on the answer, we will attribute to Kant a model similar to the European Union or to the United Nations, just to mention the two most obvious examples, thereby shaping the normative indication of the second definitive article in profoundly different manners. In the first scenario, Kant would be suggesting a strong division of the world in two main zones, one that includes the already virtuous states and another that encompasses all the others. This is obviously the picture that Rawls assumes in *The Law of Peoples*, with one significant variation, namely that the club generously opens up its doors not only to liberal peoples, but also to the good enough, the decent ones. In the second scenario, the federation will be a heterogeneous institution, where different kinds of regimes can meet and have permanent channels of diplomatic communication for the sake – mainly – of security or commercial exchange.

Democratic peace scholars – from the very beginning (Doyle 1983a) – massively opted for the first interpretation and, despite the documented protests by various Kant scholars (Cavallar 1999; MacMillan 1994), retained this view of an allegedly Kantian 'separate peace' among democracies (Russett 2001, 2006; Doyle 2011).[30] Among DPT scholars, Doyle meritoriously takes the issue seriously and attempts a reply to the criticisms of his narrow reading. Pressed to show where Kant would suggest a federation with restricted access – something taken for granted in 1983 – Doyle concedes that there are passages in favour of the more inclusive reading, but claims that more persuasive evidence of a textual and systematic nature favours the 'only republics' hypothesis. What is this evidence?

To begin with, in an inspired plea for his project, Kant says that the most suitable constitution for approaching the ideal of perpetual peace is 'perhaps that of republicanism in all states, individually and collectively [*samt und sonders*]'. On Doyle's reading,

Kant is wishing here that republicanism triumph not only inside states ('individually') but also 'among them' ('collectively'). Since Doyle assumes that relations between states can be 'republican' on condition that the federation is composed of republics only, it would follow that Kant is here precisely advocating a federation of republics.

This reading can be questioned both textually and systematically. Textually, the German expression *samt und sonders* is commonly used to reinforce the idea that a certain concept applies *überhaupt*, that is, in general to each member of a set. Instead of referring to the relations between republics, in the passage under consideration Kant seems to be reiterating the familiar hope that republicanism extends as much as possible to each polity. After all, in Kant's times republics were very few (France, the Swiss cantons, and the United States). Therefore Kant's wish is quite naturally understood as the hope that domestic republican institutions spread beyond this limited circle. Only with some stretch can one read in Kant's hope a concern for a much more sophisticated thing such as membership criteria of a yet-to-be constituted supranational institution. Systematically, even if we concede that *samt und sonders* applies to international relations between states, the expression is at best ambiguous. Kant may be referring to the opportunity to shape the procedures and decision mechanisms of the federation in line with republican principles, as opposed to prescribing the restrictive membership criteria Doyle reads into the expression. Republicanism between states may very well mean that the internal procedures of the federation are to be inspired by republican values and ideals (e.g. democratic procedures in decision-making and balance of powers), not that the members of the federation must be republics.

The second piece of evidence Doyle mentions is that the first definitive article is indeed *definitive*, by which Doyle means that 'in a formal sense, the states he [Kant] refers to later in the treaty have already "signed" the first article' (Doyle: 210). It would be unthinkable – this seems to be Doyle's reasoning – that the prescription to institute a republican constitution could be obeyed permissively, perhaps after having joined a mixed federation. A state cannot enter the federation if it has not already reformed its internal institutional structure. In order to secure perpetual peace, states must sign each of the three definitive articles, and above all, they must do it *in the order in which they are presented*.

There is little to quarrel with Doyle's idea that each of the three articles is necessary to ensure peace or that each of them is equally important. This is in fact one of the virtues of his interpretation over those who emphasize the primacy of domestic institutions over international and cosmopolitan right, thereby instituting something like a lexicographical priority of the first article over the other two. But the fact that each article is necessary does not say anything as to Kant's view on the order in which definitive articles are to be implemented. And, clearly, the order of presentation is insufficient evidence to reach a conclusion as to Kant's preferred order of implementation. Not only is this view unsupported by textual evidence, but systematically, as will be shown in a moment, it does Kant very poor service.

The last and 'more significant' piece of evidence is that, before peace has been institutionalized through the implementation of the three articles, international relations are in the state of nature and the existing 'international law' (that defined by the natural law tradition) is by itself no guarantee that states will not turn any possible controversy into a fully fledged war. Doyle reminds us that Kant lists three cases in which a state has a *right* to wage war: (1) perception of having received an injury, (2) threat posed by a neighbouring state preparing for war, or (3) threat by a neighbouring state that is alarmingly increasing its power. A mixed federation between republics and despotic states – Doyle reasons – is still insufficient to guarantee peace, especially if it is conceived of, as Kant does, without coercive powers. Only if international treaties are signed between republics does each national player know that all the others have independent reasons to stick to the treaty. And this independent and publicly known reason is people's natural aversion to war because of the costs that it brings (the utilitarian logic of the first article).

No matter how rightly construed on the interdependence of the peace-inducing mechanisms of the three definitive articles, this last argument is similarly dubious. Again, it shows at most that only the combined presence of republican institutions and the federation produces a sufficient guarantee of peace. But, leaving aside that if this were the case, then one would not see what role would be left to play for cosmopolitan right, which however Doyle seems to consider as important as the first two, this is perfectly compatible with the possibility that, in a transitional stage, when we are still striving to reach perpetual peace, the international institution that best helps this approach is a mixed federation, not the club of democracies Doyle envisions. Put differently, it is almost a truism, given Kant's logic, that a federation of democracies is a better guarantee of peace than a mixed federation. The point we are discussing, though, is whether Kant thought that a mixed federation is the best means of approaching that goal. Doyle's reminder that republican institutions are indispensable for a reliable federation is irrelevant to deciding this point.

Why then should we part company and favour the alternative view? In addition to the significant textual evidence that Doyle himself acknowledges,[31] and that therefore we shall not discuss, there are extra textual and very strong systematic reasons that suggest a mixed federation. To begin with, if the federation that is meant to improve relations between republics should already be quite peaceful (at least in the relations of its members), what *significant* role is left for the federation, that is, a role that is compatible with the status of the second definitive article wherein it is presented? What added value does the federation bring to inter-republican relations that are – by the logic of Doyle's argument – already in good shape? To be sure, even inter-republican relations, as we know from history, are subject to controversies and tensions which have in fact have been quite frequent and still occur today. Hence the permanent diplomatic channels ensured by the presence of a federation could still be of some use. But, leaving aside the fact that democratic controversies have *not* been settled by the presence of a federation (Layne 1996), if the relations between two democracies really needed the presence of a joint peace treaty to remain peaceful, then two embarrassing consequences would follow: (1) the normative logic of DPT would collapse (democracies are supposed to respect each other, not to avoid wars between them only if they find them ultimately inconvenient); (2) the role of the federation would be reduced to avoiding the rare cases in which democracies find war between them useful – perhaps in cases in which the normative dissuaders are weaker than the benefits democratic *demoi* envisage. This would be a truly diminished role for the federation, that can hardly be compatible with the status Kant assigns to the second article, namely that of a definitive article as important as republicanism within states. Much more plausible is that the Federation is thought of as providing those war-avoiding incentives when and where they are most needed, that is, in the relations between democracies and autocracies, and between autocracies. The presence of permanent diplomatic channels seems to be far more important in cases in which neither mutual trust nor mutual respect can be assumed.

Moreover – as MacMillan noticed and Doyle recognized – Kant himself indicated as an example of the federation the Dutch States-General in the Hague in the first half of the eighteenth century, to which 'the ministers of most European courts and even of the smallest republics brought their complaints about an aggression suffered by one of their numbers at the hands of another' and 'all neighboring states' (*MS*, 6:350) were free to join. Kant insisted that these ministers promisingly thought of Europe as a single federated state 'which they accepted as an arbiter in all their public disputes'. Clearly this is the example of a mixed federation, not that of a club of republics, a club that at the time Kant is referring to would have probably included only the Swiss cantons (and not all of them) and later, at the time Kant was writing, only the French Republic, the United States (north of the Mason-Dixon line), and the Swiss cantons themselves. What role would such a restricted federation play? What real contribution to world peace could it give?

But there is something more that escaped the attention of MacMillan and others. In the following paragraph Kant talks of a '*peaceful* (if not exactly amicable) international community of all those of earth's peoples who can enter in active relations with one another' (*MS*, 6:352). Here the only membership criterion that Kant mentions is the ability of peoples of the earth to enter active relations with one another (thereby creating the risk of conflict), not the justice of their internal institutions. Combined with Kant's idea that all peoples (already in his times) are in a condition to enter active relations with one another, this explicitly shows that Kant thought of a federation which *any* state can and should enter.

This brings us to the final point. If the federation is thought of as encompassing *any* willing state, its role squares much better with the logic of gradual progress towards peace that seems to pervade Kant's project. The inclusion of as many existing states as possible seems to parallel Kant's point in the third definitive article in which he clearly thinks of economic interdependence as a peace-inducing factor that should affect all kinds of states, not just the relations between republics. Moreover, only if open to any state can the federation play the role of institutional defender of cosmopolitan right, which, in the absence of a world republic, is destined to remain at the discretion of states' good will. Inclusion in the federation, from this perspective, is the first step in helping despotic states to make their spontaneous transition to more just institutions and the only instrument available to give cosmopolitan right some institutional protection.

4.2.2 Federation or World Republic?

While the issue of membership criteria is probably the hermeneutical puzzle most relevant for contemporary DPT, Kantian scholarship has for centuries widely debated the reasons that led Kant – after some hesitation – to prefer a federation over the ideal of a world republic. To be sure, this problem has a direct bearing on contemporary DPT because a proper understanding of Kant's 'recipe for peace' depends on a clear appreciation of the reasons underlying his ambivalent attitude. It is thus probably a good idea to devote some attention to this classical hermeneutical point.

Why does Kant end up favouring the federation he himself considers as a practical surrogate solution, and come close to repudiating (especially in the *Metaphysics of Morals*) the world republic, even in the quite modest form of a regulative ideal towards which we should strive?[32] The possibility that a world state could become a 'soulless despot' that abolishes differences and fails to respect the people's autonomy are Kant's official motives. An 'everlasting and continually expanding *federation* [*Bund*]" (*ZeF*, 8:357) has the disadvantage of lacking a coercive power comparable to the one national states exercise over their citizens to ensure peace, but has the seemingly far superior advantage of not constituting too high a danger to the freedom of individuals and groups. Kant thus believes that a supranational state, especially if introduced coercively and prematurely, but probably in any case, would necessarily degenerate into a dictatorship destined to violate the autonomy of the various peoples. This leads him to abandon the ideal of a world republic in favour of a more prudent target, a 'federation of peoples' with voluntary access and ability to resign.[33]

Kant's federation has often been criticized because, if one can enter and leave it voluntarily, it is not clear how it can contribute to the cause of peace. If a country desires to wage war, all it has to do is abstain from entering the federation or, at most, leave it if it is already a member. Even with a *permanent* federation, as Kant wishes, not much changes, because states can easily fall out of its jurisdiction by withdrawing their membership. Also, if the federation is thought of as non-coercive, it is unclear what the federation could do with aggressive states that have decided to remain within the league and nonetheless pursue an aggressive foreign policy. Ultimately, the existence of a league so constructed makes little if any practical difference. And if the federation makes practically no difference for the cause of peace, the normative prescription contained in the second definitive article, obviously, becomes way less important than Kant thought.

Hence we have two interpretative problems. One concerns Kant's consistency in holding a world republic right in theory while abandoning it because wrong in practice. The other is whether the surrogate of the federation, with the very limited powers Kant ultimately is ready to concede, makes a difference for the cause of peace. Let us deal with each of the problems. Regarding the first, an attractive and clean solution is suggested by Pauline Kleingeld. She argues that there is a way to reconcile Kant's defence of a voluntary league and his ideal of a world republic with coercive powers without compromising his theory as a whole. In Kleingeld's view, Kant never abandons the ideal of a world government. He merely warns against the risks of universal monarchy, which, as we said, would ultimately violate the autonomy of the federated peoples. Kant considers the world government (that would obviously be itself some sort of federation as opposed to a centralized entity) as an ideal dictated by pure reason. It is an ideal to which we are obliged to strive. Nonetheless, since the establishment of a world government cannot be imposed without violating the autonomy of legitimate entities such as states, we will have to wait until each state *spontaneously* renounces part of its sovereignty. For the idea to become real, so to speak, the geopolitical circumstances must be favourable and times must be mature. Any forced acceleration would be not only politically unwise but also morally unjust. It would overstep the autonomous decision of each people. While waiting for this unforced evolution, we have to do with a federation with voluntary membership.[34]

The problem with this interpretation is that Kant does not prefer the federation for practical reasons, but because he seems to see it as normatively better, that is, more just. Kant never says that the federation is the best solution *now*, but in the future we can and should hope that a world republic will triumph. Moreover, the pragmatic arguments – a world republic would rule over too large a territory, it would lead to anarchy, it would remove the conditions for healthy competition among peoples – are only one of three groups of arguments Kant mentions in favour of the federation. There are also arguments of a political/juridical nature: (a) states, unlike individuals, are not entities one can force to leave the state of nature, because they already embody through their constitution the overcoming of anarchy; and (b) states must keep their autonomy. There are also arguments of a logical nature that spot an alleged contradiction in the very concept of a state of states. Leaving aside the last ones, which are clearly infected by Kant's failure to see the possibility of a horizontal dispersion of powers, the political reasons seem to keep their force even if we abstract from all pragmatical considerations that make a world republic difficult to establish and even if we conceive the world state as kept sharply distinguished from a universal monarchy with an intrinsic and ineradicable tyrannical tendency. In the last analysis, if states are juridical entities and their autonomy is to be preserved, it seems that there are insurmountable *normative* reasons against a world state, even if non-tyrannical. This is not to say that a world republic with truly dispersed powers and limited functions could not adjust the juridical, political and even logical concerns Kant has. As argued by Pogge (2009), the possibility of a world republic with limited sovereignty escaped Kant because he was embedded in the modern 'all or nothing' conception of sovereignty. Acknowledging that much, though, is very different from reconciling by attributing to him the view that the federation is all right for an early stage, but a world republic should take over as soon as times are mature.

Be that as it may, the second interpretative crux, the one related to the difference the federation makes for the cause of peace, is even more relevant for the comparative analysis of DPT that we will submit in the next chapter. In fact, one suspects that the tendency to interpret Kant's federation as a club of democracies stems from the sceptical attitude on the peace potential of a mixed federation of the sort we described. But is it really true that a loose and possibly mixed confederation does not provide a significant contribution to peace and is helplessly impotent before states that by and large keep their sovereignty untouched? Kleingeld (2006) interestingly refers to a passage in the *Metaphysics of Morals* in which Kant briefly mentions the possibility for two states with an ongoing controversy to use the pre-existing diplomatic channels of the federation. Notice that the *permanence* of the federation is crucial here. The supranational institution must already be there when the controversy arises. Only if this condition of permanence is respected, will diplomatic channels and the protocols of arbitration help to avoid war. Therefore a permanent federation does have the chance to make a difference for the cause of peace, even if this is less than one could hope for. After all, we have some evidence that this is not a mere theoretical possibility. From the vantage point of two hundred years since Kant's essay, to use a famous title by Habermas (1997), we know that the UN, an institution quite similar to Kant's federation, was able to make a contribution in some crises (Trieste, Cyprus, East Timor, Macedonia) despite all its inefficiencies and weaknesses. We know that the League of Arab States defused at least six major disputes between members that had a real chance of degenerating into international conflicts (Hassouna 1975). And that it did so through the meagre means of permanent diplomatic channels, a council with only the power of expulsion of a member in case of conduct inconsistent with the principle of the federation, and the 'good offices' of the General Secretariat. We know that ASEAN (Pennisi 2012) has a similar story of success in a similarly complicated and unstable region of the world. And of course we know the success stories of IGOs commonly cited to prove the peace potential of supranational institutions: EU, NATO, NAFTA and so on. A mixed federation is no guarantee of peace between members, but it is not completely insignificant either.

4.3 The Third Definitive Article

Kant complements his 'recipe for peace' with a recommendation, as we shall see, quite novel in his political thinking, that concerns what he calls cosmopolitan right (*Weltbürgerrecht*). We read that 'Cosmopolitan right shall be limited to conditions of universal hospitality', which is to be understood as a 'right of resort, for all men are entitled to present themselves in the society of others by virtue of their right to communal possession' (*ZeF*, 8:358).

The first thing to notice is that in 1795 Kant no longer thinks that republicanism and federalism (the focus of the first two definitive articles) are sufficient to yield peace. For the first time, a specific and irreducible role is left to cosmopolitanism. To be sure, the notion of cosmopolitanism already appears in the 1784 essay *Idea for a Universal History with a Cosmopolitan Purpose*. As we saw, there Kant shows that one can reasonably look at history as the irregular yet inexorable unfolding of a plan leading to a 'cosmopolitan system of general political security' (*IaG*, 8:26). With similar intent, he talks in the 1783 essay *On the Common Saying* of a 'cosmopolitan constitution' (*Weltbürgerliche Verfassung*; *TP*, 8:310) or 'cosmopolitan commonwealth' (*Weltbürgerliches gemeines Wesen*; *TP*, 8:311). However, as we approach the later works, things change considerably. In *To Perpetual Peace* (1795) and in *The Metaphysics of Morals* (1797), Kant introduces for the first time the notion of 'cosmopolitan right' (*Weltbürgerrecht*). Right (*Recht*) is now tripartite in terms of state right, international right and cosmopolitan right.[35] The new subdivision of right concerns the rules that all nations should adopt in the treatment of foreigners, especially when they attempt to enter other countries. These rules accord visitors the *'right of resort'* (*ZeF*, 8:358) and prescribe that foreigners or stateless people be treated without hostility when they arrive on someone else's territory. Cosmopolitan right does not grant them a right to become members of the hosting country. In fact, they can be 'turned away' (*ZeF*, 8:358), if this can be done without endangering their lives. However, it does grant them a right 'to *visit* all regions of the earth' while they attempt 'to establish a community with all' (*MS*, 8:352).[36]

In *To Perpetual Peace* Kant claims that cosmopolitan right is both (a) a condition of the accomplishment of the cosmopolitan constitution and (b) a necessary complement to the unwritten code of state right and international right, that transforms it into a 'universal right of humanity as well as into something that leads to perpetual peace' (*ZeF*, 8:360).[37] If Kant now thinks that cosmopolitan right is so important, one would expect that he would give us a clear account of why the right to visit is so crucial for peace. We have been told quite eloquently why the republican form and the international federation promote peace. Are we going to be told with similar clarity why the right to visit is such a crucial peace-promoting factor? Kant explains this point in a comparatively less clear manner, and different readings are legitimate, though not all of them will prove adequate.

There are two main ways to read the causal link between the right to visit and peace. On the one hand, one can narrowly see the right to visit as a condition that enables economic interdependence, considered as the true peace-promoting factor. On the other hand, one may recognize this enabling function but read into the right to visit more than this instrumental function. Let us discuss briefly some of the readings belonging to both camps.

The most straightforward narrow reading is that without the cosmopolitan right international commerce is impossible. In fact, how could it flourish if people are not secure in their attempt to reach new markets? Only if the right to visit is enforced or at least de facto respected, can countries become economically interdependent – a step crucial for the pacification of their relations. An alternative narrow reading is that international commerce brings about advantages for all parties involved. This establishes a peaceful *modus vivendi* among them, which ends up with the recognition of the right to visit. Cosmopolitan right is nothing more than the formalization of a condition already generated by mutual interest. A different and quite sophisticated narrow reading is that proposed by Norberto Bobbio, who sees in Kant's cosmopolitan right nothing more than the anticipation of what we would now call private international law, that is, the rules that states must follow in their dealings with foreigners (Bobbio 1985: xv).[38] These rules are (again) all about the facilitation of commerce, which in turn is the true peace factor at work (Bobbio 1985: xvi).

Even among specialist Kant scholars, the narrow reading has some acceptance. Allen D. Rosen (1993) and Samuel Fleischacker (1996), for example, construe Kant as rather a naive free trade supporter. On their reading, Kant's cosmopolitan right would simply secure a prerequisite of international trade, by guaranteeing that individuals are permitted to move across frontiers. Kevin Thompson (2008) thinks that the 'commerce [*Verkehr*]' between peoples Kant secures through cosmopolitan right is exclusively economic commerce (*contra* Kleingeld 2012: 75). Recently Byrd and Hruschka (2010: 207f.) flirt with the narrow reading when they suggest that in the *Metaphysics of Morals* Kant conceptualizes cosmopolitan law in terms of the idea of a perfect World Trade Organization. But it is mainly outside the circle of professional

Kant scholars that the narrow reading has become popular, especially among DPT scholars. It is quite impressive that the very term 'cosmopolitan right' or even 'right to visit' hardly makes any appearance in the works of one of the foremost exponents of DPT, Bruce Russett. In *Triangulating Peace* (2001), co-authored with John Oneal, Russett never uses the term 'cosmopolitan'. Kant's third ingredient for peace is reduced to economic interdependence. In the founding father of liberal peace, Michael Doyle, we find a better awareness that Kant's theory includes cosmopolitan components, but when Doyle moves on to explain how cosmopolitan right promotes peace, we fall back on the familiar reduction to economic interdependence. For example, in a passage from the 1983 'Kant, Liberal Legacy, and Foreign Affairs' we read: '[t]he cosmopolitan right to hospitality permits the "spirit of commerce" sooner or later to take hold of every nation, thus impelling states to promote peace and to try to avert war' (Doyle 1983a: 231). In other words, the whole point of cosmopolitan right is to promote trade, which in turn promotes peace. Notice also that Doyle inverts the causal order. While the 'spirit of commerce' is in Kant explicitly presented as the means by which cosmopolitan right is expected to obtain recognition worldwide, in Doyle it becomes the end secured by cosmopolitan right, which remains mainly of instrumental value.[39]

What about the alternative, broad reading? The majority of professional Kant scholars favour this interpretation, whose central idea is that cosmopolitan right is something more than international trade (or a way of securing it). For example, Ripstein realizes that the right to visit is about opening up frontiers to foreigners by virtue of the 'disjunctive possession of the Earth's surface' (Ripstein 2009: 296), and commerce is only one of the many relations individuals have a right to propose to inhabitants of receiving countries. Ruyssen (1924: 355–71), Kersting (1996: 1972–212) and Marini (2001: 19–34) see cosmopolitan right as the constitutional law of a world state. Waldron (2000) interprets Kant's cosmopolitan right mainly as the disposition not to take our conceptions of justice as non-negotiable in dealing with people and peoples with different views. Taraborelli argues that the right to visit is a right that 'guarantees everyone's opportunity to become "associated" with a new nation and possibly, in some future time, to become a fellow inhabitant' (Taraborelli 2006: 153). Brown

(2009) sees a commitment to a global morality (albeit of minimal reach). Kleingeld construes cosmopolitan right as a right – ultimately springing from humans' innate right to freedom (*MS*, 236) – to attempt to initiate all sorts of communicative exchange – including, but not limited to, commercial interactions (Kleingeld 2012: 83–4). Hence, the right to visit is not merely about enabling international trade. It is also about the mutual knowledge of different peoples and the intermingling of cultures. Mutual knowledge and cultural contact decrease distrust and therefore promote peace.[40] A yet broader reading suggested by Anderson-Gold (2006) points out that cosmopolitan right is not only a negative right, about refraining from hostilities against foreigners, but a positive right to a 'dynamic interactive community of moral interdependence that is the only condition under which states could consistently adhere to international laws that are also universally just' (Anderson-Gold 2006: 138). Consonant with this approach is Derrida's famous account of hospitality as, among other things, a condition for epistemic progress thanks to the different perspectives that *l'étranger* brings into the receiving community (Derrida 2000). From this perspective, cosmopolitan right is about the creation of a global community in which various moral traditions have found common ground – Anderson-Gold's notion of 'moral interdependence', as I read it. This common normative commitment is the sole guarantee that sovereign states, in the absence of a world government, will stick to any legal obligations that they may be subject to in international institutions.

Thus far the representatives of the narrow and of the broad reading. Which reading should one prefer? There is little doubt that the broad reading's central intuition – cosmopolitan right is something more than international trade – renders Kant's thought better. To be sure, the idea that economic interdependence is good for peace is part of what lies behind the third definitive article. When Kant explains nature's guarantee of the possibility of a cosmopolitan right, he affirms that: 'Nature unites nations [...] by means of the mutual self-interest. For the *spirit of commerce* sooner or later takes hold of every people, and it cannot exist side by side with war' (*ZeF*, 8:368). There is no indication, however, that the significance of the article is limited to the peace–trade nexus. In fact, this is not even the core of the article. To begin with, the 'spirit of commerce' appears only in the section devoted to the guarantee of perpetual peace, where Kant offers reasons to believe that nature promotes the realization of each of the three branches of right. Regarding the third branch, it is the 'spirit of commerce' – a natural drive – that shows how nature 'pushes' in favour of cosmopolitan right. In other words, the 'spirit of commerce' is the means provided by nature for the realization of the end, that is, cosmopolitan right. Why conflate means and end when Kant so clearly distinguishes between them?

Furthermore, in the attempt to expand and clarify cosmopolitan right Kant talks about a right of all individuals *'sich zur Gesellschaft anzubieten'*, which may be translated as 'to offer oneself to social intercourse'. Kant seems to have in mind a right to apply to enter a new social compound that he at times calls 'a society' – as in the passage cited – but more often, and significantly, a 'community'.[41] Clearly, we are dealing here with something more than the sheer right to cross frontiers, to exchange goods and to do business in a foreign country. We rather have a right to come to know each other, to get in contact with foreigners in order to lay down the basis of a community wider than the national one. In this sense, the third article pertains to *cosmopolitan* right. It focuses on the conditions that prevent peoples' reciprocal closure. It deals with those 'good practices' needed to make sure that societies influence one another, know one another and thus decrease the level of reciprocal distrust. Mutual knowledge and the diffusion of a culture of respect for the fundamental rights of men are the primary goals of the third definitive article and the exchange of goods is just one of the means through which that end is effectively rendered.

Finally, by reducing cosmopolitan right to a mere plea in favour of international trade, the narrow reading makes Kant nearly indistinguishable from authors who before and after him praised the peace-inducing virtue of international trade: Smith, Montesquieu, Bentham, Bastiat and others, to name but a few. They never thought about using the category of *Recht* to convey their recommendation on the positive effects of economic interdependence. Nor were they interested in the specific way in which foreign traders had to be treated in their dealings abroad. Certainly, unlike Kant, they did not see international trade as a means for the realization of a normative, perhaps institutional structure that would protect certain prerogatives and rights of humans *qua* humans.

In conclusion, there are few doubts that broad readings are to be preferred over narrow ones, even if one takes Doyle's qualified and sophisticated narrow reading as term of comparison. Still, in the versions of the broad reading discussed above, the impression is that three crucial aspects remain insufficiently highlighted, perhaps even in the particularly broad reading of Anderson-Gold (2006):

1. *The relation between cosmopolitan right and a growing global moral conscience.* Cosmopolitan right rests, perhaps more than the two other definitive articles, on a moral substratum. For Kant the reason why cosmopolitan right is not 'overstrained and fantastic' (*PP*, 360) is that 'the peoples of the earth have entered in varying degrees into a universal community which is so real and well developed that 'a violation of rights in *one* part of the world is felt *everywhere*' (*ZeF*, 8:360). In other words, the existence of a universal community with a common moral conscience that condemns violations of the natural rights of human beings is the guarantee that cosmopolitan right is not a mere utopia. On the one hand, Kant thinks that humans already share some basic moral values – that a moral global conscience already exists. On the other hand, the translation of those common moral values into an article of law (cosmopolitan right understood as a part of *Recht*) is destined to strengthen and further develop the same global conscience. Given its very content – the right to cross frontiers securely – cosmopolitan right enables and promotes mutual knowledge and various dimensions of interdependence (economic, cultural, demographic) which reinforce and gradually expand that global conscience, taking it beyond the sheer recognition of a universal right to visit. In fact, although 'this natural right of hospitality, that is, the right of strangers, does not extend beyond the conditions that make it possible to *attempt* to enter into relations with the native inhabitants', it nonetheless bridges distant continents and opens up otherwise closed nations, 'thus bringing the human race nearer and nearer to a cosmopolitan constitution [*weltbürgelichen Verfassung*]' (*ZeF*, 8:358).

It is famously difficult to interpret Kant's notion of a 'cosmopolitan constitution' because this concept is destined to follow all the convolutions and reservations Kant has regarding the feasibility/desirability of a universal republic. If history is to reach a world government, as at times Kant suggests, then the 'cosmopolitan constitution' is obviously the constitutional law of such world government. But if history neither will nor should reach that end goal, as Kant more often suggests, especially in his late writings (most clearly in the *Metaphysics of Morals*), then the cosmopolitan constitution will be closer to a universal international covenant signed by all countries (similar to the two human rights treaties of the 1960s), possibly enforced by global tribunals (similar to the International Criminal Court or the International Court of Justice). In either case, the cosmopolitan constitution will include more than the right to visit, and probably will extend to the full set of rights humans would have *if* they were citizens of a world republic or, which is about the same, *if* a world republic existed. The cosmopolitan constitution and a fully developed global conscience, which in some *Reflexionen* Kant calls the 'cosmopolitan destination' of humankind, are respectively the legal and the moral side of the final stage of the progress Kant envisages for human beings.

2. *Global conscience and Kant's overall project for peace.* The complex relation between cosmopolitan right and what we have referred to as a global moral conscience reinforces the general point we have already made about Kant's path to peace. The model rests on the moral improvement of both individuals and peoples despite the fact that it invokes essentially legal and institutional reforms. While Kant's path to peace is often interpreted as leaving a marginal role to individuals' morality, we have shown that the diffusion of a culture of respect for what Kant called *Menschenrecht* is crucial for the dynamic imagined as conducive to peace.

3. *International trade and global conscience.* Kant seems to consider trade a pacifying factor only if conducted in accordance with some basic moral rules of respect and reciprocity which are already part of the global conscience. His condemnation of colonial states and their unfair business with extra-Europeans speaks quite clearly to that effect. Thus it is not sufficient to highlight, as any broad reading does, that cosmopolitan right is not merely about international trade. It is also necessary to specify that not all sorts of international trade are peace-promoting.

From the perspective of the specific broad reading we defend, this qualification is quite natural. Since on our reading cosmopolitan right is mainly about the creation of a global conscience through mutual knowledge and decreased distrust, it is almost implicit that economic dependence based on exploitation can never be considered as either peace-promoting or conducive to the cosmopolitan condition.

The three definitive articles unequivocally constitute the backbone of Kant's project. This does not mean, however, that they can be read in isolation – as they have often been – or that a proper understanding even of what Kant meant by them can bypass the context of the whole *To Perpetual Peace*, let alone the context of Kant's thought in general. One part that is clearly crucial to put the three definitive articles in the right perspective is the famous section devoted to the so-called 'guarantee of perpetual peace'. It is here that Kant displays the fruitful dialectic between objective constraints and individuals' initiatives that, on his view, is supposed to yield the final outcome of a durable universal peace. It is here, to use the contemporary jargon, that Kant begins his attack on one subtle and often unrecognized enemy of peace that is neither the despotism of internal regime nor the absence of the required international institutions. It is rather the self-authenticating prophecy of hypersceptical thinkers and realist politicians who look down on the project of a perpetual peace for its alleged utopian character. This attitude is dangerous because it serves as an obstacle to any effort at reforms of national and supranational institutions towards the standards set by the three definitive articles. By showing that perpetual peace is in a sense 'written in our destiny', no matter how blind or resilient we are to the proposed reforms, Kant is introducing an element of 'enlightened and justified optimism' that completes his project by silencing the dangerous argument of those who are not sceptical because the project is impossible, but rather make the project impossible because of their scepticism. A detailed analysis of Kant's guarantee of perpetual peace will be offered in chapter 8. For the moment suffice it to notice how the three definitive articles are inserted in a complex view of human history as a system with its own readable logic, no matter how controversial this assumption may sound.

5 • Democratic Peace Theory

1. Democracy and Peace: An Ancient Idea

The belief that democracies are, in some sense to be specified, more peaceful than any other kind of regime, is not new. For some scholars (Wearth 1998; but *contra* Robinson 2001 and 2006), this conviction was born in Greece, and indeed in the contemporary version of a separate peace *between* democracies. Ironically, it is the noble founder of realism in international affairs that first formulates this thought. In his great work on the Peloponnesian War, Thucydides notices that not only democratic city-states, but also democratic factions across *poleis* tend to come closer and never to fight each other. Never, or almost never, because already in the period studied by Thucydides one can find some counter-examples. Think of Athens, which in 415 BC attacked democratic Syracuse to secure control over Sicily. But over and above exceptions, before drawing conclusions from the alleged democratic peace in ancient Greece, it must be said that the idea of democracy among the Greeks was very different from the one we have today. Moreover, Thucydides noticed that there was the same absence of conflict among oligarchic factions and states. As Weart (1998) would put it, with a vision that also embraces the modern period, oligarchies as much as democracies tend to avoid conflicts with similar regimes. This does not mean that the regularity Thucydides noticed can be dismissed easily. He implicitly drew attention, perhaps for the first time, to the fact that foreign policy is not only determined by national players' attempt to enlarge their power and security. Identities, ideologies and solidarity between apparently similar regimes also appeared to play a role. As we have said, this is quite ironic, given that the Greek historian is considered the founding father of realism. But the irony is mitigated if one looks at the way Thucydides explains why oligarchic and democratic factions/states end up together. His preferred explanation points to factors far less noble than the defence of common political convictions and principles: mainly the search for power by individuals, groups or states. Nonetheless realist qualifications of this sort could not close the Pandora's box Thucydides had just opened. In fact, if the pursuit of power is all that counts, why is it the case that individuals or collective players always found their allies among similar political actors? Thus, not only did Thucydides notice for the first time the idea of a separate peace among democracies, but he also revealed the need for an explanation of that fact, an explanation scholars are still seeking today.

2. The Peacefulness of Democracies in Modern Times

The idea of a 'democratic peace' in the most general sense, namely the idea of a relation between *some* democratic features and peace, after a long period of latency, was rediscovered late in the modern era.[1] It makes an appearance in the eighteenth century, when countries with a parliamentary system were very few (at most three: USA, France and the Swiss cantons). It is worth noting is that – unlike today – it was not liberals that insisted on this relation, but two traditions quite far from liberalism. On the one hand, democratic thought with Jean-Jacques Rousseau. In *Jugement sur le project de paix perpétuelle* (1756) Rousseau criticized the Abbé de Saint-Pierre for having suggested, in his proposal of a federation of European states, nothing but a permanent congress of dictators as an antidote to war. Saint-Pierre failed to realize – this was Rousseau's analysis – that it was precisely their absolute and irresponsible power that was the first cause of conflict in Europe. On the other hand, it was utilitarianism, with the founder of the school Jeremy Bentham, that was perhaps the clearest supporter of the idea that popular government was the best instrument to institute peace. In *Plan for an Universal and Perpetual Peace* (1786–9/1927) Bentham argued that – to counter states' aggressive tendencies – secrecy about the operations of the minister of foreign affairs had to be abolished. This appeal to transparency comes earlier than the logic of popular checks on government contained in the first definitive article of *To Perpetual Peace*, and anticipates a point dear to another democratic thinker, Giuseppe Mazzini (Recchia and Urbinati 2009: 169–77).

It is only with Kant and Madison that the liberal school approached the thought of a causal relation between a certain kind of institutions and peace. As we saw in the preceding chapter, *To Perpetual Peace* recommends three institutional reforms (of national, international and cosmopolitan right) to remove once and for all war from human affairs. Madison, like Kant, thought that government had to be subjected to popular will to reduce the likelihood of war. And like Kant, and perhaps even better than him, Madison knew that popular rule by itself would have ensured only the elimination of those wars undesired by the people, not all wars. On the same line was another exponent of the *Federalist*. John Jay was convinced that absolute monarchs often wage wars for merely personal motives, such as 'thirst for military glory, revenge for personal affronts, ambition, or private compacts to aggrandize or support their particular families or partisans'.[2] This is precisely Kant's argument in the first definitive article.[3]

The nineteenth century has a protagonist of this intellectual history who has not been recognized until very recently. We have in mind the Italian revolutionary and political theorist Giuseppe Mazzini. As convincingly argued by Recchia and Urbinati (2009: 2–3), Mazzini, not Kant, was the first to introduce the idea of a 'separate peace' among democracies. As we shall see, *pace* Doyle (1983a), Kant never had such an idea. Rather, Mazzini takes up Thucydides' intuition that democrats recognize each other as similar and avoid conflicts. Common values and common aspirations to freedom, cooperation and privileged commercial ties, but also a common aversion to autocrats and their values would lead democracies to respect one another, enter alliances to resist authoritarian threats, and eventually merge into common supranational institutions. For Mazzini nothing could stop the progressive integration of European states, once turned democratic, into something like the 'United States of Europe'.

Two points need to be highlighted. Mazzini had a deep conviction that despots were the first rulers responsible for the ruin and suffering of peoples. Only popular government would have ensured not only consideration for the interests and freedoms of citizens, but also for other peoples' rights and prerogatives. In particular, Mazzini thought that only a people that cares about its own self-determination is in a position to respect the same right of other peoples. Hence by far the most important ingredient in his recipe for peace was domestic democratization. Uncoerced democratization, to be sure, because Mazzini, like his acquaintance John Stuart Mill (1973 [1859]), thought that any institutional change imposed by external forces would have been ineffective as well as morally dubious. The disastrous experience of the attempt to export the French Revolution by means of Napoleonic rifles suggested to both authors prudence on how to reach the desired political outcome. Still, domestic democratization was the first – in the order of execution and in the order of importance – of the necessary steps to reach a stable peace. Given Mazzini's nationalism, it comes as no surprise that the domestic element was the most important, if not the sole factor.

Notice, however, how complex was Mazzini's argument on why democracies are selectively peaceful. To use the contemporary jargon, for Mazzini peace among democracies rests both on normative and institutional factors: on the one hand, common respect for certain fundamental rights of humanity, among which are individual freedom and political self-determination; on the other, institutional mechanisms such as economic interdependence and common membership in supranational institutions. Both would have strengthened, *after the establishment of democratic institutions at the national level*, the natural respect of democratic peoples for other similarly free nations.

From Mazzini, our very brief intellectual history moves to the early twentieth century, where we find the fascinating character of Woodrow Wilson. And it is not an accidental stop in our trajectory. Wilson was profoundly influenced by Mazzini, as recognized by the president himself. In his *Remarks about Giuseppe Mazzini* (Wilson 1986: 614–15) he acknowledged his intellectual debt and considered his commitment to the cause of peace as an attempt to implement Mazzini's ideals. Actually, Wilson was influenced by Kant as much as by Mazzini. In fact, his project for a Society of Nations was explicitly inspired by the second definitive article of *To Perpetual Peace*. It is suggestive to speculate that this double source of inspiration (Mazzini and Kant) is the reason why Wilson seems to oscillate between an idea of peace among democracies, in which the crucial factor for peace is the democratization of domestic regimes, and an idea closer to Kant in which the justice of domestic institutions is nothing but one of three crucial ingredients. In this perspective, internal democratization is neither more important than the other two elements (international and cosmopolitan right), nor is it to be understood as temporally prior in the order of the reforms we need to implement. In fact, on the one hand Wilson seems to hold that peace is possible only among free states. In his opinion, representative government is the key for a real pacification of international relations. Morever, the United States and Great Britain are considered as invested with the mission to promote the cause of freedom, the necessary step to reach global peace and prosperity. On the other hand, his grand project of the Society of Nations – a project whose advocacy to the American people sapped his decaying energies during the illness that brought on his death – was open to any kind of state, and *precisely for this reason* was expected to give a decisive contribution to peace. Thus, the lesson of World War I for Wilson was that not a 'club of democracies' but a mixed IGO had to be established. It is fascinating to see how these two lines of thought coexist in the American president – quite independently of whether they really come from Kant and Mazzini. And one should not blame Wilson for failing to distinguish them clearly in his reflection, because it is only towards the end of the twentieth century that the generic idea of a nexus between democracy and peace diverges in two clearly distinguished and even competing claims: (a) the idea of a separate peace among democracies or democratic peace, and (b) the idea of cosmopolitan democracy with its plea in favour of mixed IGOs as a factor promoting international peace and domestic democratization (Archibugi 2008).

3. The Rediscovery of Kant: Doyle and the Liberal Peace

Although democratic peace theory has a generally uncontested date of birth, the 1983 publication by Michael Doyle of 'Kant, Liberal Legacies and Public Affairs', it is opportune to remember that the nexus between democratic institutions and peace, and in particular the fact that democracies do not fight one another, had been noticed long before by the American sociologist Dean Babst, who in 1964 published in the unfortunately obscure *Wisconsin Sociologist* his 'Elective Governments: A Force for Peace'.[4] Babst noticed a regularity – the absence of conflicts among democracies – that, in a field traditionally void of general laws such as international politics, had already made an impact for its scientific relevance and for the obvious societal repercussions. Doyle two decades later confirmed the regularity noticed by Babst and inserted it within a broader conceptual contest, which is probably one of the reasons why his work had an incomparably stronger impact. 'Kant, Liberal Legacies and Public Affairs' connected the fact that democracies never fight each other with the recipe Kant indicated for reaching perpetual peace, thereby constructing an explanatory framework in which an empirical regularity – otherwise significant but by itself sterile – was used to bring about a major reorientation in at least two proximate fields. In political philosophy, the paper showed that liberalism was not merely a powerful tool for defining domestic justice (what Rawls had done in 1971) but had something crucial to say also for peace studies and international justice. Within the field of international politics, it challenged the by then mainstream realist school, showing that international affairs are not fully explainable in terms of national players' search for security or power. In a nutshell, the theory was articulated in three main claims: (1) liberal-democratic values and institutions are one of the factors that influence international relations, to be added to those traditionally recognized by the realist school (security, relative power, desire for aggrandizement and so on); (2) data suggest that the 'liberal factor' is activated only when liberal peoples relate to other liberal peoples, but remain idle or even become a reason for animosity when democracies face autocracies (liberalism does not preach non-violence in all circumstances); (3) the importance of the 'liberal factor' for peace has been understood best by Immanuel Kant, whose lesson is to be rediscovered.

The definition of liberalism Doyle adopts is interesting. In his perspective, liberalism has a central thesis on the primacy of the individual over the state and over groups. This primacy is articulated in the defence of three kinds of freedom: (a) negative freedoms (conscience, association, press, property and so on); (b) positive freedoms, that is, all socio-economic rights of equal opportunity in education, right to health care and employment (considered as presuppositions of the citizens' capacity to influence public decisions competently); and (c) freedom to take part in the business of democratic representation, i.e. political rights. Worth noticing in this definition is that Doyle includes socio-economic rights, even if he is well aware that only some liberals (whom he calls welfare liberals) would be comfortable with this choice. Although Doyle is not explicit about it, the reason is that the liberal-democratic state grants an equal opportunity and the right to a minimal standard of living (health and employment) because the possession of these rights is a prerequisite for being able to exercise the other class of rights, the civil and political ones. In other words, if people possess civil and political rights on paper but are hungry and illiterate, the exercise of these rights is dubious, if not dangerous, as uneducated and uninformed people are easy prey to demagogic propaganda. We should keep this point in mind because – quite mysteriously – in the time that followed, DPT scholars tended to forget or ignore the importance of redistributive justice for the validity of the entire model. It was an omission that would make the whole theory – as we shall see – very vulnerable to criticism.

Given this definition of liberalism, Doyle shows that since the eighteenth century, when the liberal state made its first appearance, liberal democracies have never fought each other, even if their number has exponentially increased from the 3 existing in Kant's time to the 49 in 1983, when Doyle published his original papers, to the 86 of 2016, thereby reaching 44 per cent of the 195 world states, covering 2,891,158,000 people, or 40% of total world population.[5]

On the criteria used to identify liberal-democratic regimes until 1983, Doyle affirms he has looked at the presence of four main institutional features, which nicely parallel the four elements in the definition of liberalism seen above: (1) market economies based on private property; (2) national independence and sovereignty; (3) recognition of 'juridical rights' (Doyle 1983a: 212), by which the author apparently means civil, political and socio-economic rights; and (4) representative government (whether republican or monarchical). Moreover, to be considered liberal-democratic, a state needs the following features: (a) wide male suffrage (30 per cent) or at least open to anyone who becomes a taxpayer or the head of a household; (b) female suffrage conceded within one generation from the introduction of male suffrage; (c) primacy of the legislative power (over the military and in foreign policy); and (d) stability (a regime in charge for at least three years).

Given these definitions, here is the already mentioned historical regularity: despite the considerable rivalries between democracies in the nineteenth and twentieth centuries, and their often coming to the verge of open conflict, especially in the period of imperialism, democracies have never fought each other. As examples of controversies short of war, Doyle cites the negotiation between the USA and Britain on the American northern boundary, the tensions between these two states related to the close ties between the British aristocracy and the landlords of the South, for reasons of class affinity and economic interdependence (cotton trade), the non-violent resolution of the Anglo-French Fashoda crisis (1898), the numerous colonial rivalries between France and Great Britain that not only never degenerated in open conflicts, but did not prevent the two states entering an *entente* to stop imperial Germany before the First World War. Other examples are the choice made by liberal Italy to abandon the triple alliance with two autocratic states (Austria and Germany) to side with the liberal *entente* in the First World War and the alliance between the USA and Britain before the same war despite decades of acute tension and commercial rivalries.

The reason why such controversies, and others one could cite, remained 'cold' is for Doyle the mutual recognition naturally developed by states habituated to respect the freedoms of their citizens. The idea is that, being liberal, these states care about popular sovereignty and certain basic individual rights of their citizens. This naturally led them also to respect the rights of foreign citizens and their self-determination. Moreover, this relationship of mutual respect facilitates commercial exchanges, which render a war more costly than it would be in the absence of such dependence, and cultural exchanges, with scholars establishing a web of relations that bolster 'sentiments of public respect' (Doyle, 1983a: 213). Doyle thus comes to formulate that regularity – no longer as a historical fact, but as a scientific prediction – that others (Levy 1988: 653) would have labelled the closest thing we have to a law in international politics: although in absolute terms liberal regimes get involved in conflicts as much as other types of regime, they never fight each other.[6]

Political realism, the school of international relations dominant at the time, was seriously challenged by such finding. Realism could explain the reasons for war but was hard put to cope with the stunning fact of so long a peace. The very existence of a liberal zone of peace and security without an overarching coercive power constituted a considerable problem, because the familiar realist explanations of peace, based on some versions of the balance of power account or on the existence of some fortunate common interest in peace, appeared incapable of accounting for 200 years of competing, even rival, yet peaceful, relations among democracies. Liberal states seemed to have abandoned that state of anarchy that political realists since Hobbes had predicted as the necessary condition of international relations. The idea of a systematic and ineliminable – unless through the constitution of a world state – condition of war latency, of structural anarchy and insecurity seemed to be superseded by the liberal peace.

Besides realism there was another school of international relations that was targeted by Doyle: Marxism. For the Marxist-Leninist school, peace and war are determined only by the evolution of the capitalist economy. If the interest of the economy of one or more capitalist states is to wage war (either for raw materials or to open new markets) and if – obviously – the power relations allow it, war will certainly follow. The liberal peace poses a challenge to Marxism because democracies have always had competing economies. In fact, they have often been on the verge of war, especially during the time of imperialism. And yet the disputes have never escalated to open conflicts. The existence of a zone of peace in which fiercely competing economies have coexisted peacefully appears as too huge a regularity to ascribe to mere chance. In sum, two points were particularly problematic for Marxism: (1) it underestimated the force of liberal ideas and values (considering them mere 'superstructure'; (2) it excluded the possibility that the capitalist processes (accumulation, production and expansion) could unfold within a context of common rules without aggressive wars, at least against other competing capitalist economies.[7]

This was the theory of democratic peace in its original form, together with its main targets. Going back in the history of ideas, Doyle found in Kant the noble father of the theory, and described him as a forerunner who had the genius to predict a model that only two centuries later we would have enough data to confirm. Only Kant had clearly seen that 'liberal' institutions and principles would generate peaceful international relations and ultimately lead to perpetual peace. Kant was thus rediscovered as the philosopher of peace *between* democracies, as the one who foresaw a 'liberal peaceful union' that would have expanded in proportion to the acceptance on a global scale of the three definitive articles. Not only was Kant the philosopher who foresaw why democracies do not fight each other, but he was also considered capable of explaining why democracies were aggressive towards illiberal states. To be sure, the last claim would be later repudiated by Doyle (2005) who realized that Kant could have never accepted imperial or colonial wars.[8] But the other claims remained valid. Kant's theory of peace is the anticipation, in the form of a philosophical model awaiting empirical confirmation, of democratic peace theory.

Since the publication of Doyle's article, more than thirty years have passed. The hypothesis that democracies do not fight each other and the explanation of that fact have become among the most studied themes in political science, with obvious repercussions on normative philosophy and Kant scholarship, not to mention its influence on the foreign policy of major democratic states. Already in 1982, Reagan proclaimed before the British Parliament that governments founded on a respect for individual liberty exercise 'restraint' and 'peaceful intentions' in their foreign policy. Margaret Thatcher in 1990 explained that the rise of democracy in eastern Europe was in the interest of the West because 'Democracies don't go to war with one another' (quoted in Encarnation 2006). In his 1994 State of the Union address, Bill Clinton said: 'Ultimately, the best strategy to ensure our security and to build a durable peace is to support the advance of democracy elsewhere. Democracies don't attack each other' (quoted in Encarnation 2006). George W. Bush affirmed repeatedly the link between the spread of democracy and the prospects of peace, especially when defending his decision to invade Iraq. In a speech in London's Whitehall Palace in November 2003, after the fall of Baghdad, he claimed: 'Democracy and the hope and progress it brings are the alternative to instability and to hatred and terror. Lasting peace is gained as justice and democracy advance' (quoted in Encarnation 2006). In 2005 he repeated: 'It should be clear that the advance of democracy leads to peace, because governments that respect the rights of their people also respect the rights of their neighbors' (quoted in Purdum 2005). And he concluded his 2004 debate with John Kerry by declaring his faith in 'the ability of liberty to transform societies, to convert a hostile world to a peaceful world' (quoted in Purdum 2005).

4. Five Versions of DPT

There are many versions of this intuition underpinning DPT, which in turn have taken countless shapes. Firstly, there is a *utilitarian* argument that echoes Kant's first definitive article, as well as the ideas of thinkers of Kant's own time such as Bentham and Madison. Citizens usually have a pro-attitude towards peace because they have to bear the costs of a militarized dispute. Another approach insists on *institutional* constraints. Here the emphasis is not on the dispositions of citizens, but on the constitutional design of *liberal* democracies. So, for example, transparency and the slow process of decision-making in constitutional systems characterized by checks and balances is thought to mitigate the security dilemma in the international arena, in particular the fear that a state will be subject to sudden attack (Russett, 1996). Similarly, others (Bueno de Mesquita et al. 2003) have pointed to institutional features related to the electorate (winning coalition, private/public goods) to explain the distinctive democratic behaviour. Thirdly, there is a *normative/moral* argument according to which democratic *demoi* strongly value life and human rights. Unlike peoples living under authoritarian regimes, citizens of a democracy are socialized in a way that builds in them the habit of resolving their controversies in peaceful ways. Democracy habituates its members to the idea that a conflict *can* and *must* be settled in a non-violent way. This 'second nature' is also operative in democratic rulers as well as in the public opinion of democratic countries when it comes to settling disputes with other peoples. The violence-free composition of controversies operative within democracies is then externalized to international relations, at least towards those who share the same culture (Maoz and Russett, 1993). War is ruled out unless aggression forces democracies to fight for their survival. Precisely because wars are often fought for 'good' reasons and are backed by popular endorsement, democracies are also likely to win the military operations they are involved in (Reiter and Stam, 2003; *contra* Desch, 2001). Fourthly, democracies 'signal' their intentions more accurately and reliably. Finally, a related perspective emphasizes that democracies are better able to make credible institutional commitments to carry out international agreements (Lipson 2003; Martin, 2000).

A last point of division among scholars, that cuts across the five versions just seen, refers to the question whether democracies should be considered as more peaceful than other types of regime in absolute terms, or more peaceful only when they relate to other democracies. These are known respectively as the monadic and dyadic interpretations of DPT, and they deserve, along with other specific divisions treated in the following sections, special attention.

5. Dyadic and Monadic

In its original form (Doyle 1983a and b), DPT was presented as a dyadic regularity. Democratic dyads are more peaceful than any other kind of dyads (democracies/autocracies or autocracies/autocracies), but in mixed dyads democratizing states may be more likely to enter a military dispute than autocracies (Mansfield Snyder 2005, 2009; *contra* Narang and Nelson 2009). On this interpretation, strictly speaking, there is nothing inherently peaceful about democracies. The peculiarity they have is displayed only in inter-democratic relations.

The dyadic interpretation has been and still is largely majoritarian[9] up to the point that some scholars (Archibugi 2006) argue that the very label democratic peace is misleading. We should talk of 'inter-democratic peace', or 'peace among democracies' because Doyle's theory does not stipulate in the least an intrinsic peacefulness in this kind of regime. In fact, given the high frequency of conflicts of democracies with other types of regimes – conflicts that only in certain cases can be reasonably classified as cases of self-defence or human rights protection – one can legitimately ask whether inter-democratic peace is consistent with democratic ideals. If the principle of non-aggression (arguably one of the pillars of democracy) is so often betrayed, is there any difference, going back to Thucydides, between a democratic peace and an autocratic one?

Although the dyadic interpretation is still mainstream, recently some scholars have moved from the dyadic interpretation (Russett 1993) into qualified acceptance of the stronger thesis that democracies are more peaceful *absolutely* (Russett and Oneal 2001; Russett 2009). According to the monadic interpretation, democracies are inherently more peaceful. Especially so if we consider, for any war, which state initiated the militarized dispute, the context when they became involved, and the severity of inflicted violence (Rummel 1995; Rousseau 1995). Is democracy to exert an influence primarily on dyadic relations (democracies acting peacefully towards one another) or monadically (more peaceful in general than autocracies)? In a world consisting mostly of autocracies, the great majority of democracies' interactions would be with autocracies. One empirically established fact of modern international relations is that democratic/autocratic pairs of states are more conflict-prone than autocratic pairs, and much more conflict-prone than democratic pairs. Coupled with contemporary theory about states' interactions, that makes sense. If democracies are reluctant to fight, whether from institutional or normative restraints (or both), then they will expect other democracies to be similarly reluctant. But they will not expect autocracies to be so restrained. Indeed, autocracies may seek to take advantage of democracies' reluctance, and hence push for greater gains than they might expect from another autocracy. Consequently in terms of relative frequency of conflict, democracies may not appear to be very peaceful from a simple monadic perspective. A common procedure in many analyses (e.g., Huth and Allee 2002; Oneal 2006) has been to use as the unit of analysis so-called directed dyads; that is, to indicate which state in a pair initiates a military confrontation, or which one escalates an existing conflict to an actual use of military force. While it may be difficult to say objectively who is 'to blame' for the conflict, there is evidence that when democracies engage in conflict with autocratic states, democracies are less likely to be either the initiators or the escalators. In other words, democracies are more peaceful in general, but this feature does not appear in statistics because they have been often 'forced' by one or more autocratic states to enter a conflict, for reasons that range from self-defence, legitimate defence of a national interest and (lately) human rights protection.

The monadic interpretation is still scarcely supported by evidence. Those who believe that democracies are more peaceful in general are at pains to ground this intuition on data because, as we said, democracies have been involved in wars as much as any other type of regime. If there is evidence in this sense, it is probably the case that it can be found only if one moves beyond the counting of countries' involvement in wars as such and differentiates between legitimate and illegitimate involvement, which presupposes the availability of moral criteria for distinguishing legitimate (or just) and illegitimate (or unjust) wars. Normative theories have of course been proposed to draw just that distinction (Walzer 1977), but so far political science has quite mysteriously decided to ignore them. This is unfortunate because nobody would seriously believe that the allies' involvement in the Second World War should be counted as evidence of their lack of peacefulness. Conversely, nobody, I hope, would be ready to construe the second war against Iraq as a case that should *not* be counted against the peacefulness of the USA and of all democracies that participated in that embarrassing adventure.

Be that as it may, the monadic interpretation still lacks empirical support, which, we suspect, it will never have until data on wars are collected without engaging in moral arguments. It should be noticed, though, that it enjoys a logical advantage over the dyadic interpretation, because it appears as more consistent. The dyadic interpretation, in fact, has a normative dimension that explains the separate peace among democracies in terms of a commitment to non-violence, respect for human rights, and habituation to a peaceful settlement of disputes. Now these values are probably compatible with the use of military force for self-defence or the protection of human rights (in certain circumstances), but they are not compatible with an indiscriminate and morally dubious use of force against other states simply because they are not democratic. Arguing that a democratic aggression is compatible with the very idea of a democratic peace simply because the opponent is autocratic is an ad hoc move of gigantic proportions. It would follow that democratic peace is compatible with bloody wars of expansion simply on condition that the invaded country is not democratic. Proponents of the dyadic interpretation (Doyle 2011), especially if pressed by critics with hard cases of democratic aggression, appear at times attracted by this easy way out. A solution that risks turning a theory proposed as capable of showing the intrinsic validity of Kant's model for peace into a grand *ex post* justification, among other things, of colonialism, imperialism, US-led overthrow of democratic regimes during the cold war and other democratic atrocities. Therefore, if democratic peace is to retain some meaning, this solution is to be avoided, and the model must make room for democratic violence only in certain well-specified cases (self-defence and human rights protection, again in certain well-specified circumstances). This means that democracies must have a peaceful attitude independently of the kind of regime they face, which in turn means that any dyadic interpretation must ultimately rest on some version of the monadic one.

6. Determinists and Probabilists

Another interesting point of controversy in DPT concerns the epistemological weight to be attached to the relation between democracy and peace. Some – let us call them the determinists – consider the presence of democratic institutions in a dyad as a sufficient condition for avoiding any risk of war. Others, more modestly, believe that shared democracy makes war less likely, not impossible, and we will call them probabilists. One form of determinism is the historical thesis formulated by Spencer Weart (1998). In reconstructing the relations between democratic and republican regimes since ancient Greece, including the free cities in medieval Italy (the *comuni*), the Swiss cantons, and up to the whole twentieth century, Wearth notices two regularities: (1) well-established democracies never fought each other; and (2) well-established oligarchies have rarely waged war on one another. Weart however does not merely notice these regularities but attempts an explanation, thereby moving to the level of social laws with a predictive value. Weart's explanation turns on the general human tendency to classify individuals either as insiders (those who are within our group) or as outsiders (those who are perceived as others and alien from us), with the ensuing feelings of trust or diffidence respectively. Weart in fact cites a substantial amount of psychological literature to back up the thesis that we look unconsciously at outsiders as inferiors, thereby justifying their exploitation – a treatment that we would not mete out to insiders. Democratic citizens and rulers perceive other democratic citizens and rulers as insiders and therefore respect them, while disrespecting non-democratic individuals. Oligarchic citizens and rulers respect other oligarchic individuals while disrespecting democratic outsiders.

Can we thus conclude that shared democracy is a sufficient condition to avoid conflict in democratic dyads? Very few scholars today would follow Weart down this path. For example, Russett flirts with the deterministic thesis (Russett and Oneal 2011: 48) but more often embraces the claim that shared democracy decreases significantly the probability of conflicts (Russett and Pevehouse: 2006). Thus the majority opinion among scholars is that shared democracy will make a conflict between two democratic states unlikely, but in and of itself this will not be a guarantee of peace.

7. Rationalists and Constructivists

Some scholars (Owen 2004) have recently found it useful to organize the various orientations of DPT independently of the peace-promoting mechanisms they focus on, but by reference to the categories of rationalism and constructivism. Constructivists emphasize the importance of values, beliefs, identities and self-identities in explaining the foreign policy of states (Risse-Kappen 1995; Hampton 1998/9; Kahl 1998/9; Wendt 1999). Rationalists assume that national players follow a value-free cost/benefit logic and that, given any international dispute, there is always a negotiable solution preferable (even for the eventual victor) to a war. It follows that the explanation of any international controversy must include an account of why the Pareto optimal solution was or was not reached (Fearon 1994). In explaining the absence of wars between democracies, these scholars point to features of democracies that facilitate bargaining and negotiation. For example, Fearon (1994) argues that democratic rulers cannot easily bluff during international crises: they would suffer high 'audience costs'. They are constrained to show a more reliable face during the crisis. And from this it follows that democratic dyads have a high probability of signalling to each other reliably, which in turn determines why their controversies, free of misunderstandings and bluffs, are always brought to a peaceful composition. This readability of democratic intentions is not present in any other dyads. This is for the rationalists why wars are more likely in these cases. Ultimately, it is a higher degree of 'rationality' typical of democratic controversies that explains both the absence of conflicts and also the relatively few cases in which controversies have escalated only one step short of war. Quite simply, democratic leaders avoid at all costs escalating and then stepping back because their *demoi* would punish them severely for their poor performance.

The constructivist/rationalist dichotomy has the virtue of highlighting the two sets of causal factors appealed to by DPT scholars.

On the one hand, we have an impersonal institutional mechanism (e.g. the structural transparency of democracies). On the other hand, an irreducibly normative/cultural/moral element, peculiar to democratic *demoi*, that ultimately yields – through a fairly complex causal chain – distinctive forms of behaviour on the international scene. The factors grouped in the two sets are obviously not incompatible with each other and they are assumed to work together towards an explanation of the fact of the democratic peace.

8. Sceptical Concerns

Each version of democratic peace theory has been subject to fierce criticism from scholars of different orientations. In what is widely considered the most powerful attack launched against DPT in recent years, Sebastian Rosato (2003, 2005) argues quite forcefully that democracies avoid fighting one another not because they are democracies, but because of other factors independent of regime type. Not only realists (Layne 1994) but other theoretical standpoints in IR theory have felt the need to reply to DPT (Garztke 1998; Owen 2004; Archibugi Koenig and Archibugi 2006). Critical-theoretical scholars, traditionally suspicious of research programmes broadly inspired by Enlightenment ideas, as well as neo-Marxist authors, traditionally suspicious of liberalism, have also expressed their concerns. The contributions collected in the volume edited by Barkawi and Laffey (2001) are all inspired by the conviction that liberalism is at best a self-indulging practice of liberal democracies and at worst a viciously ideological attempt on the part of the West to reinforce the pillars on which its supremacy rests. Some, including Bruce Cumings, Marck Rupert, Michael Mann (author of the controversial *The Dark Side of Democracy*, 2005), David Blaney and Timothy Kubik question the extent to which the countries that do not fight one another are democratic. Joining the small group of those sceptical even of the *fact* of democratic peace, Barkawi argues that if one uses Clausewitz's definition of war (roughly an extension of politics by other means) instead of that used in the Correlates of War Project, much of the empirical basis on which the theory rests is destined to vanish. Martin Shaw (2005) emphasizes that both the notion of democracy and that of peace have changed over the last two centuries so that the historical continuity presupposed by DPT is dubious. In what follows it is useful to organize the criticisms DPT has received in two main categories: (1) criticisms of the fact of the democratic peace, in which we include also all points raised to question the statistical significance of the fact itself; (2) criticisms levelled against the normative and the institutional logics of DPT.

9. Is it Really True that Democracies have Never Fought Each Other? And if True, is it Significant?

The historical fact of a 200-year-long absence of war between liberal-democratic states has been questioned mainly in two different ways. On the one hand, some scholars (Archibugi 1997, 2008, 2010; Layne 1996) have pointed to conflicts that in their opinion constitute counter-examples. Others have contested the definition of 'liberal state' used by Doyle as well as the statistical significance of the regularity, given the very small number of democracies present in the pre-Second World War period (Spiro 1996).

Archibugi, for one, notices how DPT supporters tend to exclude major war events such as the American Civil War or the First World War with dubious and quite ad hoc arguments. Regarding the first, it is said that it was a domestic conflict and that the Southern states were not fully democratic before the abolition of slavery. It is unclear, however, whether the democratic differential between the North and the South of the USA was big enough to justify the inclusion of the two parties in two fully distinct categories. Moreover, it is unclear why a bloody war between two democratic factions does not constitute a problem for DPT. Why, in other words, do only interstate conflicts matter? Finally, it should be taken into account that each member of the Union before the war enjoyed a considerable amount of autonomy up to the point that one could talk of a war between two democratic leagues as opposed to a domestic conflict.

Regarding the First World War, again the basis for conceptualizing the war as a conflict between a democratic coalition and an autocratic one are shaky. France, the United Kingdom and Italy are considered as liberal democracies, while Germany and its allies as autocracies. Now, how less democratic was Germany compared to France or the UK? To begin with, neither the UK nor Germany had reached male universal suffrage by 1914, while both had parliaments and parties competing for power. This does not mean that there was no difference. The military class in fact was significantly more powerful in Germany than in the UK. Largely populated by cadets coming from the high bourgeoisie with interests in industry and international commerce, the military class, prone to support Kaiser Wilhelm's war plans, was certainly the leading group in Germany. Moreover, the country had been permeated by an aggressive nationalist rhetoric. Finally, at the institutional level a significant difference was that the ministry of war was not, like in the UK, under the control of the parliament. The question is thus whether these undeniable differences are sufficient to include Germany and the UK in two opposed political categories. Analogous concerns could arise if the term of comparison is no longer the UK but France (universal suffrage but strong nationalism) or Italy (male suffrage limited to 9 per cent until 1913, and raised to 24 per cent for the 1913 elections, weak nationalism compensated by the bellicose inclination of the Salandra government). Similarly, Doyle's way of dealing with the 1812–15 Anglo-American war is to say that at that time only Great Britain was not 'democratic'. And this is true given his definition, but is the thin democratic difference between the USA and Great Britain sufficient not to consider the war a counter-example?

Another difficult case (of smaller proportions) is the war between the USA and Spain in 1898. Spain was then a constitutional monarchy, but the constitutional guarantees were quite limited. The king appointed the senators, had the power to revoke laws and was the commander-in-chief of all armed forces. The parliament was scarcely representative because only the interests of certain sectors of the bourgeoisie were protected. Despite all these democratic deficits, to what extent was Spain less liberal-democratic than the USA, where, for example, there was still a de facto segregationist policy in the Southern states? Other controversial cases are the 1849 repression of the newborn Roman Republic by republican France, the wars between Serbia and Croatia (1991–5) and the 1999 air raids against Serbia led by NATO. Concerning this last event, it should be recalled that Milošević's leadership had been the outcome of elections which international observers had recognized as free, even if not fully competitive. In fact, no equal access to mass media had been guaranteed to all parties before the elections, but very few found this a sufficient reason to call into question the legitimacy of the procedure.

A different yet very significant case is that of so-called *covert actions*. These are indirect hostile actions, often carried out by secret services, that some democracies (in particular the USA) took against other democracies, as is now known by the admission of the very people who ordered them. The best-known case is perhaps the operation, inspired and later admitted by Nixon, that the USA conducted against the newborn Chilean democracy. Salvador Allende had regularly won free elections but was a socialist (not even a communist or a friend of the USSR), and for that very reason was regarded with suspicion by the USA. The CIA backed and perhaps organized the counter-action by conservative forces (within the larger 'plan Condor') that culminated in the seizing of the Casa Rosada in 1973 and the killing of Allende. Telling are the words attributed to Nixon before the coup of 11 September 1973. Kissinger apparently said: 'I don't see why we need to stand by and watch a country go communist due to the irresponsibility of its people. The issues are much too important for the Chilean voters to be left to decide for themselves.'[10] No doubt, a statement of allegiance to democratic ideals by the government of the world's oldest constitutional democracy.

Other covert actions can be cited. As pointed out by Rosato (2005), on at least five more occasions the USA has – indirectly but heavily – interfered in the internal affairs of countries that, by Doyle's own definition, were democratic, causing a reversion to autocracy: Iran (1954), Indonesia (1957), British Guyana (1961), Brazil (1961, 1965), Nicaragua (1984). Certainly democracy in these countries was not well established at the time of the US interference, and the fact that these actions were and had to be carried out secretly says something in favour of DPT logic (Forsythe 1992; Russett 1993: 120–4), but up to what point?

Finally, there are the so-called 'near-wars', that is, diplomatic crises between democracies that came close to erupting in armed conflicts. In these cases, it is crucial to understand: (a) why democratic peoples and rulers who are supposed to share the same ideals of respect and non-violence came near to war; (b) why and how they finally stopped at the last minute before hostilities. If in fact the crisis was solved through that mediation invoked by DPT as one of the habits of democracies, or because of the respect originating in the mutual recognition of shared values, then these near-wars become significant pieces of evidence in favour of DPT. However, if the reasons leading to a peaceful composition had nothing to do with these mechanisms, and much to do with the usual balance of power or merely strategic calculation by national players, then the same events seem to become a problem. Layne (1996) offers a fairly detailed analysis of four profound diplomatic crises (or near-wars) between democracies: (1) the 1861 Anglo-American crisis known as the Trent Affair; (2) the 1895–6 Anglo-American crisis in Venezuela; (3) the 1898 Anglo-French Fashoda crisis, related to control of the Nile river; and (4) the Franco-German 1923 crisis over the Ruhr area. Layne shows (and no DPT supporter to my knowledge has contested this reconstruction) that fully realist factors led to the peaceful settlement of the crises. There is no evidence of moderation due to democratic factors, of an institutional or moral nature. Even less was it the utilitarian logic of Kant's first definitive article that helped to secure a peaceful outcome. Instead of having a democratic people checking a war-prone attitude in the leaders, in some cases just the opposite happened, with rulers restraining the bellicose spirits of their populations. Similar conclusions are reached by Stephen Rock (1997), who analyses Anglo-American relations between 1845 and 1930 to show that respect based on recognition of common values played little or no role in the avoidance of war between the two major and oldest democracies in the world.

As we have said, the fact of democratic peace has not only been contested through the citing of potential counter-examples. Perhaps a more intriguing and fundamental objection targets the definitions used in DPT. Zeev Maoz (certainly no opponent of DPT) has, for example, come up with a list of liberal-democratic regimes very different from the one adopted by Doyle. This has been used by critics of the theory such as David Spiro to challenge the accuracy of the definitions on which, obviously, much if not all of DPT robustness depends. Spiro also notices that DPT supporters call the 'good' countries at times 'liberal' and other times 'democratic'. Doyle for example focuses more on liberal elements (it is not accidental that he talks of a *liberal* peace) and is comfortable with the exclusion of entire sectors of the population from the right to vote, up to the point that a 'wide' suffrage of 30 per cent of the male population is considered sufficient to label a country as liberal-democratic (Doyle 2013: 212; Spiro 1996: 207–8).

There is finally a more technical objection that centers on the statistical relevance of a two- centuries-long absence of wars between democracies. Spiro (1994) tries to show that the 'zero war' fact could be accidental, hence insignificant. Given the list of liberal states adopted by DPT, Spiro calculates the number of possible dyads (pair of states) for each year and shows that the number of wars between democracies is not significantly different from the one generated by sheer chance. In other words, given the number of wars fought in a certain year and the number of possible dyads, the likelihood that two liberal states were at war is so low that the result of 'zero war' between liberal countries is not statistically significant. It is not different from the fact that in a family nobody has ever won a lottery. No serious scholar would start an investigation to explain why nobody in a family has ever won a lottery. Why – we could ask paraphrasing Spiro – should we then be concerned with explaining the 'fact of the democratic peace'?

10. Rosato. How Solid is the Logic of the Democratic Peace?

Concerns about the fact of the democratic peace are important, but only up to a point. On the one hand, most of those who deny a flawless regularity are ready to acknowledge that democratic dyads have experienced militarized disputes significantly less than any other dyads. Or, which is not the same thing but comes close to it, that democratic dyads have a lower probability of engaging in militarized combats in the future. On the other hand, even if the evidence in favour of a positive correlation between states' shared democratic features and peace is less robust than one thought, the causal relation that DPT suggests could nonetheless be true. We would merely have to wait and see if the low frequency of conflicts between democracies holds true in the future. Finally, Russett (1996) provided a fairly compelling reply to Spiro's charge of statistical insignificance.

We owe to Sebastian Rosato (2005) what remains today the strongest and most articulated criticism of what he calls the 'causal logics' of DPT. Rosato in fact does not challenge the fact of the democratic peace. He recognizes that, despite the attempts by Farber and Gowa (1997), Layne (1996), Spiro (1994) and – we could add – Archibugi (1997, 2008), the generalization remains robust, as also shown by the replies of Maoz (1998), Oneal and Russett

(1999), Weart (1998). He challenges the evidence in favour of the various causal relations (the 'logics' in his language) suggested by the theory to explain the fact of the democratic peace. Rosato first enucleates the various logics suggested by DPT scholars (and this is already a great intellectual increase of clarity) to show that the available evidence does not support and at times directly falsifies them.

What, then, are these logics? Rosato distinguishes six causal relations of which one relates to values and the remaining five to institutional features. The causal scheme that applies to all is: Democracy (D – independent variable) generates (or yields) a factor x that generates another factor y, which is in turn generates Peace (P – dependent variable). Briefly, $D \rightarrow x \rightarrow y \rightarrow P$. Table 1.1, which we take almost exactly from Rosato (2003), summarizes the six logics:

Table 1.1

Logic	Independent variable	Factor x	Factor y	Dependent variable
Normative	Democracy	Internal non-violence	External non-violence	Peace
Normative	Democracy	Commitment to liberal values	Trust and respect	Peace
Institutional	Democracy	Accountability	Public constraint on government	Peace
Institutional	Democracy	Accountability	Group constraint on government	Peace
Institutional	Democracy	Accountability	Slow mobilization	Peace
Institutional	Democracy	Accountability	No surprise attack	Peace
Institutional	Democracy	Accountability	Transparency	Peace

Unlike Rosato, who identifies one normative logic only, we distinguish two: one captures the democracies' alleged tendency to externalize the internal norm of peaceful settlement of disputes. The other deals with the respect and trust that democracies should show each other on the basis of common values. In fact, Rosato himself (2003: 586) distinguishes norm externalization and trust/respect as two components of the same logic. But what exactly are the values democracies share? The normative logic insists on the fact that democracies value violent-free dispute settlement, trust other democracies to do the same, and in general respect them for sharing the same values. Even if Rosato is not explicit about it, at the heart of the normative logic lies the intuition that a democratic regime refuses to use violence as a way of solving controversies. This stance suffers exceptions only in a very limited number of circumstances: (a) the necessity of self-defence and (b) the protection of human rights in the face of serious and massive violations committed by other governments against their citizens.

It is debatable whether these values are compatible with aggressive policies neither dictated by self-defence, nor inspired by human rights concerns. The historical example usually cited to support this claim is John Stuart Mill's permission to intervene against 'barbarous' peoples even if they pose no threat to civilized countries. As he puts it,

> there assuredly are cases in which it is allowable to go to war, without having been ourselves attacked, or threatened with attack ... To suppose that the same international customs, and the same rules of international morality, can obtain between one civilized nation and another, and between civilized nations and barbarians, is a grave error. (Mill 1973 [1859])

There is much to say about the internal consistency of Mill's liberalism, but in any event it is unlikely that any definition of liberalism acceptable *today* is compatible with this permission to conduct aggressive foreign policies against non-liberals. The normative logic, as originally presented by Doyle, rests on the idea that what liberals respect in other liberals is a common commitment to tolerance, respect for individual liberties, attachment to the ideal of non-violence.

The other five causal relations are institutional in kind and have in common a focus on elites' accountability. Reminiscent of Kant's first definitive article, it is stipulated that war between democracies is impeded by some form of popular control on the decisions of government, or by other mechanisms ultimately related to popular constraint. Democratic elites have to justify their decisions before electors if they are to have any chance of being re-elected. This general feature of accountability generates five features that are supposed to make wars between democracies unlikely. They range from the people's opposition – at least as default stance – to wars because of the material and moral costs they entail, to the anti-war attitude of some specific groups (think of the groups with interests in the country targeted as the potential enemy). Additionally, the necessity for democracies to discuss publicly and openly any decision to go to war eliminates the risk of sudden attack (slow mobilization and transparency). Finally, because democratic elites cannot afford to bluff on the international scene (their electors would make rulers pay dearly for such a poor showing), democracies tend to send clear and reliable signals to other states. Moreover, if a democracy does decide to wage war, it usually has strong support from the population, which makes it a particularly difficult enemy. Democratic threats are therefore usually taken seriously and, during inter-democratic controversies, the parties have no interest in exacerbating the confrontation, knowing that the potential enemy is both ready to go down the path of war if no other solution is offered and that it will be a strong and determined enemy (Bueno de Mesquita et al. 1999: 802–3; Schultz 1998: 840–1; Reiter and Stam 1998; Fearon 1994).

The same democratic characteristics are used to explain why democracies are so often at war with autocratic regimes. Briefly: (1) democracies do not respect and trust autocracies; (2) public opinion by and large supports wars that are perceived as just; (3) groups usually interested in peaceful conditions favourable to business may turn in favour of wars that are considered either inevitable or supported by strong reasons; (4) autocracies may launch a sudden attack and this favours preventive moves on the part of democracies; (5) autocracies do not provide reliable information on their intentions; (6) autocracies are perceived as intrinsically unstable and therefore weak, because the population is expected to oppose the regime. Each of these reasons, and often a combination of them, weakens the anti-bellicose nature of democracies, thereby explaining why mixed dyads are statistically as war-prone as autocratic dyads.

So, what's wrong with the logics of the democratic peace? Let us start with the normative logic. On Rosato's interpretation, it rests on the externalization of domestic norms of peaceful conflict resolution. Since democratic citizens and rulers are socialized in an environment in which conflicts are processed and settled in a non-violent way, they tend to adopt the same attitude towards international controversies. A negotiating attitude is thus the default position of democracies which – this is the gist of the normative logic – avoid violence except in very limited and well-defined cases, namely self-defence, protection of basic human rights or some combination of the two that may suggest a forced democratization for protecting the human rights of the population and prevent future aggression by autocratic regimes.

If this is the normative logic, it is easy to find evident counter-examples that discredit any explanation based on it. To begin with, democracies have fought many wars that are not even remotely motivated by self-defence or human rights protection. From 1815 to 1975, from a total of 108 registered military events, democracies have fought 66 of them, of which 33 were of an imperial nature, that is, against independent peoples, and 33 of a colonial nature, that is, against peoples already subjugated. Examples range from wars of conquest to more strategic aggressions carried out to guarantee that other powers would not occupy a geopolitically significant region. Even if few of these 66 wars can be considered as self-defensive because they have not been initiated by democracies, the number of clearly 'unjustifiable' conflicts for which democracies have been responsible is so high that the normative logic appears irreparably damaged. The only partially valid reply (Russett 1995), as we shall see in detail later, will insist that the democratic habit of settling controversies in a non-violent manner is only one of the factors that contribute to the 'special' behaviour of democracies in the international arena. Taken in isolation, it is neither necessary nor sufficient to determine democracies' decisions. At most it is a factor that lowers the probability of democracies' engagement in wars (Caranti 2006c).

If we look at the second normative logic, things seem no better. Do democracies really trust and respect each other? Rosato shows that when interests collide, these regimes are far less respectful than DPT assumes. We have already cited the covert interventions by the USA against newborn democracies. To be sure, one could contest Rosato's historical assessment of the democratic nature of the regimes targeted by the USA. For example, it is taken for granted that Allende's regime was not communist or deeply linked to the USSR, and therefore immune to the logic of the cold war. This is true if one thinks that Allende was a social democrat and at first not interested in a relationship with Moscow. But after the first difficulties Allende did ask for support from the USSR and this obviously meant the possibility that the USA's competitor could gain a strong foothold in Latin America. Seen from this perspective, one could say, the USA's covert actions were directed not against Latin American democracies, but indirectly against the USSR. Still, it remains undeniable that geopolitical considerations – no matter how well grounded – prevailed over the respect that one democracy was expected to have for another. Recall Kissinger's words: 'I don't see why we need to stand by and watch a country go communist due to the irresponsibility of its people. The issues are much too important for the Chilean voters to be left to decide for themselves.' Interestingly, this remark combines cold war logic excusing such an intervention (given DPT logic) and a readiness to ignore those democratic ideals on which DPT normative logic rests.

Something very similar to Chile could be said about British Guyana in the sixties when the CIA intervened to avoid the election of the allegedly communist Cheddi Jagan of the People's Progressive Party as prime minister. Moreover, one should not forget that at times the 'covert action' was targeted not at young and fragile democracies, with some dangerous inclination towards Moscow. Rather they were aimed at fairly consolidated regimes that were giving no sign of falling into the sphere of influence of the USA's world competitor. Think of the cases of Guatemala in 1954, when the army of Col. Carlos Castillo – organized and fuelled by the CIA – invaded the Republic of Guatemala from Honduras and El Salvador to overthrow the democratically elected government of the *liberal* president Árbenz Guzmán. Tellingly, the justification was again the fear that Árbenz Guzmán would turn Guatemala into a USSR puppet state. Yet it is hard to believe that the interests of the multinational United Fruit Company – damaged by Guzmán's land reforms – played no role in the CIA plan.

Finally, the 1964 coup in Brazil that ultimately overthrew President João Goulart. Again, the reason for the intervention was Goulart's 'socialist' policy of redistribution of the profits of foreign and local multinationals. Led by the armed forces and supported by the United States, the coup began a twenty-year autocratic rule in Brazil that ended only in 1985. Hardly an example of sincere commitment to democratic ideals by the most powerful democracy of the time. Even less a sign of trust and respect for fellow democracies.

All in all, even if the targeted regimes were not full and ideal, let alone old liberal democracies, it is certain that they were more so than their predecessors and clearly more so than the *juntas* the USA contributed to installing after them. The fact that these actions had to be kept secret, among other things to avoid criticism by the American people, is of little significance. The normative logic is in fact that both peoples and rulers in a democracy trust and respect other democrats. In this context, one should not omit the analyses by Layne (1966) and Rock (1997) that we mentioned above. In the near-wars between democracies, what prevented the parties from escalating to a militarized dispute were reasons very different from mutual trust and respect. Even if one grants, with some hermeneutical charity, that the normative logic does not make mutual trust and respect a sufficient factor for avoiding conflict, we should still be able to see at least some hesitation on the part of the attacking democracy due to the recognition that the target is a fellow democracy. But alas, no such sign is evident. Regarding the first normative logic, democracies have solved controversies merely for purely realist reasons – interest and mutual advantage – while there is no evidence of some restraining force exercised by virtue of a shared non-violent attitude. Regarding the second normative logic, the two contending countries do not seem to have been constrained even a little by the similarity of their values.

What about the institutional logic? As we saw, here Rosato distinguishes five mechanisms, but at a closer look one can reduce the variety to two main causal relations. On the one hand, public opinion's pacifism is in this context not of a deontological nature (otherwise it would fall into the normative logic), but is based on the legitimate interest the population has in avoiding the costs of the conflict. Similar interests move the groups Rosato refers to. If I do not want a war against a country because it is there that my investments are concentrated, we are still within the same logic and it seems reasonable to group these two mechanisms under the same logic that goes back to Kant's first definitive article. On the other hand, slow mobilization, no surprise attack, and transparency all descend from the necessity for democratic elites to build popular consensus for a military operation (at least for those not covert).

What is wrong with these two logics? First of all, Rosato doubts that democratic leaders are more 'accountable' than autocrats. He thus calls into question a sort of dogma that has been taken for granted since Kant's time. If one looks at the available evidence, it does not seem that democratic leaders are under stronger constraints than their autocratic counterparts when it comes to deciding whether their country should enter a war. At least, if one looks at the costs leaders face in case of defeat, autocratic leaders risk much more (prison, exile, execution) than democratic ones (at most they lose the next election and/or have their political careers ruined). Regarding the alleged 'interested pacifism' of democratic populations, the pacifying factor should work independently of whether democracies face similar or dissimilar regimes. But, as we know, democracies fight wars in absolute terms as much as autocracies, and only on rare occasions has this happened for reasons of self-defence or human rights protection. What is left, then, of Kant's intuition in the first definitive article? Obviously today wars are very different from those imagined by Kant, who – not accidentally – despised mercenary armies. The widespread abolition of conscription in contemporary democracies, which in some countries went so far as to 'subcontract' military operations to private corporations (the USA heavily relied on subcontractors for the 2003 war in Iraq), made it easier for bellicose democratic leaders to bypass popular control. Just to mention one figure, if one excludes the two world wars, of all wars fought by democracies, only in 6 per cent of the cases was more than 0.1 per cent of the population involved in the military operations. Professional armies have thus – as predicted by Kant – greatly diminished the peace potential of democracies.[11] Moreover, we know that the alleged pacifism of democratic *demoi* can easily be overcome by nationalistic feelings, more or less generated by regime propaganda. The wars in the former Yugoslavia dramatically bear witness to that. Finally, one should not underestimate the fact that democratic leaders have a direct interest in mobilizing the country because the constraints to which they are subject in times of peace are usually weakened during a war. The executive branch, on the verge of or within a war, increases its power and operates virtually without control by the legislative.

Regarding the pacifist groups which should stop the war, things are not very different. On the one hand, history shows that often pro-war groups have overcome pacifist groups in the public debate preceding a military event (Owen 1997; Snyder 1991).[12] On the other hand, it is not clear why this peace-inducing mechanism is not operative in mixed dyads. To be sure, groups in autocratic regimes have less leverage than that exercised by groups in democracies. However, for the reasons seen above, powerful groups favoured by the autocrat usually risk much more than democratic groups in a war. Moreover, in autocracies those in power need to compromise with groups currently excluded from power if they want to buy their support for the war. And this constitutes an additional disincentive to military adventures peculiar to autocracies.

On slow mobilization and surprise attacks, Rosato adopts a study conducted by Rourke (1993) that shows how US presidents have easily bypassed the authorization of Congress to use military force. In 200 cases, only 6 times had Congress the opportunity to authorize the intervention *ex ante*. Most of the time it did it *post factum* or not at all. For example, during the first Gulf War, President G. H. W. Bush had no preventive authorization form Congress. Moreover, he later declared that, even had Congress objected, he would have gone ahead anyway. Similar considerations could be advanced for France. For example, in March 2011 President Sarkozy launched air strikes against Gaddafi's forces in Libya without consulting the French Assembly. To be sure, presidential or semi-presidential systems can launch surprise attacks more easily than parliamentary systems. The recent (August 2013) refusal by the British parliament of Prime Minister Cameron's proposal to engage the UK in military action against the Syrian government shows that parliamentary democracies work differently. Nonetheless it remains true that the institutional logic, resting on division of powers and the mechanism of checks and balances, does not always work as predicted. Since the end of the Second World War, ten major surprise attacks have taken place in the world. Two of them were launched by democracies: (1) the joint attack by France, UK and Israel (1956) and (2) the six-day war initiated by Israel (1967). In these cases the executive power has been quite efficient in hiding its intentions not only from the enemy, but also from public opinion in its own country.

Regarding transparency, understood as readability of foreign policy plans, to which democracies are allegedly tied by virtue of the need to have a public debate before a war, Rosato notices that a distinction must be drawn between the accuracy and the abundance of the information. When a democracy debates the opportunity to enter a war, it rarely does so with one coherent voice. The parties that support the government and opposition, opinion makers and media often diverge on the opportunity to engage the country in military operations. It is therefore difficult for an external observer to understand exactly what a democracy will do. Recent events again offer a good example. In September 2013 nobody knew what the USA or France would do about Syria, despite an official statement by President Obama on the necessity to intervene. In fact, in the end the USA did *not* intervene against Assad. Even when public opinion is largely and consistently against the war, this is not a reliable guide. Rosato cites the following cases: Madison decided on war against England in 1812 despite the opinion of the Federalists. Truman entered the Korean war despite the opposition of some Republican senators. The UK 1956 attack on Egypt was opposed by the Labour party. Some Democratic congressmen were against the first Gulf War (1990). We can add various examples of democracies sending unreliable signs on the occasion of the second Gulf War. If public opinion in the USA was divided about the opportunity to attack Saddam Hussein, it was clear that public opinion in European democracies was largely opposed to the war, but this did not prevent some of their governments (Italy, Spain, UK) following George W. Bush and joining the so-called Coalition of the Willing. To sum up: *often* democracies do not send reliable signs.

The conclusion to which we are pushed by Rosato's analysis is that, once all arguments put forward by DPT proponents to explain the fact of democratic peace are carefully distinguished and confronted with available evidence, none of them stands. This obviously does not mean that democracy and peace are unrelated. While Rosato seems to believe precisely that, preferring an explanation that looks at the hegemonic role of the USA in the post-Second World War period, the more modest conclusion his critiques lead to is that the fact of democratic peace still has no convincing explanation.

11. Liberal Replies

Predictably, Rosato's articulate criticism generated a variety of replies. In a forum hosted in the 2005 issue of the *American Political Science Review* Doyle and others offered interesting arguments that do not discredit the evidence cited by Rosato, but mainly point to alleged misunderstandings of the very logic of DPT that Rosato targets. Kinsella (2005) insists on the dyadic logic of the theory that – he thinks – Rosato fails to take into due consideration. Rosato is wrong, for example, when he assumes that the externalization of pacific norms of controversy resolution entails a democratic attitude to fighting wars only for reasons of self-defence and to avoid aggression. This is not DPT's normative logic. Democracies externalize their peaceful method of conflict resolution only when they can expect that other states will do the same in return. In all cases in which they do not know enough, or are under the impression that they have insufficient knowledge about the political process in other states, sheer uncertainty may lead democracies to wage wars against such 'black boxes'. The same failure to pay due attention to the dyadic logic – continues Kinsella – leads Rosato on the wrong path in his evaluation of the other logics. For example, when Rosato notices that democratic public opinion is not as peace-prone as expected, he fails to consider that in the vast majority of the cases democratic *demoi* have supported a war when the enemy was autocratic.

Is Kinsella's reply convincing? The impression remains that, given any reasonable interpretation of the normative logic, democracies should avoid all wars that are not clearly fought for reasons of self-defence, and should limit preventive wars according to the same logic of self-defence. To assume that it is permissible for democracies to attack states about which they do not know enough is equivalent to assuming that a policeman is allowed to shoot a criminal because he *could have* a gun and *could plan using it*. Since any reasonable liberal would condemn the second act as unacceptable violence, should she not do the same about the first? Moreover, we know that democracies' colonial and imperial wars have not been motivated by ignorance of the internal political processes of the targeted states; even less by the possibility that such states or peoples could constitute a threat to security. Obviously, if in the notion of self-defence one includes also the protection of colonial interests by liberal groups or individuals, then pretty well anything becomes a war of self-defence. But such an ad hoc move does not deserve much attention. Finally, and most importantly, to assume that an attack by a democracy motivated by uncertainty or ignorance about the intentions of an opponent is compatible with DPT opens the path to those 'ambushes' rightly feared and denounced by Russett (2006) after George W. Bush's attempt to use DPT as a legitimation of the second Gulf War. If the cost of a convincing reply to Rosato is that of making DPT an ally of democratic aggression and a tool in the hands of irresponsible democratic leaders, the price is obviously too high.

Doyle's reply to Rosato fortunately follows a different path and points to the real weakness of his criticisms, which is Rosato's separate treatment of each pillar of the theory. Liberal-democratic domestic government, international IGOs (which strangely in this reply Doyle turns into 'respect of some basic human rights') and transnational interdependence should not be understood as being each sufficient to explain peace between democracies. Since the very beginning (Doyle 1983a and 1983b) the idea has been that the combination of all three factors yields peaceful inter-democratic relations, but none of them separately is to be considered as sufficient. In Doyle's own words: 'No one of these constitutional, international or cosmopolitan sources is alone sufficient, but together (and only where together) they plausibly connect the characteristics of liberal politics and economies with sustained liberal peace' (Doyle 1983a: 232). Thus, when Rosato attacks the normative logic and shows that the USA had little hesitation in striking (more or less covertly) at other democratic regimes (see the list above), he forgets to check whether there were common memberships in sufficiently developed IGOs and a sufficient level of economic (and possibly cultural) interdependence. Or, when Rosato attacks the institutional logic relative to the reliability of signals that a democracy sends out, he again forgets to check whether these signals were inserted in pre-existing stable diplomatic channels (IGOs), and whether there was interdependence between the state sending and the one receiving signals.

Liberal institutions and values dominant within states, IGOs based on reciprocal respect of members which see each other as reliable, transparent and treaty-respecting partners, and high levels of economic interdependence are the three factors that promote peace. While each of them gives a contribution, it is only the combination of all three that *guarantees* peace. It follows that none of the following scenarios can be considered as a counter-example of DPT: (a) wars in mixed dyads if either economic interdependence or common membership in IGOs is lacking (or *a fortiori* if both are lacking); (b) inter-democratic wars or even disputes if the two democracies do not share permanent diplomatic channels (IGOs) or are not interdependent; (c) a democratic aggressive foreign policy against an illiberal state, as in the case of colonial or imperial wars. In this case, Doyle argues (2005: 465), the crucial factor was the merging of material interests (protection of property abroad) and liberal ideologies linked to the *mission civilisatrice*, that is, a sort of paternalism *à la* Mill. In the absence of mutual recognition among liberal peoples, material interests coalesce with paternalistic ideologies, given that the colonized were perceived as not deserving respect and incapable of self-government.

How convincing is Doyle's reply? While Doyle is certainly correct in emphasizing the insufficiency of each of the three pillars of DPT, and therefore the necessity that all three work together to yield the predicted result, there are at least two points that remain unaddressed. To begin with, Doyle's strategy to defuse the problematic phenomena of liberal colonialism and imperialism is surprising, to say the least. If liberalism were a theory committed to non-violence, respect for human rights, and self-government *only towards other liberals*, it would be a rather strange theory, close to schizophrenic. It simply does not make sense to say that you are committed to non-violence and basic civil, political and economic rights *and* that you are allowed to colonize other people for exploitation and/or paternalism. Not accidentally, the Kantian model that will be proposed in the next chapter as an alternative to DPT is not committed to this unpleasant theoretical result and has plenty of space for condemning old or new forms of colonialism, imperialism and sheer aggression. Secondly, it should be noticed that in all the cases of covert actions mentioned above, the USA and the targeted countries (British Guyana, Guatemala, Brazil, Chile) were co-members of at least two significant IGOs: the UN and the OAS. Shared membership in the OAS is particularly significant. The membership of this IGO has always been largely democratic. Hence it is the paramount example of the kind of IGO that should promote peace (Russett and Pevehouse 2006).[13] Also consider that the level of economic interdependence was high, up to the point that one of the motivations behind the CIA operation was the protection of US multinationals' interests in the targeted countries. So one need not consider CIA covert operations in Latin America as splendid counter-examples of DPT, even in the enlarged understanding of the theory defended by Doyle, only at the price of failing to consider them wars. And this is correct, given the standard definition of war assumed by DPT scholars.[14] But, even if covert operations are not wars, one can hardly believe that they do not impact on DPT normative logic.

The conclusion to which we are led is thus that Doyle's reply to Rosato, despite its opportune insistence on the interconnection of all three pillars of the Kantian peace, falls short of restoring DPT's full credibility. The necessity of a rethinking of the whole theory, in particular with regard to its normative underpinning, suggests itself quite forcefully. A way to carry out this reformulation will be provided in the following chapter, where DPT and Kant's model, as reconstructed so far, will be compared, contrasted and evaluated.

6 • The Two Models Compared

In the preceding chapters we have reconstructed the Kantian model (chapter 4) and the model of democratic peace (chapter 5). Even if we have already mentioned some points of differentiation in the course of the exposition, it is useful to have a synoptic view that sums up the major differences. This will also help the evaluation of the policy indications that derives from the two models. The political agendas suggested by the two models are significantly different. What follows is not a mere intellectual exercise. We have already seen how DPT has heavily influenced the foreign policy of Western countries, the USA in particular. On our interpretation, Kant offers an alternative set of policy indications, thereby giving us the possibility of rethinking the foreign policy of democratic countries in the twenty-first century. We touch here on the part of the Kantian legacy that may have the strongest impact on reality, if taken seriously and understood properly.

1. Democratic Peace Theory: Normative Indications

Since there are, as we saw, various versions of DPT, it is difficult to infer from them a coherent and unified set of policy indications. However, we can significantly reduce the variety if, taking advantage of the criticisms levelled against DPT that we briefly discussed in chapter 5, we adopt the following stratagem. We focus on the version that remains credible even after all major critiques have been duly taken into consideration. One can hardly doubt that Doyle's version of DPT, refined and further clarified over the years, is by far the best equipped to rebut criticisms. As often happens in major research programmes, the original is better than the copies. The great virtue of Doyle's theory is that he insists from the beginning on the necessity of all three peace-promoting factors he reads in Kant.

Doyle reiterates this relation of mutual dependence in reply to Rosato's criticism that, it will be recalled, put under scrutiny *separately* the various pacifying factors invoked by DPT. Analysed one by one and never considered as parts of a causal story that guarantees peace only when all factors are operative, Rosato had an easy victory. Colonial and imperial wars waged by democracies, bellicose democratic peoples willing to wage wars even when the government is hesitant, inter-democratic relations far from being inspired by mutual trust and respect, wars between countries that could be considered 'liberal-democratic' by modifying slightly Doyle's definition, peace-inducing institutional mechanisms stronger in autocracies than in democracies are all wonderful counterexamples that discredit the idea that each of the factors invoked by DPT is sufficient to guarantee peace. They hardly prove, however, that their combination does not yield the expected result. The best defense for DPT is evidently that of returning to the original intuition of factors sufficient to guarantee peace only if simultaneously present.

Let us then focus on the version of DPT that, very briefly, goes as follows. Liberal-democratic values and institutions within states; presence of IGOs largely, if not exclusively, with democratic members; a high level of economic interdependence: these are the three factors that promote peace and explain the fact of democratic peace. While each factor makes its contribution to pacifying international relations, only the simultaneous presence of all three guarantees peace. Obviously, this is compatible with the fact that one factor in specific circumstances is sufficient to avoid conflicts. For example, despite all sorts of tensions between the USA and China (accusations of commercial fraud, unfair currency exchange policies, infringements of intellectual property), and despite the enormous difference of the domestic political regimes, the two countries have not come even close to fighting. The high level of economic interdependence has clearly facilitated this result. Possibly, also shared membership in IGOs where they enjoy *equal status* (their reciprocal veto power in the UN Security Council) has contributed. In the 1970s and 1980s, despite their considerable commercial rivalry, Japan and the USA avoided military confrontation because of a good level of economic interdependence (although lower than the interdependence today of the USA and China) and a sense of reciprocal trust generated by the fact that Japan was no longer an autocratic state. Autocratic states such as the Arab states, with a low level of economic interdependence but great interests in the natural resources (oil, water, land) of neighbouring states, have avoided a high number of conflicts by virtue of their common membership in the Arab League (Hassouna 1975). It follows that potential falsifiers of the theory are not inter-democratic wars per se (assuming that there are some), or wars between highly interdependent states per se, or wars between co-members of an IGO per se. Potential falsifiers are wars that happen despite the combined presence of the three factors mentioned above.

This is thus the best version of the theory. What normative indications can be inferred from it? First of all, DPT does *not* suggest any coerced democratization of the world. Self-interested democratic leaders such as George W. Bush may have exploited the theory to justify an aggressive foreign policy, but of similar 'bushwhacks' – to use a witty title by Russett (2005) – DPT is a victim, certainly not the culprit. What DPT suggests is rather the creation and spontaneous enlargement of a federation comprising all liberal democracies in a sort of exclusive club. DPT also recommends integrating the economies of member states, so that the third ingredient for peace is operative. This creates a zone of peace meant to expand as the 'wage' of (uncoerced) democratization continues and new countries turn to liberal-democratic values and institutions.

But let us now turn to the relations with the part of the world that remains outside the 'zone of peace'. Here the normative guidance of DPT is puzzling. In the first place, the theory affirms that disrespect for those outside the 'liberal golden circle' is fully compatible with the 'liberal internationalism' practised in the 'good' part of the world. This internationalism (still of a Kantian nature?) that Doyle (1986) distinguishes from 'liberal pacifism' and 'liberal imperialism' is also compatible with an attitude of exploitation towards illiberal peoples. This is the surprising answer Doyle (2005) gives to Rosato's point about colonial and imperial wars. As we saw, Doyle believes that a combination of paternalism, disrespect for non-liberal states and economic interest is what led liberal democracies to aggressive wars of conquest. It follows that even today, according to DPT it is perfectly legitimate for a liberal democracy to wage wars that are not even remotely connected to self-defence and protection of human rights.

Notice the paradox: on Doyle's reconstruction, DPT would not justify controversial wars such as the second Iraq War with the argument that the spread of democracy is what the world needs to become secure – which was in fact the moral George W. Bush's administration readily drew from DPT. DPT would rather explain the war as an attempt to protect the interests of liberal countries in a region unworthy of respect. DPT would therefore unmask the real motivation behind the war, but only to legitimize it from a different and even more embarrassing normative perspective. This sort of pre-Westphalian standpoint would legitimize the war in Iraq as an instance of the natural disrespect liberals have towards illiberal regimes and (perhaps) illiberal peoples.

Even if we refrain from drawing such paradoxical conclusions, the least one can say is that DPT offers no clear indication regarding the path to follow to improve world security. Moreover, the few clear indications we receive are problematic:

1. States that have already become liberal-democratic do not have to do much to improve themselves; in the best versions of DPT, they have to improve their record of respect for socio-economic rights for the sake of better political participation; this is the (forgotten) lesson that comes from Doyle's insistence, already present in his seminal essay (Doyle 1983a), on the necessity that not only civic and political rights, but also socio-economic ones be respected for the theory to work. The same lesson is to be found in the 'more precise idea of the democratic peace' that Rawls (1999) defends, by spelling out certain conditions that need to be met to ensure that the mechanism foreseen by DPT (people limiting rulers' aggressive policies) is operative. Other than that, there is really nothing liberal democracies need to do. In particular, it is not clear whether the diffusion of a republican ethos, which goes beyond a generic 'respect for individual freedoms' and includes the rejection of wars unmotivated by 'good reasons' (self-defence or human rights protection), is thought of as a goal liberal democracies need to pursue. In other words, nothing is said about the preconditions that need to be met to ensure that liberal peoples and rulers do more than respect only other liberal countries and adopt foreign policies compatible with democratic principles.

2. Illiberal states are excluded from the IGO that covers the 'zone of peace' between liberals. On a version of DPT built on Rawlsian principles, the exclusion would be mitigated by the acceptance of 'decent' peoples (Rawls 1999). Obviously,

the idea is not that liberal countries should never enter into IGOs with illiberal states. They could do so, for example, to facilitate commerce with those states. The idea is rather that IGOs become effective as an instrument of peace mainly, if not exclusively, if their membership is largely democratic (Russett and Pevehouse 2006). Supranational organizations are not thought of as means to increase the security of the relations with illiberal countries, let alone as means that contribute to democratize them.

3. A disrespect by liberals towards illiberal countries (and perhaps peoples) is not considered an unwelcome reflex that needs to be cured, but elevated to a natural and therefore legitimate moral disposition.

4. Commercial exchanges not inspired by fair terms of cooperation, and potentially biased to favour powerful countries, are accepted. The rules currently governing trade and intellectual property, which clearly favour rich, powerful countries (Pogge 2008), would therefore (a) be considered in line with liberal-democratic values and (b) no less peace-promoting than rules that establish fair terms of co-operation.

5. Regarding the ways in which liberal countries are supposed to treat foreigners, and in particular the citizens of states whose access to the federation is precluded, DPT is probably committed to legitimize an attitude of indifference or even disrespect. In any event, no mention is made of the fact (at the centre of the UN insistence on human rights) that protection of human rights is, besides being something intrinsically good, an instrument to prevent wars. Not accidentally, the content of Kant's third definitive article, centred on the 'right to visit' and on respect for what we today call basic human rights, is reduced to the recommendation to make economies interdependent. Moreover, it is not clear whether interdependence is considered capable of promoting peace only among liberal democracies or in general.

6. In terms of security policy *stricto sensu*, wars can be waged against illiberal regimes for reasons that include paternalism,

protection of commercial interests, self-bestowed permission to violate basic rules of international law. Again here the crucial text is Doyle's reply to Rosato who, it will be recalled, argues that colonial and imperial wars, far from violating DPT logic, strengthen it.

2. The Kantian Model: Normative Indications

Using the reconstruction advanced in chapter 4, let us move to the policy indications we can derive from the Kantian model. At a very general level, Kant suggests to peoples and countries that they adopt, spontaneously and without coercion, a few basic rules (the preliminary articles) of good policy and reciprocal respect aimed at containing and limiting the inevitable sense of reciprocal diffidence and latent animosity of the international arena. Diffidence and latent animosity are inevitable until three major reforms (the definitive articles) of domestic, international and cosmopolitan right are implemented: (1) states need to adopt domestic republican institutions (where by 'republican' is meant something different from liberal-democratic); (2) interstate relations concerned with security and possibly other areas need to be filtered through the permanent channels of IGOs, with regional or global reach, to which all kinds of states (not only republics) are allowed to participate as members with equal status; (3) international trade and cultural exchange need to expand in a context of fair rules in such a way as to build a cosmopolitan civil conscience that each individual develops and cultivates along with regional, national and supranational identities.

Notice that, contrary to a common interpretation, Kant does not suggest that the definitive articles are to be implemented only when the preliminary ones have been fully realized. Nor does he think that the second and third definitive articles concern only those states that are already in line with the prescription of the first. And so on. The preliminary articles ensure that international relations are not in a condition so difficult that the implementation of the definitive ones is impossible. Intuitively, we need to avoid building a huge threatening mercenary army if we want to share common membership in a security IGO with a neighbouring state. Similarly, we need to avoid interference in the internal political affairs of a neighbouring country if we plan on building a high level of economic and cultural exchange or a common membership of IGOs. It follows that a responsible politician should attempt to realize *as much as possible* both sets of articles *simultaneously*. In fact, there is no incompatibility between the two sets. Rejecting mercenary armies at home and refraining from undue interference in the affairs of neighbouring states is compatible with the attempt to build an IGO. Avoiding a huge public debt for the sake of future military campaigns is not only compatible with the effort to bring one's state closer to republican standards but is clearly functional to that goal. And so on.

Having clarified that much, let us proceed to list the six normative indications one receives from Kant. To facilitate the comparison, they parallel the six indications from DPT we identified in the preceding section:

1. No existing republic can be satisfied with the level of normative and institutional development achieved. Rather, there should be a tension to approximate an ideal of political excellence that foresees, among other things, the moving away from the reduction of a republic to a regime in which individual freedoms and rights are guaranteed and used strategically by citizens merely to protect and maximize their interests. Most importantly, a republic cannot be satisfied if, in expressing preferences, citizens pay no attention to the moral quality of the political outcome, where by 'moral quality' is meant attention to ensuring that decisions are taken with an eye to building, preserving and strengthening the *equal* status of citizens. This is possible only if large socio-economic inequalities and asymmetrical powers are progressively removed and all citizens are given the chance of an active and informed participation in the political life of the country. This is the essence of the distinction between liberal democracy and republic that we drew in chapter 4.

2. *All* states need to enter regional or global IGOs to overcome a lawless condition and establish a juridical framework to handle possible disputes through permanent diplomatic channels and possibly an independent judge. This is particularly urgent for the relations between republics and despotic regimes and for the relations of despotic regimes among themselves, because

in these cases the republican peace-inductive mechanisms – of an institutional and normative nature – are entirely absent or seriously limited, and certainly not present, as in the case of republican dyads.

3. Interference in the internal affairs of despotic states, let alone military campaigns to promote economic interests, are incompatible with republican standards. To be sure, a moral condemnation of the injustice of despotic regimes is permissible. Freedom to criticize one's own rulers in writing is allowed. A fortiori – although Kant is not explicit about it – the right to criticize foreign regimes should be guaranteed. Nothing beyond this moral condemnation is permitted, and any aggressive attitude the republican people may have to be cured through the participation of citizens in political life. With the passing of time, rejection of violence as a means to settle disputes, and something to be used only for self-defence – typical of republican institutions – will become second nature to republican citizens.

4. Economic interdependence and cultural dialogue are to be promoted not only between republics but also in mixed or autocratic dyads. But the increase in the percentage of international trade between two countries will have pacifying effects only when trade is inspired by fair terms of cooperation.

5. Over and above economic interdependence, what most efficiently promotes peace is an attitude of respect towards foreigners, which includes a disposition to create the condition for a common global conscience and a commitment to respect for the 'rights of mankind'.

6. Colonial and imperial wars are to be banned absolutely, including those in which the promotion of interest has been coupled with 'noble ends' such as the civilizing mission of republican powers. Far from making republics closer to their natural vocation, these adventures violate the most fundamental values on which they rest, and are nothing but embarrassing, blameworthy episodes. Republics that wage such wars, far from reinforcing the normative and institutional logic on which they rest, betray their nature.

3. Synoptic Visions: The Two Models Compared

It is perhaps useful to summarize what we have said to make sure that the considerable distance between DPT and the Kantian model is made as clear as possible. In table 2.1 we compare the different pillars on which the two models rest. In 2.2, we compare the different policy indications.

Table 2.1 The pillars

	DPT model	Kantian model
Domestic pillar	Democracy. Institutions inspired by welfare liberalism and liberal internationalism.	Republic. Institutions based on 'representation' and citizens with internalized republican ethos.
International pillar	IGOs, regional or global, with access limited to liberal democracies.	IGOs, global or regional, with open access.
Cosmopolitan pillar	Economic interdependence.	Right to visit. Respect for human rights as instrumental to economic interdependence and the construction of a global civil conscience.

Table 2.2 Normative indications

	DPT model	Kantian model
Domestic institutions	All states should become spontaneously liberal democratic– no forced democratization. Not only civil and political, but also socio-economic rights need to be ensured to all citizens. The condition of international politics is more or less independent of the quality of domestic liberal democracy.	All states should become spontaneously republican – no forced republicanization. All material conditions that generate relations of dependence among citizens need to be removed. Without an adequate international and cosmopolitan context, a republic will never be in a condition to reach its perfection.

(continued)

	DPT model	*Kantian model*
Domestic values	Non-violence and tolerance, but only towards fellow liberal democrats. Intolerance, exploitation and disrespect are permitted dispositions towards non-liberals. Citizens are expected to express their individual interests, not the general good, through the vote.	Universal principles of respect, non-violence (except for self-defence). Vote as subjective interpretation of the general will.
IGOs	IGOs are effective in promoting peace only if their membership is largely democratic.	IGOs based on equal status for each member, even if with mixed membership, promote peace, either directly if their mission is security, or indirectly if their mission is the facilitation of trade among members.
Interdependence	International trade promotes peace. It does not matter whether trade is ruled by fair terms of co-operation.	*Fair* commercial trade and cultural dialogue leading to the creation of a global civil conscience promote peace.
Human rights	Liberal internationalism makes room for the possibility that liberals violate them in their relations with non-liberals.	They can never be violated. The 'rights of man' need to be respected in all circumstances.[1] Even if serious violations occur in despotic countries, republics are not allowed to interfere with their internal affairs. However, if the state collapses, or if it is barbaric, intervention is allowed.
Use of force	Liberal states can use military force not only for reasons of self-defence, but also to protect their economic interests.	Permissible only for reasons of self-defence. Human rights can be protected through military operations only if violations occur in collapsed states.[2]

4. DPT and Normative Thinking

DPT was born as a theory that aimed to explain the fact of the liberal peace. One easy way to avoid confrontation with the less than attractive normative implications we have just highlighted would be to say that DPT – quite simply – contains no normative implication. It is a merely descriptive theory that shows how liberals behave in world affairs. Whether this is attuned to our comprehensive moral judgements today or to the accepted political ethos of international relations is beside the point. In other words, liberals behave in the way DPT describes, and this is sufficient to explain *their* peace. However, those convinced by DPT do not have to embrace any normative implications one may want to draw from it.

Is this really so? Let me first clarify that 'normative' here does not mean 'moral'. 'Normative' is used in the modest sense of a hypothetical prescription: 'if you want to reach a certain goal (in this case, peace), you must do X.' So, for example, I argued that DPT infers from its descriptive part that you must restrict access to IGOs to liberal democracies if you want IGOs to make a significant contribution to peace. Or, I argued that DPT says that if you want peace you need to promote economic interdependence (quite independently of how these dependencies are fair or not).

Having said that, there are three reasons why DPT cannot simply disown its normative dimension. To begin with, one can hardly doubt that Kant's project was *essentially* a set of normative implications. It follows that, to the extent to which DPT professes itself as Kantian, it is strange that no normative implications can legitimately be inferred. Secondly, descriptive theories often entail – more or less willingly – normative implications. And this is clearly the case of DPT. For example, in *Purpose and Policy in the Global Community*, Russett compares DPT to epidemiology. In the same way in which epidemiology tells you that you need to avoid smoking if you want to decrease the likelihood of lung cancer, so DPT tells you that you need to do X (where X stands for all the causal links it established in the descriptive part) if you want to reduce the likelihood of conflict in the future (Russett 2006: 233–4). In fact, Russett suggests incorporating 'Russia and China in the Kantian System' (Russett 2001: 286), that is, to engage them according to the causal links explained as decreasing the likelihood of war with them. This sounds like normative reasoning. In general, it is undeniable that if we ask DPT or the Kantian model what – in the light of the theory – one should do to make the world more stable, the implications would be considerably different. Once again, just think about what we would be told of the opportunity to establish or strengthen IGOs with autocracies, of the ways in which our liberal states are supposed to use force, of the role of a common cosmopolitan conscience – inspired by the human rights culture – for the promotion of peace. Thirdly, and lastly, DPT has already been used to draw normative implications on foreign policy. Doyle himself reminds us of Reagan's calling for a 'crusade for democracy' as a way to expand the zone of peace (Doyle 1986). And Russett (2005) alerts us to the fact that the second war in Iraq has been justified by a reference to the democratic peace. It does not matter whether US presidents have legitimately interpreted DPT or are rather responsible for a 'bushwhacking'. What matters is that DPT lends itself naturally to indications for the foreign policy of liberal states. This suggests that we had better get our hands dirty with normative work to avoid potentially disastrous distortions of the Kantian legacy.

**Part III:
Progress**

7 • Kant's Early Teleology in *Idea*

The first two parts of this book dealt with Kant's accounts of human rights and peace. We now focus on his reasons to trust that the world is not inhospitable to the political reforms meant to realize both political goals. This chapter and the next one deal with Kant's teleology as presented respectively in *Idea for a Universal History a Cosmopolitan Purpose* and in *To Perpetual Peace*, in particular in the (in)famous section devoted to the 'guarantee of perpetual peace'. Needless to say, Kant's view of progress has been one of the most debated topics in all of Kant scholarship. What follows is by necessity a cursory treatment of an issue that should have a far more refined analysis. Our limited goal is to explain how one can defend Kant's progressive teleology from the most serious weaknesses it has been charged with, and how, as a consequence, we can remove the spectre of a world intrinsically and objectively non-amenable to the reforms suggested. The last chapter hosts a discussion of Kant's account of how a political actor should act to promote political progress effectively. Kant's interesting yet often neglected account of political agency will thus complete our reconstruction of his progressive view of history.

Let us then start with Kant's account of history as presented in the 1784 *Idea*. After decades of quick dismissal on the part of scholars, the essay seems to have been enjoying renewed attention combined with a more benevolent attitude (e.g. Flach 2005, 2006; Fiegle 2014). Among the questions currently debated is the status of Kant's teleology and in particular: (a) whether it is meant to have theoretical validity (Kleingeld 1995: 31; Kleingeld 2001: 210) or, like the postulates in the second critique, its use is only practical (Wood 2005: 111–12; Guyer 2000: 372–407); (b) whether its theoretical ambitions are the same as those of any empirical science (Kaulbach 1975: 65; Rauscher 2001: 51) or do not extend further than the regulative function played by the ideas of reason

(Williams 1983: 20; Kleingeld 1995: 110–16); (c) whether we have today any reasons to believe the progressive view of history Kant proposes (no matter whether for theoretical or practical purposes), given past and present atrocities, as well as the worldview currently offered by science.

The reading we are going to defend here argues that Kant's teleology in *Idea* can be salvaged only if the mechanism of social unsociability, considered as the true centre of the essay, is (a) detached from the – by contemporary standards – hardly defensible notion of 'natural dispositions' and (b) understood in conjunction with general premises about human nature and the world that Kant takes as self-evidently true. From this perspective, Kant's teleology is reduced to the affirmation that, given certain constant features of human beings (mainly, limited benevolence and ability to see their best interests through experience) as well as relatively constant objective circumstances in the external world, an approximation of human affairs towards the 'cosmopolitan constitution' is more likely than its opposite or a condition of stagnation. Contrary to all previous interpretations of *Idea*, it will be argued that the status of this thesis extends beyond the merely regulative function of guiding our historical research towards some unity. The chapter affirms that Kant's goal in *Idea* is more ambitious: the goal is that of providing reasons to believe that non-linear progress towards the cosmopolitan constitution, rather than regress or stagnation, is the most likely development of human affairs.

The chapter is structured as follows. The first section focuses on the preliminary methodological remarks Kant offers before the nine propositions of *Idea*. The second section analyses, criticizes and discards the first three propositions. The third section, devoted to the last six propositions, introduces the 'Separability Thesis', i.e. the hermeneutical suggestion that the mechanism of social unsociability, with all the far-reaching consequences it generates for human affairs, can be reformulated in such a way that it becomes independent of the first three propositions. The fourth and final part reformulates the last six propositions of *Idea* with no reference to the idea of 'natural dispositions'. This reformulation is also offered as the most plausible teleological argument one can construct out of the material Kant offers in the essay.

1. The Methodology of 'Universal History'

In the introductory remarks to the essay, Kant sketches what seems to be a methodology for 'universal history', a project whose ambition he himself no doubt recognizes as problematic. Kant draws our attention to the rates of births, marriages and deaths in (large enough) societies to show that even phenomena that seem *par excellence* left either to sheer chance or to the free choice of individuals are influenced by objective factors, and as such are predictable with a certain degree of precision. We know in fact that birthrates, for example, are greatly influenced by the policy that a country adopts for young people in terms of accessibility to the job market, public nurseries, subsidies for maternity leave, level of women's education, religion and so. Hence, at least regarding whether they are going to increase or decline, birthrates are as predictable as any other natural phenomenon.[1]

The existence of such regularities opens up the possibility of looking at the whole of human affairs as a *system* in which certain general tendencies can be identified. This identification presupposes that we have a rough knowledge of what humans are and of what the institutions in which they live can become, to paraphrase Rousseau. It also presupposes that the objective circumstances in which they live are constant enough. However, if these conditions are met, there is no a priori reason that rules out the possibility of looking at history (the totality of human events) as a system in which regularities can be detected. With this crucial methodological caveat in mind, let us approach the nine propositions through which Kant attempts to show that history is moving towards a cosmopolitan end.

2. The First Three Propositions

As reconstructed by Kleingeld (1995; 126–8), Kant borrows the first steps of the validation of his progressive view of history from the biologist J. F. Blumenbach. Blumenbach modified the then dominant biological paradigm, known as 'Evolutionismus' or 'Theory of individual pre-formation'. He denied that organisms develop from miniature versions of themselves that already include all characteristics we observe in a grown-up individual. Rather, individual development is conceived as the result of the interaction between prefixed, God-given specific dispositions and the environment in which the individual grows up.[2] Clearly, both the concept of a set of capacities implanted by God in each species, as well as the formation of new characteristics as a result of the encounter between this set and the natural environment resonate in the first three propositions. They in fact state that: (1) the natural dispositions of all natural creatures are destined towards a full and complete development; (2–3) in human beings, the chief natural feature, to which all other human dispositions are subordinate, namely reason, is best developed only in society. God gives humans reason, but only through interaction with a specific natural environment (civil society, best if of a republican sort) can this natural capacity fully develop.[3]

There is a lot to quarrel with in Kant's first three propositions as they are presented. Just to mention one problem, they set the whole proof of *Idea* on a circular path. In the first proposition, in fact, Kant assumes that all natural dispositions of a creature are 'destined' to develop fully and in conformity with their *telos*. The subsequent propositions spell out the necessary conditions that enable that development. The argument thus seems to be moving from a teleological premise to a more specific teleological conclusion: from the assumption that nature has an end for all species (the full development of their pre-formed natural dispositions) to the identification of the specific end for the human species (the development of reason), and to the means nature provides to reach that end.

Leaving aside the circularity of the argument, there is a simple reason why we, readers of the twenty-first century, should dismiss Kant's first three theses. They are incompatible with the now dominant scientific paradigm, i.e. Darwinian or neo-Darwinian evolutionary theory. Contemporary science can account for the differentiation and evolution of the species without making any reference to a pre-fixed, God-given set of characteristics for each species. What Kant called 'natural dispositions', and we now call 'genetic materials', are not fixed and can change through the combined influence of the two key factors of contemporary biology, which are mutation and natural selection. In the context of a Darwinian biology, especially if amended by later developments (e.g. Mendel), the by-and-large creationist model Kant operates with is denied and there is no room for his talk of pre-fixed and constant 'natural capacities of a creature'.[4]

So far, so obvious. What is perhaps less evident is that contemporary biology is so distant from Kant's scientific horizon that it enables what for Kant is utterly impossible. In a famous passage of the third critique (§75), Kant argues that mechanical natural laws alone 'unordered by any intention' will never be able to explain 'how even a mere blade of grass is produced'. Actually, Darwinian biology can account for the 'production' of all features that constitute a specific kind of grass from merely mechanical laws, resting on the combined effects of mutation and selection, and without resorting to any 'intention' by nature, God or the like. As Kleingeld succinctly puts it, '[Darwinian theory] has removed teleology from biology' (Kleingeld 1995: 130). This is important because it already places constraints on any foundation of a progressive view of history that wishes to remain faithful to contemporary science. Any prediction of the future state of human affairs, any 'universal history' we might dare to write today, will have to refrain from attributing to individuals or species any pre-established end. It follows that it will have to arise out of a mechanical consideration of human interactions, combined with very general causal laws about human beings and the environment (physical and political) in which they live. In other words, any 'teleology' acceptable to contemporary standards will have to avoid the circularity of starting from teleological premises (like those noticed above in Kant's argument) and arise from considerations of human affairs viewed in a systemic perspective.

3. The Last Six Propositions

Fortunately, Kant does offer in *Idea* systematic considerations of the kind just mentioned. We can abandon the outdated view of nature as tending towards the realization of all pre-fixed 'natural dispositions' and retain the mechanism of unsocial sociability with its consequences for the evolution of human institutions, at the domestic and international level. To be sure, in proposition 4 Kant connects the mechanism of social antagonism to natural dispositions by saying that nature employs the former to enable the full development of the latter. However, the series of predictable social transformations brought about by social unsociability would occur even if there were no 'natural dispositions' which need to develop. All that is necessary for the mechanism in question to work is that humans truly, as Kant says, 'cannot bear' their neighbours, who compete with them for scarce resources, and whom they 'yet cannot bear to leave' (*IaG*, 8:21). In other words, for the mechanism to be triggered it is sufficient that humans and the environment in which they live be conceived according to rather uncontroversial and solid assumptions concerning the fact that we do not live in a world endowed with infinite resources combined with our limited benevolence (the circumstances of justice), and our capacity to see what is in our best interest while learning from past mistakes.

This is what could be called the Separability Thesis: the theory of 'natural dispositions' and the theory that spells out the consequences of social unsociability are separable and independent. One can believe in social unsociability (proposition 4) as well as accept the account that spells out the predictable institutional repercussions of such a mechanism (propositions 5–9) without endorsing the 'natural dispositions talk' in which they are embedded. Not accidentally, Kant himself will introduce the concept of unsocial sociability in the First Supplement of *To Perpetual Peace* after an account of nature completely different from the one introduced by the first three propositions.[5]

Detaching social unsociability from natural disposition is obviously still insufficient to ground a progressive view of history. At most, we have removed one obstacle. Something needs to be said to prove that the causal story and the chain of conditions of possibility envisaged in propositions 4 to 9 are plausible. Three crucial points, however, are already clear. To start with, the only teleology that can be defended within *Idea* is, so to speak, a teleology without natural purposes. Holding that history has a predictable (albeit non-linear) development is fully compatible with saying that nature does not have any plan for us. In fact, the reformed and de-dogmatized teleology we are about to defend is closer to predictions concerning the evolution of complex systems (e.g. the distribution of molecules of gas in a controlled environment or changes in birthrates caused by certain policies in large societies, as in Kant's example) than to providential perspectives on our destiny. Secondly, precisely because this new teleology rests on empirical causal mechanisms, its validation cannot stop with the proof that such a perspective is necessary for finding some unity in the otherwise lawless aggregate of human events. Its validation will have to rest, quite simply, on the truth of those mechanisms. Finally, even abstracting from the last point, there is a general reason why we have to reject all readings (e.g. Williams 1983: 20; Kleingeld 1995: 132; Fliege 2014: 167) that construe the status of Kant's teleology merely in regulative terms. The idea that without a progressive view history would be an aggregate non-amenable to reason is simply false. In fact, a view that attributes to history a *regressive* tendency would be as useful as Kant's for that purpose. It would 'systematize' history just as well. It follows that the justification of any progressive view of history (including Kant's own) needs more than the simple thought that such a view is 'good for science' or the like.[6] What is needed, quite simply, is a good argument showing that progress (measured in terms of approximation to the cosmopolitan constitution) is more likely than regress or stagnation.

4. Towards a Reconsideration of Kant's Teleology

With this much clarified, let us have a fresh look at the reasons Kant offers in the last six propositions to prove that history is progressing. This is our central question: once Kant's propositions are purged of all references to 'natural capacities', are we left with a material that enables us to construct a compelling argument? The reformulated argument can be constructed in six steps.

1. Unsocial sociability is 'obviously rooted in human nature' (*IaG*, 8:20) and dictates the necessity to live in society. Through competition it fosters the development of human talents.
2. Intellectual talents lead humans from barbarism to culture, which in turn is the first step towards moralization. What used to be an aggregate of amoral individuals who stick together because they cannot afford to live in isolation gradually becomes a society in which individuals accept the limitations of their freedom according to a universal law: 'a *pathologically* enforced social union is transformed into a *moral* whole' (*IaG*, 8:21).
3. A 'perfectly just civil constitution' (*IaG*, 8:22) which assigns equal spheres of freedom to all consociates is the institutional

setting that best enables human coexistence and best coheres with the growing moral capacity of individuals.
4. This institutional achievement is difficult to reach and yet nothing in human affairs rules it out as impossible.[7] Actually, given humans' capacity to learn and to improve from culture to morality, the outcome is dictated by objective factors.
5. There cannot be any 'perfectly just civil constitution' in one state without a 'law-governed external relationship with other states' (*IaG*, 8:24). Some form of global institution is necessary to remove anarchy from international affairs and this is in turn necessary to establish a just domestic regime. A 'federation of peoples' therefore serves the interest of individuals and states. It follows that it is reasonable to assume that a lawful, peaceful yet competitive international system (*IaG*, 8:23) will be reached one day.
6. Experience already gives us *some* hints that the system of international relations has certain features that facilitate that achievement: (a) 'The mutual relationships between states are already so sophisticated that none of them can neglect its internal culture without losing power and influence in relation to others' (*IaG*, 8:27); (b) civil freedom can no longer be so easily infringed without disadvantage to all trades and industries, and especially to commerce (*IaG*, 8:27); (c) conflict is generally against commerce, which makes the peaceful, diplomatic resolution of international controversies not only in the interests of the conflicting parties, but also of other states that are linked to them by relation of economic interdependence. In sum, experience shows some signs suggesting that the 'system' of human affairs tends towards a 'universal *cosmopolitan existence*' (*IaG*, 8:28).

Nothing in this long argument makes a reference to natural ends or to ends of nature, let alone to a plan of providence. All we have comes from consideration of human affairs as a system in which certain forces will exercise their effect, *if certain general circumstances remain stable*. The mechanism of social unsociability, combined with general premises about the environment in which humans live, suggests that our world, the world of human actions, with all its unintended consequences, is a world biased towards the cosmopolitan constitution. The argument is not only compatible with contemporary science, but asks us to accept rather uncontroversial assumptions regarding our nature (mainly our limited benevolence and our ability to learn) as well as to consider certain features of our environment as constant. If one rejects the argument, it should be shown which of the mechanisms that Kant relies on does not apply or fails to yield the expected effects. An a priori rejection of such a view on the grounds that it is 'metaphysical', too ambitious or (worse) incompatible with critical standards, is not acceptable.

This is obviously not to say that Kant's 'universal history', even if reconstructed most charitably as we have attempted to do, is free of difficulties. It is debatable, for example, whether it relies on a thought that, encompassing the totality of experience, is in tension with the limitations imposed on our cognition by the first critique. In fact, without an all-embracing stretch of one's cognition, how could one rule out the possibility that the same natural mechanisms that today make progress more likely will not change in the future? Or, even if we assume that human nature is stable, it could be that the same mechanisms become inert or even counterproductive because they are inserted into a new set of objective circumstances (for example, a dramatically insufficient amount of vital resources for the world's population). And what if some passion were to become so dominant in the constitution of future human beings as to impede the perception of their best interests?

These and other objections are fully legitimate and should be addressed. The goal of this chapter, though, was to find a teleological view that is not ruled out by our best science from the outset, i.e. even before doubts regarding the specific mechanisms Kant appeals to arise. Secondly, the goal was precisely to draw the boundaries of the field in which the confrontation with the critics should occur. In our reconstruction, the battlefield is that of systemic analysis of complex systems.[8] Thirdly, the goal was to show that *Idea* is mainly about the objective grounds we have to adopt a progressive view of history. On our reading *Idea* is neither about the heuristic opportunity to endorse a certain perspective, nor about the necessity, for practical purposes, to do so. Subordinating the ambitions of the essay to the attempt to make a case for the regulative or practical importance of adopting such a view is far from prudent. As we have seen, it exposes Kant to too obvious retorts.

8 • *To Perpetual Peace*: A Secular Guarantee of Progress?

If we abstract from the views on moral progress in the 1793 essay *On the Common Saying*, discussed above in chapter 5, Kant's major text on progress after *Idea* is the First Supplement of the 1795 essay *To Perpetual* Peace. Here Kant introduces one of the most controversial and criticized tenets of his entire philosophy, namely the claim, which we shall call here the 'Guarantee Thesis', that nature ensures that humans will one day achieve a condition of perpetual peace. Many have read this prediction as nothing but an example of simple-minded faith in the progress of mankind, typical of an Enlightenment style of thinking. Recent sympathetic interpreters of Kant (Guyer 2006; Ludwig 2006) have attempted various strategies for watering down Kant's claim and for separating his peace project from the Guarantee Thesis, since the latter is judged to be incompatible not only with contemporary epistemology but also with Kant's own fundamental theoretical principles. One simple reason for being suspicious of this approach is that Kant's writings on history – where various versions of the Guarantee Thesis appear – all belong to the critical period. Another reason is that Kant never abandoned his progressive view of history, which is – if anything – stated more forcefully in the last significant writing that Kant devotes to history, *The Contest of the Faculties* (1798).[1]

This chapter tries to show that, properly understood, the idea that there is a guarantee of perpetual peace is both compatible with Kant's critical philosophy and less embarrassing than usually assumed. The chapter proceeds by introducing three main concerns raised against the Guarantee Thesis, here labelled the epistemological, the anthropological and the moral concerns. After dealing with each of them, the chapter offers an interpretation of the Guarantee Thesis which should appear to contemporary readers as purged of dogmatism but also as not completely void of epistemic significance.

1. The Guarantee Thesis

In his political writings Kant often claims that the achievement of a condition of perpetual peace among nations is guaranteed by nature. In one form or another, this thought recurs from *Idea for a Universal History with a Cosmopolitan Purpose* (1784) to the late *The Contest of the Faculties* (1798), albeit with interesting variations.[2] Perhaps the clearest, strongest, and therefore most controversial version of this thought is to be found in *To Perpetual Peace* (1795) where Kant writes:

> Perpetual peace is *guaranteed* by no less an authority than the great artist *Nature* herself (*natura daedala rerum*). The mechanical process of nature visibly exhibits the purposive plan of producing concord among men, even against their will and indeed by means of their very discord. This design, if we regard it as a compelling cause whose laws of operation are unknown to us, is called *fate*. But if we consider its purposive function within the world's development, whereby it appears as the underlying wisdom of a higher cause, showing the way towards the objective goal of the human race and predetermining the world's evolution, we call it *providence*. (*ZeF*, 8:360–1)

Thus nature brings about peace 'even against their [men's] will and indeed by means of their very discord'. But how exactly does it do so? Nature's plan seems to unfold in two steps. To begin with, nature exploits human beings' tendency to fight each other in order to spread them to all areas of the world, 'even the most inhospitable' (*ZeF*, 8:362). Forced by war, humans form into groups that spread all over the finite surface of the earth in such a way that no human group can live in complete isolation. Secondly, precisely because they live in as 'many independent adjoining states' (*ZeF*, 8:367), and thus in a condition of potential war, each of them has the tendency to seek security by dominating their neighbours, and, if possible, the entire world. This tendency towards some sort of universal, monolithic despotism is, however, challenged by nature itself. As Kant claims, 'nature wills it otherwise, and uses two means to separate the nations and prevent them from intermingling – *linguistic* and *religious* differences' (*ZeF*, 8:367). These may be the cause of hatred and violence, of course, but as culture grows and men gradually move towards greater agreement over their principles, they lead to mutual understanding and peace. And unlike the universal despotism which saps all man's energies and ends in the graveyard of freedom, this peace is created and guaranteed by an equilibrium of forces and a most vigorous rivalry. (ZeF, 8:367)

As the very reference to an equilibrium of forces makes clear, however, this peace is anything but stable. As Kant famously put it, 'a permanent universal peace by means of the so- called *European balance of power* is a pure illusion' (*TP*, 8:312). To overcome this unstable condition nature uses her last trick: she exploits the greed of humans and uses the spirit of commerce that 'sooner or later takes hold of every people, and cannot exist side by side with war' (*ZeF*, 8:367). Kant's claim that the spirit of commerce cannot coexist with war is certainly not a new one, as it belongs to an already long tradition of liberal thought that started at least with Montesquieu's thesis of *doux commerce*. The claim has an objective and a subjective component. Respectively: (a) international trade is impossible in wartime, while economic interdependence among states decreases the likelihood of war; (b) the habit of bargaining and negotiating habituates people to resolving their disagreements in a non-violent manner (the reference to the *spirit* of commerce). Thus Kant concludes:

> In this way, nature guarantees perpetual peace by the actual mechanism of human inclinations. And while the likelihood of its being attained is not sufficient to enable us to *prophesy* the future theoretically, it is enough for practical purposes. It makes it our duty to work our way towards this goal, which is more than an empty chimera. (*ZeF*, 8:368)

2. Three Concerns

The Guarantee Thesis has been called into question from a number of different standpoints. The following criticisms seem to be those most worthy of attention:

1. *The epistemological concern.* It is highly dubious that predicting the development of human affairs and the end of history is compatible with the limits Kant's critical philosophy imposes

on human knowledge. Most importantly, even if we grant compatibility, what reasons (of an empirical or theoretical nature) does Kant have to be so confident that perpetual peace is the goal towards which humanity – willingly or unwillingly – is going? Quite simply, how does he know? (Guyer 2006:162–5).
2. *The anthropological concern.* If man is radically evil – as Kant claims in *Religion within the Limits of Reason Alone* – in the sense of having a disposition to prioritize self-love over morality, even assuming that there is a plan of nature favourable to peace, how can there be a guarantee that this plan is not subverted by humans' propensity to evil? (Guyer 2006: 166–8).
3. *The moral concern.* If nature does the job of bringing about peace *despite us*, the *duty* to promote perpetual peace risks becoming void. Not only *ultra posse*, but also *pro necessitate nemo obligatur*.³ Duty in this case would be void not because it is impossible to conform to it, but because it is impossible not to⁴ (Ludwig 2006: 185).

3. Reply to the Epistemological Concern

It is useful to rephrase the epistemological concern into two subtheses, a strong and a weak one. The strong version attributes to Kant the idea that we can know that a state of affairs (perpetual peace) will take place. We may ignore precisely when (there is no prophecy of the future), but we know for sure that a state of perpetual peace will be reached. The weak version interprets the guarantee as the idea that we know (or that there are grounds to be confident) that we are constantly approaching that desired goal. In the former case, we are supposed to be able to predict a future state of affairs; in the latter we are supposed to know only an existing tendency. But this tendency is quite compatible with the possibility that the final goal will never be achieved or, what is roughly equivalent, that we can only be certain that we are progressing towards that goal *asymptotically*. The weak version can be further weakened if progress towards that goal is meant not as certain but as probable (see the reference to the 'likelihood' in the earlier quotation). In other words, the thesis would be that, all things considered, the likelihood that the world is evolving to perpetual peace is higher than the likelihood that it is evolving in the opposite direction or in no direction at all.

One problem with the strong version is that such a prediction seems to be well beyond our cognitive powers. A state of perpetual peace, unlike an event without a cause, is certainly a real possibility (in the technical sense of being an object of possible experience). Hence, there is no problem in this sense. But predicting its taking place – something that would include certainty that, once reached, that state will not be reversed[5] – comes problematically close to the inferences of the mathematical antinomies before Kant's critical cure. In both cases, the attempt would appear to be that of embracing the totality of experience. In the present case, one assumes a complete knowledge of all historical events, as required by the idea of a 'final goal of history' and even more so by the idea of non-reversibility.

Kant himself, however, often suggests the weaker and less problematic version. Two passages make this quite clear. The first is in *To Perpetual Peace*. In the concluding remarks of the essay, Kant states:

> If it is a duty to bring about in reality a state of public right (albeit by an infinite process of gradual approximation), and if there are also good grounds for hoping that we shall succeed, then it is not just an empty idea that *perpetual peace* will eventually replace what have hitherto been wrongly called peace treaties (which are actually only truces). On the contrary, it is a task which, as solutions are gradually found, constantly draws nearer fulfilment, for we may hope that the periods within which equal amounts of progress are made will become progressively shorter. (*ZeF*, 8:386)

In other words, there are 'good grounds for hoping' that we are approaching perpetual peace. This is sufficient to establish the meaningfulness of our duty to realize a condition of public right (at the domestic, the international and the cosmopolitan levels), but it is still compatible with the possibility that that final goal will never be reached. In expressing the weaker thesis, Kant at times affirms just the opposite of the strong version, i.e. that we know that perpetual peace will *not* be reached. For example, in the section devoted to the 'Right of Nations' in the *Metaphysics of Morals* (1797) Kant inserts the following comment:

> It naturally follows that *perpetual peace*, the ultimate end of all international right, is an idea incapable of realisation. But the political principles which have this aim, i.e. those principles which encourage the formation of international alliances designed to *approach* the idea itself by a continual progress, are not impracticable. For this is a project based upon duty, hence also upon the rights of man and of states, and it can indeed be put into execution. (*MS*, 6:350)

Let us leave aside that Kant here seems to argue in the wrong direction. From the sheer fact that there is a duty to realize public right he infers that public right *is* realizable, which is the opposite of what the argument is supposed to show. In fact, the Guarantee Thesis should prove that a duty to realize the conditions of perpetual peace is legitimate (it does not violate *ultra posse nemo obligatur*) because perpetual peace is realizable, not the converse. The important point for us is rather that Kant acknowledges that perpetual peace is 'an idea incapable of realisation'. If this is so, it clearly follows that it does not make sense to affirm that we can predict the future occurrence of that state of affairs. It would be equivalent to saying that we can see in the future something that – we know – will never happen. Kant's point now seems to be that those natural mechanisms we discussed above ensure *progress* towards a goal that nonetheless will never be fully reached. Or even more modestly, natural mechanisms do not guarantee progress either. They simply make progress more probable than a condition of stagnation or even regress.

How solid is this weaker version? Well, much depends on whether we accept the assumptions about human nature and the system of international affairs *from* which Kant seems to argue. In fact, if one looks at the whole argument of the Guarantee Thesis, it becomes evident that Kant relies on the truth of some basic empirical claims, for which, like in *Idea*, no explicit argument is given, probably because they are taken as self-evident: (1) human nature is stable enough to allow some generalizations, e.g. that all humans strive towards happiness and the fulfilment of the material conditions that make happiness possible; (2) these material conditions can be met by means other than the instrument of war, e.g. by trade in conditions of peace; (3) these alternative means are prudentially better in that they do not endanger lives and wealth (at least not in the same degree as armed conflicts); (4) the obstacles to the adoption of these better means, such as uncertainty about the intentions of other players in the anarchical system of international affairs, can be removed by feasible reforms of the international order.[6] If (1)–(4) are true, it does seem to follow that the 'system' of human affairs tends towards one determined end. The main idea is that humans are not asked to renounce war and the goods they expect from it for the sake of morality. Rather, they are simply asked to realize that much, if not all, that they expect from war can be attained by different, better means. Here the analogy with the prudential argument that shows how even a 'nation of devils (so long as they possess understanding)' (*ZeF*, 8:366) would abandon the state of nature in favour of the civil condition suffers no limitations. In fact, the two cases are disanalogous not because the interests of individuals or countries in leaving the state of nature are substantially different, but because countries, unlike individuals in the state of nature, are juridical entities that must survive even after the establishment of supranational institutions. Incidentally, this is the principal reason why Kant rules out a world government, even aside from practical difficulties (Mori 2010: 118–23).

A different analogy, now with a physical system, may contribute to clarify further the plausibility of Kant's thesis. In very much the same way as we know that the molecules of a gas have an objective propensity to reach a certain internal organization, given certain physical laws and background conditions, we know that human beings, given certain general laws reflecting their nature and stable background conditions, have an objective propensity to evolve towards a certain political organization at the national, international and global level. (Of course molecules do not have free will, but this is a problem we defer to the discussion of the next concern.) If the analogy holds, Kant's prediction is no bolder than any thesis about the probabilistic evolution of complex material systems.

Still, despite its relative modesty and the defence we have just offered, the claim that natural mechanisms make progress towards peace more likely than any other outcome poses serious problems. Two such problems have already been mentioned at the end of the preceding chapter in relation to *Idea*, but it is useful to repeat them here. To begin with, it is not clear how this thesis does not rely, very much like the stronger one, on a thought that tries to encompass the totality of experience. Without an all-embracing stretch of one's cognition, it is not clear how Kant can rule out the possibility that the same natural mechanisms that make progress more likely today will not change in the future. We can be confident that human inclinations will constantly push in a certain direction only if we 'prophesy' that human nature will never change significantly. Or, even if we assume that human nature is stable, the same mechanisms may become inert or even counterproductive by being inserted into a new set of objective circumstances (for example, an irremediably insufficient amount of vital resources for the world's population). Secondly, if the thesis is reduced to an evaluation of chances, we need to abandon the very idea of a guarantee. As Guyer puts it,

> that the probability of precipitation today is ninety or ninety-five percent does not guarantee that it will rain today at all nor even that there will be a misty condition approximating to full-blown rain; it just says that on ninety or ninety-five out of a hundred previous days with initial conditions like today's it has in fact rained. And just as in meteorology some minor or even imperceptible difference between today's conditions and those prevailing on ninety or ninety-five similar days when it did rain can undermine the inference from the probability of perception to actual precipitation today, likewise we know all too well that some minor incident could precipitate an unpredictable chain of events leading to war even in conditions that we might otherwise have thought were unfavourable to war. So natural conditions that would make peace more probable would not seem to guarantee anything at all, whether the complete realization of perpetual peace or asymptotic approximation to it. (Guyer 2006: 165)

Therefore, Kant's thesis in the First Supplement would boil down to a rhetorical move that promises a certain outcome of human affairs as guaranteed while, at best, it would be merely probable. The language of a 'guarantee' may be useful for motivating peace activism and proper reforms but it would still be epistemologically groundless.

Let us start with this second charge. While Guyer is right that the probabilistic thesis is incompatible with the very idea of a guarantee – by definition, something that is only likely is not guaranteed – it seems that he does not take into due consideration the distinction between a subjective and an objective probability (or as Popper (1959) aptly puts it, a *propensity*), as well as the distinction between the probability of one event as opposed to the probability of a series of events. If Kant's point is to make any sense, it is quite clear that he means that something in human nature combined with the factual conditions he describes – call this the political world system – causes a certain *propensity* towards republican government, an international federation and a cosmopolitan condition. Asserting that there is such a propensity is clearly compatible with the possibility that the system will produce, on certain occasions, outcomes that run against that propensity. In the long run, however, if there is such a propensity, it will not fail to lead the system towards the 'intended' goal.

To see this point, compare Kant's assertion of a propensity to the case of a rigged dice. If the dice is loaded towards outcome six, this does not mean that six will always be the result of throwing that dice. Nor does the loading guarantee a bet on a single outcome. It merely guarantees that six, *given a high enough number of throws*, will come up more often than any other outcome. *How many more times* depends on how heavily the dice is loaded. If the natural mechanisms Kant describes really are at work, this does not guarantee that, given any international controversy, the result will be the peaceful resolution of the crisis. But it does guarantee that, in the long run, the system will evolve in such a way that peace will be the more frequent outcome. The analogy with dice throwing of course has limits, but these limits merely reinforce Kant's point. While the probability of outcome six remains the same no matter how often six has already occurred, any given approximation to the final goal of peace decreases the likelihood of future wars. In fact, if – as our working hypothesis has it – human inclinations are better served by a condition of peace, and human beings equipped with understanding can learn this lesson, then any progress towards the conditions that make peace stable will be positively reinforced by the individual and societal benefits thereby occurring. While the outcome 'six' merely confirms a given, fixed propensity, the success of peace makes its propensity higher. Unlike the loaded dice, peace is a self-reinforcing process, a process that builds on its own success.

What can we say about the first, more difficult charge? Does not the Guarantee Thesis rely on the illegitimate ambition of grasping the totality of (historical) experience? Remember that the core of the objection is that human nature or the background conditions conducive to peace could change. In other words, the objection does not challenge the effectiveness of the natural mechanisms Kant appeals to. Rather, it merely doubts that they are stable enough to license a prediction regarding a trend in human affairs. What if, for example, the goals humans set for themselves are better served by means other than peaceful, cooperative international relations? Imagine that we discover that there are simply not enough resources for all humans on earth and no way to come to a shared principle of redistribution. And what if some passion were to become so dominant in the constitution of future human beings as to impede the perception of their best interests? And what if we were to discover that Marx was basically right and capitalism (or the market in general) is based on the exploitation of some groups, in such a way that there is no reason to believe that competitive yet peaceful international relations will bring about prosperity for all? If any or all of these were to become true, then we would be evidently less confident that the system is biased towards peace.

Four points need to be made against this last objection. To begin with, notice how the objection challenges the Guarantee Thesis at the level of the general *empirical* laws on which it rests, thereby acknowledging that Kant is not engaging with metaphysical premises or dogmatic clichés. In other words, the critic implicitly grants that Kant's teleology is in principle no different from the attempt to predict the evolution of a physical system on the basis of knowledge of background conditions and empirical laws. The critic thus concedes that Kant is advancing a thesis about the evolution of human affairs founded on nothing else than empirical science, general premises about human inclinations and a fairly uncontroversial assumption about humans' capacity to learn what is in their best interest. Now, securing the view that Kant's teleology is similar to uncontroversial scientific predictions would already be a good result against those who find the guarantee an embarrassing bit of dogmatism.

Secondly, the mechanisms to which Kant appeals could certainly change, but how is that different from the possibility that well-tested empirical laws will be falsified by an unexpected future change in the structure of the universe? How is that different from being concerned that nature may deviate from the most stable regularities we have observed? And, above all, how is that more dogmatic than the belief that planets will keep following a certain course or that the natural laws on which astrophysicists base their predictions as to the likely evolution of the universe will no longer be valid in the future? Thus, leaving aside the question of free will for a moment,[7] if there is no difference between Kant's prediction and, say, a prediction about the evolution of the climate of this planet, why is the former a piece of dogmatic metaphysics of history and the second something we should take very seriously?

Thirdly, let us use the distinction drawn by one of the strongest critics of historicism, Karl Popper (1961), between unconditional and conditional predictions. An example of the former kind is the foreseeing of an eclipse. Such predictions are unconditional because they allegedly hold independently of the occurring (or remaining true) of specific background conditions. They merely presuppose the truth of astronomical laws. Such predictions are rare in science. More common are conditional predictions of the form: 'if X applies, given Y, then Z will occur', where X is a set of stable background conditions, Y a set of empirical laws, and Z the predicted evolution of the system. One error of historicism is to believe that one can come up with an unconditional prediction about the course of history, for example the prophecy of a revolution which will occur no matter what the surrounding background conditions are. But is Kant doing something that even remotely looks like predicting unconditionally? If one looks at the invoked mechanisms, he seems to be engaged in an uncontroversial, albeit very broad, conditional prediction, which is fully legitimate even for Popper. Again we have the form: 'if X applies given Y, then Z will occur', where the stable background conditions (X) are basic facts about human nature and the world, empirical laws (Y) suggests among other things the incompatibility between the spirit of commerce and war, and the predicted trend of the system (Z) is an approximation to perpetual peace.

To be sure, Popper would still consider Kant's prediction as a piece of bad historicism because Kant seems to be confident in considering human affairs as a *system*, that is, something stable enough to lend itself to a description in terms of fixed background conditions and general empirical laws. Popper would protest that the whole of human affairs is not an isolated, stationary and repetitive system. Human history, quite simply, is not a system at all, because it is constantly changing, and it continually undergoes rapid, non-repetitive development. In the most fundamental sense possible, every event in human history is discrete, novel, quite unique and ontologically distinct from every preceding historical event.

However, as we saw in our analysis of Guyer's objection, Kant does not deny the peculiarity and uniqueness of any *singular* historical event and would therefore agree that no specific historical event can ever be predicted (again: there is no prophecy of the future). He would insist, though, that human affairs are not as irregular as Popper assumes, and to demonstrate the existence of an identifiable trend he would again point to the natural mechanisms we have cited: humans seek happiness, do it in the least costly way, are characterized by limited benevolence, can learn that the world allows them to obtain through cooperation what they have sought through war, and so on. Either these general premises are true or they are not. If they are not, then there is no reason to believe in a trend to perpetual peace. If they are, then they do allow a prediction of a trend although no prediction of specific historical events. After all, Popper himself does not deny that one can detect trends in history. It is not clear why a trend to perpetual peace should be particularly problematic.

Finally, leaving aside the issue regarding the nature and the epistemological legitimacy of Kant's Guarantee Thesis, what can we say about the solidity of the general empirical premises on which it rests? Is war really something irrational that can be wiped out through a better understanding of our options? Is it just a question of blindness on our part about the possibility of reaching what we want by better means? Is the life of a (still growing) population of seven billion people on a resource-limited planet really compatible with a decent level of wealth and opportunities for each human being? Is finding a fair distribution of resources merely a question of good will and political imagination, or is there something in human nature or in the features of the world we inhabit that is inherently incompatible with peaceful relations? These and other fairly obvious questions are all legitimate, and I believe they cannot be easily dismissed. However, if we confine our view to what has happened since Kant's time, many signs appear to confirm that peace and prosperity go hand in hand *as long as* certain institutional reforms are implemented. Liberal democracies – the political systems we have that are closest to Kant's republics – are wealthy and peaceful (at least towards one another). International organizations (global and regional) have been developed and play a role that was unthinkable in Kant's time. A culture of human rights is rapidly taking hold of the global community. These may not be good enough 'signs' of the direction in which we are moving for the sceptic, but it is quite likely more than Kant himself would have hoped for two centuries ago.

4. Reply to the Anthropological Concern

Scepticism about the Guarantee Thesis does not stop with epistemological considerations. Critics also question the compatibility of the very idea of a guarantee of perpetual peace with Kant's doctrine of radical evil (Guyer 2006). If human beings are radically evil – in Kant's technical sense that they have an inexpungible tendency to prioritize self-love over morality (*RGV* 6:32) – how can there be a guarantee that the mechanisms of nature favourable to peace will not be subverted by humans' evil inclinations? No matter how strong these natural mechanisms are, the radically evil human being can always overcome them. After all, this seems to be just the dark side of Kant's strong notion of transcendental freedom. In much the same way as the moral person can resist the strongest human inclination (such as self-preservation) for the sake of duty and, to echo Kant's famous example, refuse to give false testimony at the cost of her life (*KpV*, V:30), the radically evil person can resist even the strongest incentives nature provides in favour of peace and give priority to a short-sighted conception of her own interests.

Unlike the epistemological concern, this line of thought is quite easy to refute. To begin with, it comes close to sheer inconsistency. *Ex hypothesi*, nature makes the interest of individuals and groups better served by peace (in our example, enrichment is attainable through peaceful commercial relations). Moreover, it is stipulated that the radically evil person deviates from morality out of self-love. Now, why should she subvert the course of nature to bring about a condition that is contrary to her own self-love? Of course, even if the mechanisms that Kant details are at work, it may be that while the interest of humankind in general, or even of a nation as a whole is better served by peace, war is still in the best interests of a particular individual or group. For example, rulers may have all sorts of individual interests in favour of war and be capable of fooling their citizens. It should be noted, however, that this is not the anthropological concern. The problem is no longer that individuals can fail to listen to what morality *and* self-love suggest. The problem is rather that Kant's mechanisms do not seem to be sufficient to exorcise well-known cases of the manipulation of public opinion, elitist degenerations of democratic systems and the like.[8] In other words, Kant's mechanisms may be insufficient to ensure that the particular interests of a few people do not trump the general good. But even if these cases are certainly possible – as the second war in Iraq clearly proves – one could wonder how long the deception can last. Above all, one would expect that such cases become rarer as the learning process, foreseen by Kant's mechanisms, reach higher stages of sophistication and the institutional settings prescribed (republican institutions) are gradually implemented and strengthened.

This also puts us in a position to go back to a problem that we put to one side during our discussion of the epistemological concern. We introduced the simplifying hypothesis that humans behave in ways similar enough to molecules while – quite obviously – molecules, unlike humans, do not have free will. But we can 'discharge the hypothesis', to use the language of logicians, by noticing that, if Kant is right in the description of how certain natural mechanisms work in favour of perpetual peace, human freedom, even of the transcendental kind, does not really change the picture. If individuals come more and more to realize that their (even egoistic) interests are realized by certain institutions and practices (that happily are the same as those dictated by morality and justice), insisting that their free will could subvert the natural unfolding of events would be tantamount to being concerned that facing a choice between easily saving a baby and thereby getting a reward, and leaving the baby to drown, individuals would seriously consider the latter. Even if this could happen in rare cases of maniacs, should we really worry about it? Would not these absurd preferences – from the point of view of historical development – be diluted in the ocean of rational preferences? If morality and self-interest really converge, as Kant assumes and the anthropological concern does not deny, freedom of the will does not seem that much of a threat.

5. Reply to the Moral Concern

If nature really makes peace more profitable than war and thus makes evolution towards peace inevitable, why does Kant insist that we have a duty to promote the conditions that favour its realization? Where is the space for moral action in a world that has been described as steadily inclining to perpetual peace? In the words of Bernd Ludwig:

> If nature does the job in the near future, the *duty* to promote perpetual peace would be void. Nobody has a duty to promote a course of nature that will occur anyhow in proximity. If we were told that our duty is to make the night follow the day, this would set no restraint to our actions since we would not know what we could *do* to fulfil our alleged duty. There is no compulsion, no 'ought,' and thus no Imperative, and hence no duty at all. (Ludwig 2006: 184f.)

As in the case of the anthropological concern, there is a fairly easy way out of this problem. And the solution is suggested by Kant himself in his discussion of the Eighth Proposition of the *Idea* essay, which can be rightly considered the ancestor of the Guarantee Thesis. Recall that this proposition states that, '[t]he history of the human race as a whole can be regarded as the realisation of the hidden plan of nature to bring about an internally – and for this purpose also externally – perfect political constitution' (*IaG*, 8:27). Kant first compares his tentative prediction about the future development of human affairs to equally insecure and yet valuable astronomical predictions about the path of our solar system within the larger system of fixed stars.[9] Then he claims that, 'it appears that we might by our own rational projects accelerate the coming of this period which will be so welcome to our descendants' (*IaG*, 8:27).

Our rational (that is, freely chosen) plans can accelerate the coming of a 'period' that would be – no matter what – the final destination of human affairs. Nonetheless, our failure to act may unduly delay it. And since war is connected to human suffering and to political injustice, it is not difficult to see why we have a strict political and moral duty to remove all conditions that delay the realization of this earnestly desired goal. The purposive plan of nature leaves plenty of room for human responsibility. In fact, there are a number of things we can do to speed up the process. We can get involved in a political process directed to the transformation of our state into a 'republic' if we live under a despot. Or our efforts could focus on approximating our real republic to the ideal of a republic. Also, we could do everything in our power to convince our government to transfer portions of its sovereignty to a federation, and we can contribute to the affirmation of cosmopolitan right, either in the form of the defence of human rights or through the removal of all protectionist trade barriers that limit an ever-increasing economic interdependence between peoples. The duty to promote perpetual peace is, therefore, by no means void. It is no more void than the duty to work for the overthrow of a dictatorial regime that causes deaths and suffering simply because we know that the regime is on the verge of collapsing.

6. Empirical, not Metaphysical

What we have argued is that research on the Guarantee Thesis has fallen prey to a hermeneutical cliché. Instead of taking seriously Kant's reference to empirical features of our world – the natural mechanisms he describes and the background conditions he points to – with an eye to testing the explanatory power of such mechanisms, interpreters have recently been eager to repeat that Kant's view of history is a relic of old metaphysics incompatible with his mature philosophy. A feature of Kant's teleology that makes it nearly indistinguishable from Hegel's doctrine of the cunning of reason.

Even sympathetic interpreters of Kant have chosen to water down the Guarantee Thesis by emphasizing how the reference to a natural plan gradually gave way in Kant's political writings to the more modest consideration that such a plan is a regulative ideal that we adopt to render human history intelligible (Mori 2008: 59).[10] If I am right, though, the Guarantee Thesis legitimately wants to be something more than a regulative principle. In fact, I showed that there is nothing a priori wrong or dogmatic in focusing on certain fairly stable human inclinations (such as the pursuit of happiness or self-love), as well as on certain very general and uncontroversial empirical facts about the world, to infer from them a thesis about the likelihood of a certain evolution of human affairs. What we have been suggesting is that Kant's Guarantee Thesis mainly rests on a logic that is already accepted in much empirical social science: the logic of unintended consequences. Economics, for example, tells us that prices in a free market are determined by the unintended consequences of the choices made by consumers. For example, If I buy a house for my family in a city, I contribute to raising the price of real estate property in that area, even if I do not want that effect. Similar examples can be found in politics (domestic and international), sociology, ecology and even psychology. If we do not find the doctrine of unintended consequences in these sciences problematic why should we find Kant's predictions, based on much the same logic, embarrassing? More importantly, why should we let the self-interested political moralist win his intellectual battle and thereby delay the coming to be of the condition in which humanity will stop what Voltaire liked to call the self-inflicted tragedy of mankind?

As we have said repeatedly, one can doubt that the mechanisms Kant describes are sufficient to ground a propensity in human affairs to perpetual peace. But it would already be a substantial improvement, and this chapter would have reached its goal, if interpreters started focusing precisely on these mechanisms instead of remaining secure in the thought that they are not worth serious attention. If this were done, the Guarantee Thesis would no longer appear as the *locus* where Kant's path crosses that of two equally embarrassing travelling companions: the old metaphysics that he wanted to silence with the critical cure, and the soon-to-come new metaphysics – mainly Hegel's philosophy of history – that he would have hardly recognized as a legitimate offspring.

9 • Progress and Political Agency

Contemporary scholarship, both in the field of political philosophy and in that of international relations, has focused more on Kant's theory of right than on his account of how politicians, activists and concerned citizens are to act to bring about the reforms necessary to achieve a rightful condition. In other words, Kant's theory of politics (not of political justice) has thus been by and large ignored. This has generated a certain degree of confusion on the independence Kant is ready to grant to politics in relation to morality and right, with negative repercussions on the comprehension of Kant's system as a whole. Kant's view of politics, however, is crucial for our purposes because no account of progress in Kant can do without a treatment of the way political actors need to act in order to enable or perhaps merely accelerate progress. In what follows, we offer our reading of the place politics and political agency occupy next to morality and *Recht* in Kant's system. Our task is particularly complicated by the ambiguous status Kant himself attributes to politics, at some times considered as merely derived from morality and at others as enjoying some autonomy. Nonetheless, our reading will attempt to make Kant's account of politics both meaningful in its own right and consistent with other parts of the system.

1. Politics, Morality and Right: Agreement, Subordination, Autonomy

In the first section of the Appendix to *To Perpetual Peace* with the title 'On the Disagreement Between Morality and Politics in Relation to Perpetual Peace', Kant defines politics as an 'applied branch of right' (*ausübende Rechtslehre*) and morality as a 'theoretical branch of right' (*theoretische Rechtslehre*). With these definitions, he immediately clarifies two essential points. First, by morality, whose possible agreement with politics is the object of the whole section, he does not mean merely the system of ethical principles or the system of virtues (*Tugendslehre*) but also and above all the system of juridical principles (*Rechtslehre*). In particular, he means the principles of public, international and cosmopolitan right. These principles, even if one reads them as grounded in the moral law, are clearly different from the moral law itself, with prescriptions and domains different from those of the Categorical Imperatives. Yet they are not the principles of politics, which evidently stand in need of a different universal principle (if there is one). Thus Kant's definition institutes, from the very beginning, a difference between right and politics. The former deals with rational, abstract and universal principles. The latter deals with the application of such principles to reality, with all the difficulties that this transition entails, and, so to speak, with no specified and perhaps no specifiable principle to guide this transition. Moreover, while right, as much as morality, prescribes abstract universal principles with no regard for the consequences that may derive from their application, politics 'as an applied branch of right' needs to take them into consideration. Actually, the hallmark of (good) politics consists precisely in the ability to apply *well* the principles of right to the changing concrete circumstances that present themselves before the political actor.[1]

Kant then moves to the discussion of how politics submits to right, but provides in that very context interesting hints to capture the autonomy politics enjoys notwithstanding such subordination. To begin with, in line with what he had done earlier in *On the Common Saying*, Kant attacks the idea that moral precepts cannot be put into practice, namely used in real-life circumstances. According to realists, cynics and opportunists, real life has its own logic that is not captured by the moral laws. Even if human beings can do what they ought to do, they will never *want* to do what is mandatory from a moral point of view and at the same time necessary to reach perpetual peace. Abdicating this position would be tantamount to denying the practical reality of the moral law, which Kant proved in the second critique, not without fatigue and effort, with his words: '[I]f we have once acknowledged the authority of this concept of duty, it is patently absurd to say that we *cannot* act as the moral laws require. For if this were the case, the concept of duty would automatically be dropped from morals (*ultra posse nemo obligatur*).' In the moral writings, duty had been characterized as a command of a faculty (reason) that discovered its autonomy through the consciousness of its ability to overcome even the strongest natural instincts (including that of survival) to follow the moral law. There is therefore no room for doubt about the possibility, for beings such as ourselves, to put in practice the precepts of morality and, a fortiori, those of right.

That does not mean, however, that morality and politics can be conflated with one another, let alone that politics can be reduced to a mere application of the precepts contained in morality. Actually Kant recognizes that their principles are and must be different. Citing the maxims of politics and morality, respectively 'Be ye therefore wise as serpents' and '[Be] harmless as doves', Kant does not mean that the second should replace the first. Rather he means that they need to come together in a single, unified and possibly consistent commandment. The prudence/expediency of politics must not be cancelled out by the innocence of morality. How this is supposed to happen and how this is going to generate clear and definite guidelines for the work of the moral politician is precisely the central question Kant addresses in this section of *To Perpetual Peace*. The idea – at this stage only announced – is that politicians must be 'wise as serpents', but at the service of morality. Thus, from the very beginning Kant warns us that tricks, clever and manipulative games, astute stratagems, namely the toolbox of ordinary politicians, are not necessarily elements to be removed by the cleaning that morality ensures. In any specific circumstance, good politics, one could say, must be able to manipulate the existing forces to facilitate the happening of the state of affairs required by morality and right. This is in fact part of the official definition of the moral politician, who – Kant says – 'conceives of the principles of political expediency in such a way that they can co-exist with morality' (*ZeF*, 8:372).

To the moral politician, Kant opposes the political moralist who 'fashions his morality to suit his own advantage as a statesman'. Worth noticing in this definition is that the political moralist is not necessarily a self-interested opportunist. At least, Kant's words are open to a different reading. He may have in mind someone who – in good faith – thinks that there is moral worth in shaping a morality to the service of *raison d'état*. Or more precisely, that it is all right that morality is reinterpreted if this operation is carried out by the (responsible) statesman. We are thus still far from the case of those who surreptitiously 'try to cover up political principles which are contrary to right, under the pretext that human nature is incapable of attaining the good which reason prescribes as an idea' (*ZeF*, 8:373). For people of this sort, in fact, Kant has a different term: 'moralizing politicians' (*ZeF*, 8:373). They are much more harmful than political moralists because they 'make progress impossible, and eternalize the violation of right' (*ZeF*, 8:373).[2] With the political moralist we are dealing with someone far nobler than such a self-interested agent. He believes in good faith that *raison d'état* has a normative status superior to that of the moral law. He is a sort of Machiavellian prince who rules according to the amoral suggestions of the Florentine secretary not merely because this is what it takes to rule, but because he sincerely sees in the preservation of the state a moral value to be defended, even to the detriment of common-sense morality. The problem with the political moralist does not rest with his lack of scruples (he could very well be a dove, and in fact Kant will say that he may have the goal of perpetual peace). Even less is the problem greed, lust for power or sheer astuteness. The problem is rather the belief that morality can be shaped according to the interests of statesmanship, no matter how well-meaning this project may be. A morality at the service of a higher normativity is for Kant a non-sense. This is probably why he never says that the political moralist is despicable, or dangerous. He is simply 'unthinkable'.

Thus the political moralist inverts the hierarchical order between morality and politics, the order that only the moral politician understands correctly. The moral politician does not deny that in the business of applying morality or right to reality one must take into consideration concrete circumstances. He does not deny the autonomy of politics and the existence of an authentic problem of determination of the correct political conduct, even when it is crystal-clear what morality and right demand. It is precisely to solve this problem of determination that the moral politician will need to be prudent, and if necessary, wise as a serpent.

2. The Foresight of the Political Moralist and That of the Moral Politician

Seen in this perspective, the space that Kant assigns to politics seems to be clear and in line with his thought. Morality shapes right and rules over politics. But politics retains some degree of autonomy when it comes to deciding (prudently) the best means to turn abstract normative principles into concrete political actions. The principles politics applies are not self-given, but the way in which they are applied is the specific domain of politics, and no higher authority can provide guidelines or principles. In sum, subordination but with a certain degree of autonomy. Unfortunately, this is too simple a picture and conceals significant conceptual tensions that we need to face instead of passing in silence.

Let us start by considering the Kantian metaphor of the two gods, the god of violence (Jupiter) and the god of morality. The first in this context is the god of those who act guided by a merely instrumental reason. The second is the god of those who have a higher normativity (obviously that of the moral law). If we pay attention to the details of the present metaphor, one sees that the approximate reconstruction we proposed starts crumbling apart. The passage reads:

> The god of morality does not yield to Jupiter, the custodian of violence, for even Jupiter is still subject to fate. In short, reason is not sufficiently enlightened to discover the whole series of predetermining causes which would allow it to predict accurately the happy or unhappy consequences of human activities as dictated by the mechanism of nature; it can only hope that the result will meet with its wishes. But reason at all times shows us clearly enough what we have to do in order to remain in the paths of duty, as the rules of wisdom require, and thus shows us the way towards our ultimate goal. (*ZeF*, 8:370)

Jupiter is a god with limited power because, as in Greek cosmogony, he is still subject to fate, namely to the chain of material causes, too complex to be grasped by a human or divine mind. In contrast, the god of morality does not suffer these limitations because (this seems to be what Kant has in mind) he is stronger even than fate and capable of escaping its rule. In fact, preferring honesty over any possible advantage neither presupposes nor requires the ability to predict all natural mechanisms. All it takes is a free, autonomous decision to act from duty. This is why the maxim 'honesty is better than any policy' does not fear confutation from experience, while the maxim 'honesty is the best policy' unfortunately does, as we all know. The first maxim 'transcends all objections' because it merely depends on the decision of a free autonomous agent to prioritize morality over self-love. In contrast, the second, like any maxim ultimately resting on a hypothetical principle, depends on the truth of the causal mechanism that links the ends one desires to the means one *thinks* are needed to achieve them. Honesty must really bring more happiness than dishonesty. It therefore depends on whether one has rightly calculated how all relevant events will unfold. Since predictions of this kind are hazardous, the maxim is vulnerable to various sorts of counter-examples. While reason in the search for happiness is an uncertain guide, Kant believes that it utters crystal-clear suggestions on what one should do 'in order to remain in the path of duty, as the rules of wisdom require, and thus shows us the way towards our ultimate goal' (*ZeF*, 8:370).

Kant here reiterates his familiar thesis that duty is for us knowable, practicable and obligatory even if it runs against our natural search for happiness.[3] But he seems to be doing it in a context in which he has just affirmed that good politics, i.e. politics inspired ultimately by the moral law, must be wise as a serpent. As we saw, this means essentially the ability to manipulate reality in such a way as to convey forces and actors towards the desired outcome. Such an ability, however, presupposes precisely that predictive power that Kant has just denied to reason. And the picture gets even more complicated when we are told that the duty Kant has in mind here is not any duty but 'our ultimate goal', that is, perpetual peace. The duty not to give false testimony is relatively easy to follow. But things are quite different with the duty to approximate perpetual peace. In this case, one hardly knows what needs to be done in detail and in each circumstance. And to make things worse, Kant insists that our efforts to comply with the duty to approach perpetual peace must be carried out 'as the rules of wisdom require'. This presupposes the ability to predict most of the effects of our actions, if not all of them. In other words, it presupposes a good deal of *accurate* knowledge of the world and of its laws. If the moral politician is, like Jupiter, still subject to fate, and therefore not immune from failures, what does it mean to talk about a wise and carefully calculated effort to bring about the necessary reforms? If our reason is not enlightened enough to predict all future effects of our actions, why does Kant indicate that faculty as an irreplaceable counsellor of the moral politician? To be sure, the same faculty cannot be trustworthy depending on whether it is used by the political moralist or by the moral politician.

Kant himself provides a first hint on how to avoid the impasse. He affirms that the political moralist can be seen as someone who assumes that 'man will never want to do what is necessary in order to attain the goal of eternal peace' (*ZeF*, 8:371). In other words, the political moralist, who is now presented in the more familiar guise of the realist, denies that human beings, either considered as individuals or as peoples, will ever spontaneously agree to limit their freedom in order to bring about the condition of perpetual peace.[4] The implementation of these reforms is indeed difficult, not only because humans have their well-known tendency to prioritize self-love over morality, and thus to prefer a condition of anomy as long as this suits their interests, but also because it must be guaranteed – at the level of individuals or states – that if one adopts the republican principles, others will do the same. Otherwise, the well-meaning individual or state may suffer a condition of self-restraint in an environment populated by lawless actors. This is why at the beginning right must be imposed by force. The juridical, republican condition needs at the beginning a despotic moment at which all relevant actors are forced to conform to the principles of right (public or international). Once a constitution is established, the next institutional improvement is made even more difficult. It is not certain (actually it is quite unlikely) that those who have taken power will spontaneously decide to limit their prerogatives by introducing reforms inspired by republican principles.

These difficulties are real, and Kant has no intention to deny them. The point is rather that they become insuperable, and with them the political moralist's scepticism, if 'there is neither freedom nor any moral law based on freedom, but only a state in which everything that happens or can happen simply obeys the mechanical workings of nature' (*ZeF*, 8:372). If this is the case, then politics is reduced to a technical problem of calculation, and realism has its theoretical victory. As Kant puts it, politics would be reduced to 'the art of utilising nature for the government of men' (*ZeF*, 8:371). The political moralist does not escape the destiny that he attributes to mankind in general. He 'will never want to do what is necessary in order to attain the goal of eternal peace', including some personal sacrifice for the sake of a higher ideal.

If however one takes the reality – from a practical point of view – of human freedom seriously, and specifically that peculiar kind of freedom that is autonomy, then the picture changes. If autonomy – and therefore morality – is real, then there will be moral politicians who will not limit themselves to the manipulation of natural mechanisms to keep the status quo. Moral politicians will harmonize the principles of political expediency 'in such a way that they can co-exist with morality' (*ZeF*, 8:371). They will use the same mechanisms as the political moralist uses to rule the state, but they will use them to 'push the system' in the required direction. The moral politician, by virtue of his freedom from natural mechanisms, will know how to overcome the difficulties mentioned above (men's radical evil and the prisoner's-dilemma condition of well-meaning politics). Given the defects of the existing constitutions or the sheer absence of institutional structures where they should be present (the international/global level), the moral politician will want to 'ensure that these political institutions are made to conform to natural right, which stands before us as a model in the idea of practical reason', and she will be able to do so even if 'selfish interests have to be sacrificed' (*ZeF*, 8:371). The possibility of perpetual peace thus rests on the moral politician's good will and his free decision inspired by duty is explicitly considered a necessary element of the progress towards that goal.

3. The Moral Politician and the Guarantee of Perpetual Peace: Two Problems

Kant's appeal to the morality of individual politicians is quite interesting. We find here a novel element in the architecture of Kant's theory of peace that the essay to which the Appendix belongs had not made clear up to this point. In particular, the Appendix seems to complement the picture that Kant had given us in the first supplement to perpetual peace where the idea of a 'guarantee' of stable and durable peace is introduced. There Kant attempted to show that even if the preferences of individuals are never inspired by morality, but always only by self-love, perpetual peace will still come about thanks to the happy interplay of certain natural mechanisms that accompany the well-intentioned efforts of those who work to approach perpetual peace. This interplay pulls along even those who more or less willingly oppose progress (*fata volentem ducunt, nolentem trahunt*). Quite to the contrary, we discover here that morality and political ideals play a central role in the progress to perpetual peace. In fact, if they were ignored by all political actors, Kant has just told us, 'the concept of right would then be only an empty idea', politics would never be reconciled with morality and right, there would be no institutional improvement, either at the national or international level, and – as a consequence – we would never reach perpetual peace. Kant's project, as we have said, turns out to depend not only on favourable natural mechanisms but on the good will of individuals, in particular of politicians.[5] There is always work to do to reform existing institutions and to make them more in line with the ideal set by pure reason. To do that, one obviously needs a moral disposition, especially on the part of rulers, favourable to the adoption of the necessary reforms.

The good will of some rulers and statesmen thus grounds the possibility of moral politics, which in turn is discovered as a precondition of progress to perpetual peace. This appeal to a freely adopted moral disposition on the part of politicians, however, generates new problems for Kant's account. In the first place, it weakens the novelty of his proposal in relation to the tradition of preceding peace projects which, as with Saint-Pierre, rested mainly on the moral improvement of European rulers.[6] Then, and most importantly, it does not solve the problem from which we started. Actually it seems to make it worse, if read in conjunction with the Guarantee Thesis. On the one hand, natural mechanisms seem at times knowable (otherwise could one have a guarantee of perpetual peace?) and at times unknowable (the intrinsic and irreparable short-sightedness of politics as mere technique). On the other hand, it becomes unclear what is the role of morality in the progress to perpetual peace if this is guaranteed by natural mechanisms (assuming they are knowable).

The second problem is reminiscent of what we called the moral concern in the preceding chapter. As we saw, natural mechanisms lead to perpetual peace independently of the moral choices of individuals, but they do it in a costly way and at an unnecessarily slow pace. Their way is costly because it presupposes the (possibly repeated) experience of war, destruction and human suffering. It is unnecessarily slow because humans could accelerate the course of history by voluntarily adopting the necessary reforms, without waiting for a new proof of the atrocious and irrational nature of aggressive wars.⁷ After all, the intuition that we could accelerate the process had already been announced in *Idea for a Universal History with a Cosmopolitan Purpose* (1784). There Kant affirmed that 'it appears that we might by our own rational projects accelerate the coming of this period which will be so welcome to our descendants' (*IaG*, 8:27). The moral politician therefore accelerates a progress that would take place anyway while political moralists – with their scepticism – would do nothing to sustain it. Individual choices and natural mechanisms are thus not incompatible but can actually cooperate to reach the desired goal. Moral responsibility still has a significant role to play within a strongly teleological view of history such as the one Kant suggests.

The first problem is more difficult to handle, because Kant is unclear on the relation between knowledge and political agency, and therefore on the relation between expediency and moral politics. At times, he seems to hold that the expediency of the moral politician rests on certain and sufficiently complete knowledge. Without knowledge of the context on which our reforms are to impact, there can be no good politics, but only a well-meaning amateurish disposition, or – even worse – despotic moralism, namely the blind application of the commands of practical reasons. Despotic moralists, in fact, 'act contrary to political prudence by adopting or recommending premature measures'. At other times, however, Kant considers knowledge fully dispensable, up to the point that he seems to fall precisely in the position of the despotic moralist. For example, he points out that political expediency, by itself, will never be able to solve the problem of how to advance the cause of perpetual peace, even if this is the goal that the prudent politician sets for himself. For the solution of this problem, in fact, 'much knowledge of nature is required, so that one can use its mechanism to promote the intended end' (*IaG*, 8:377), a kind of knowledge that – Kant thinks – alas, we do not have. When it comes to determining the best means to approach perpetual peace, theoretical reason is insufficient: 'all this is uncertain so far as its repercussions on perpetual peace are concerned, no matter which of the three departments of public right one considers' (*IaG*, 8:377). If it is uncertain whether one people's prosperity and virtue is advanced by the rule of one, few or many, 'it is even more uncertain in the case of an *international right* supposedly based on statutes worked out by ministers' (*IaG*, 8:377). And after having dismissed the potentiality of political prudence, which Kant had praised a few lines above, he recommends to politicians something that sounds very like an article of faith: 'Seek ye first the kingdom of pure practical reason and its *righteousness*, and your object (the blessing of perpetual peace) will be added unto you' (*IaG*, 8:378). And, to emphasize even more the fideistic, almost irrational inclination of his thought at this moment, Kant continues:

> For morality, with regard to its principles of public right (hence in relation to a political code which can be known *a priori*), has the peculiar feature that the less it makes its conduct depend upon the end it envisages (whether this be a physical or moral advantage), the more it will in general harmonise with this end. (*IaG*, 8:377)

The 'political face' of morality, that is, the principles of public right, are to be applied and obeyed with scant or no attention to the end one pursues. Perpetual peace is more easily obtained if one cares about realizing justice (as defined in universal terms by practical reason applied to public right), without too much worrying if the effort is fully justified by the objective conditions one encounters. This is already quite shocking to hear from someone who has just recommended prudence to the politician. But Kant goes further. He claims that one should not be preoccupied with the attempt to determine the best means to reach that goal. Finally, he endorses the motto '*fiat iustitia, pereat mundus*'.[8]

All this seems to contradict the prudence Kant had praised as a central virtue. We are now told that the politician must only apply the commands of pure practical reasons, turned into juridical principles, rather than finding a place for 'the principles of political expediency in such a way that they can co-exist with morality' (*IaG*, 8:372). To be sure, Kant insists that the path to perpetual peace 'cannot be realised by violent and precipitate means, but must be steadily approached as favourable opportunities present themselves' (*IaG*, 8:378). It is not clear, however, how this prudence is to be practised if we are asked to worry *only* to seek 'the kingdom of pure practical reason and its *righteousness*' (*IaG*, 8:378) while resting assured that by so acting 'your object (the blessing of perpetual peace) will be added unto you' (*IaG*, 8:378).

4. Moral Politics: Between Prudence and Faith

Is there a consistent account beyond these tensions and oscillations? Does Kant have a compelling and consistent theory of the relation between morality and politics in general, and of the relation between politics and predictive capacity in particular? Let us recall a few hermeneutical difficulties that we have already overcome in the course of our analysis. The moral politician correctly attends to the hierarchical relation between morality and politics. Far from being a moral fanatic, however, he knows that the forceful and premature 'republicanization' of institutions is both contrary to right (the denial of the right to rebellion) and most of the times counterproductive. The good politician must therefore be prudent in this sense. And perhaps in another: she must know well the reality on which she operates in order to introduce those reforms that the context is ready to accept. The politician's wisdom does not have to become the arrogance of the one who believes he can identify *all* relevant variables to manipulate them towards the desired goal (even if that goal is perpetual peace). Our reason is significantly below that standard. Hence, Kant seems to be saying, sometimes we are asked to introduce or merely propose reforms without a clear and complete foresight of the consequences of our initiative. And this should not paralyse us. Even if we cannot prove beyond any reasonable doubt that such and such reforms will produce an advance towards our goal, at times we have to support them anyway, as long as we know that they are inspired by 'righteousness'. Even less one should give a hearing to the moralizing politician who ridicules our reforms because he knows how the world goes. Like us, the moralizing politician cannot predict the consequences of our reforms, and cannot exclude the possibility of progress. The first criterion for political action must thus be the intrinsic justice of our initiative, not the availability of a fully reliable prediction of what is going to happen. This is why Kant underlines that even if the political moralist and the moral politician had the same objective – perpetual peace – their agency would nonetheless be different. The former considers the task as a merely technical problem, which is often irresoluble given the limited power of our predictive power. The latter conceives of her task as having a moral dimension. From this perspective, that Kant now calls that of 'political wisdom', the solution 'presents itself as it were automatically; it is obvious to everyone, it defeats all artifices, and leads straight to its goal' (*IaG*, 8:377–8). In sum, the moral politician must merely make sure that the reforms are what right requires and which are not evidently premature and/ or only realizable by violent means. If the envisaged reforms pass this preliminary test, she should not hesitate to try to implement them even if it is impossible to foresee all repercussions of such an attempt. Their intrinsic justice is a sufficient justification for doing all in our power to realize them.

It remains unclear what ensures that our reformist effort, in the absence of a complete knowledge of its effects, 'leads straight to its goal', as Kant boldly affirms. To be sure, the part of Kant's essay that we are examining, the Appendix, closely follows the First Supplement, devoted to the guarantee of perpetual peace. Kant probably feels authorized to subscribe to what would otherwise appear nothing more than a leap of faith because he has just provided a macro-analysis of the system of human affairs in which perpetual peace turns out to be the necessary outcome. Our reforms thus find a fertile terrain; they accompany and accelerate a process that is unfolding anyway. But the appeal to the guarantee does nothing but reproduce the deep difficulty that surrounds the role that Kant assigns to knowledge (in particular the capacity to predict the future) in his ideal view of politics. One more time, it seems that predictions are more or less reliable depending on whether they come from the moral politician or from the political moralist (or any other subtype). If the moral politician makes the prediction, then we are able to read a direction in history. We are even in a position to provide a guarantee that this tendency will triumph (one day). If the political moralist dares a prediction, however, then the efforts becomes magically vain and our reason goes back to its condition of insufficiency and weakness. Are we dealing simply with a double standard by which Kant awkwardly attempts to discredit the political moralist, or even in this case is there a way to reconstruct a coherent account?

Probably the solution is to be found in the distinction between macro- and micro-predictions. The prediction of the First Supplement is obviously a macro-prediction, as it encompasses the end-goal of history. It is like a picture taken with a wide-angle lens, where what is represented is fairly clear but distant details are out of focus. For example, we have no idea exactly *when* perpetual peace will come.⁹ This prediction embraces the totality of all human relations and extends towards an indefinite point in the future. From so distant a perspective, although still 'internal' to the world (no God's eye point of view), Kant believes he can get a glimpse of a historical tendency, by combining very broad anthropological and sociological assumptions on the whole system of human affairs.¹⁰ We do not know when perpetual peace will come, but we can read certain promising signs, both in historical events and in the human soul that seems to enjoy the vision of individuals and peoples who fight for and obtain their freedom (the repercussion that the French Revolution has on the soul of the spectator Kant describes in the *Observations on the Beautiful and the Sublime*).¹¹

The political moralist's predictions, in contrast, are most of the time about well-determined events meant to happen in the near future. They are predictions with a telephoto lens, or perhaps even better with the microscope: what will happen if my country applies protectionist measures to trade with emerging countries? What will happen if I raise taxes? What consequences will there be if I favour this or that social class? Obviously with such predictions one needs to have an exhaustive view of all variables present in the field of intervention. The whole chain of the predetermining causes must be known. And there is nothing inherently wrong with this. Good politics in fact rests on how accurate and complete is my knowledge of the reality I intend to reform. It is the extension of this 'micro' model, useful for short-term politics, to the problem of determining the general orientation of politics that generates a short-circuit for the political moralist. Because she cannot have complete knowledge of the entire causal chain, she will always have to deal with 'twists and turns' (*IaG*, 8:375) in the attempt to find a formula – alas, for her as much as for anyone else too complex – that would guide the manipulation of the forces towards the desired outcome. Thus, even if the political moralist has the best intentions, and pursues the goal of perpetual peace as much as the moral politician does, she will do it in the wrong way, namely by conceiving of the problem as a merely technical task. Like a realist of international relations, she will think that in politics there is nothing to do other than steer pre-existing forces and interests – assumed as unchangeable and deaf to the call of morality – to lead them in the desired direction.

In contrast, the moral politician enjoys greater freedom from the obligation to predict all consequences of her action. This is because she does not see the reality on which she operates as a closed, predetermined system. She sees it as modifiable through the initiative of moral individuals such as herself. And in this she is comforted by her grand view of history as leading in a certain direction. It is the partial detachment from the world – a consequence of her being a *moral* politician – that generates an equally partial permission to ignore the limitations of our predictive capacity when it comes to deciding a political course of action. Such a permission is not absolute, obviously, and she will have to put to use her (limited) knowledge of 'how things are'. Prudence, expediency, sheer experience help the moral politician to avoid the two forbidden paths described above: violence and rashness. But a *general* vision of history makes sure that her initiatives to reform national and international institution in a republican sense, even if ultimately unsuccessful, will be recognized by all impartial spectators as aimed to the right goal. Moreover, the sheer fact that someone has attempted such reforms constitutes a victory over the scepticism of political moralists, with their potentially self-fulfilling prophecies, and – perhaps more important – over the scepticism of moralizing politicians, with their awkward and interest-based attempts to give a moral justification for the conservation of the status quo.

There is a further difference between the moral politician and the political moralist who wish for the realization of perpetual peace. By conceiving this goal as a duty, the former will work for it in a stable and constant manner. In contrast, for the latter, the adoption of such an end is the result of a cost-benefit calculation. The enlightened political moralist has come to understand that it is in the best interest of her country (and of herself) to strive for the overcoming of the lawless condition that characterizes the international arena. Her loyalty to the cause of perpetual peace thus depends on the persisting of the conditions that led her to make such a calculation, or more simply to her making the calculation in such a way that the most beneficial outcome, all things considered, is indeed perpetual peace. If doubts arose on the accuracy of the calculation that led her to embrace that cause, her loyalty would be seriously put at risk. Analogously, if the interest of the group or people that she represents would be better served in the short term by political actions that delay or damage the prospects of perpetual peace, it is unclear why the political moralist should not abandon the 'right' path momentarily to embrace it again when morality and interest will no longer be divergent. To use language introduced by Rawls, the moral politician tends to perpetual peace 'for the right reasons' whereas the political moralist embraces the cause as a *modus vivendi*. Once again, if circumstances or the information at our disposal change, and the interest of the group she represents appear better served by a goal other than perpetual peace, the political moralist has no difficulty in abandoning the cause. Conceived as a duty, the loyalty of the moral politician is not exposed to these changing conditions. For her, the fact that interest – in the long run – coheres with morality and right is not a precondition for her loyalty. At most, it is a reassurance that the duty to work for perpetual peace is practicable for sentient beings such as ourselves and does not run contrary to our natural search for happiness.

5. Politics and Judgement

Our analysis has shown so far that the moral politician's task is considerably more difficult than the mere – almost mechanical – application of principles dictated to politics by external normative sources (morality and right). The ideal politician for Kant must do whatever is in her power to conform existing institutions to the universal and unchangeable principles of state, international and cosmopolitan right. But she must do it prudently, namely by choosing the appropriate means to such an end. In particular, she must avoid violence and rashness. Interestingly, however, we have just discovered that she must do it also with a healthy dose of disregard for the consequences of her action, that is to say with a certain degree of courage. This means at least that the moral politician must live with the consciousness that she will not be able to predict all the consequences of her initiative (let alone whether it will be success). Kant seems to rule out the ideal of politics as a science despite his insistence on the importance of knowledge and competence (the premises of prudence) for responsible political action. He wants to have a knowledgeable and prudent politician who is however free from the illusion that the art she practises can be reduced to an exact science. In sum, good politics rely on the ability to read a particular situation to find a way to make it as close as possible to pre-fixed standards of justice, with a clear consciousness that prudence is a necessary yet also not a sufficient condition for success.

If this is the task Kant assigns to the moral politician, the faculty of judgement seems to play a key role. We cannot complete our analysis without clarifying how judgment enters the overall picture. Recall Kant's tripartition of the higher faculties: understanding, reason, judgement. The first thing to notice is that there is no good politics without the skilful use of each of the three. Understanding, as Kant famously puts it, is the faculty of a priori concepts and principles that constitute the structure of all possible experience, but also of the empirical concepts and laws that constitute the fabric of the world as it is in its determination. Understanding is necessary because the politician must know the social and anthropological laws that govern humans' behaviour in society. A policy blind to these regularities can have success only by sheer chance. The moral politician needs to know the best social science available in her time. Without this knowledge, her decisions would hardly be prudent, still less wise.

But of course the same politician also needs to rely on reason, both in its theoretical and practical function. On the one hand, at least as regulative ideal, she needs that all-encompassing *idea* of history that provides inspiration and reassurance regarding the prospects of her actions. On the other hand, practical reason with its law serves as *ratio cognoscendi* of that freedom from natural mechanisms that, as we saw above, is an essential component of political/institutional progress. Finally, and most obviously, reason is what makes the moral politician moral; it is the seat of the ultimate normative source from which all principles of right descend.

The faculty, however, that seems to be most characteristic of the work of the politician is judgement. Judgement, understood both as determinant and reflective, is what gives the politician the opportunity to display a skill that is not as central for the social scientist or for the good, well-intentioned human being. As determinant, judgement helps the moral politician to read the reality through the lens of this or that already given political concept. For example, in the evaluation of institutions (past or existing), determinant judgement classifies political regimes either as republics or despotisms (or any intermediate level). Notoriously for Kant, the determination of the *casus legis* is a prerogative of judgement that cannot be discharged by understanding. We can have all predetermined categories, for example, of democracy, anocracy, autocracy and so on, but only determinant judgement can make the bridge between such abstract concepts and the concrete political system we need to evaluate.[12] The talent to know when a certain rule/concept (already given and provided by the understanding) is to be applied is indeed determinant judgement. Irreducible to mechanical rule/concept application, judgement concerns itself both with universals (the concepts it applies) and particulars (the sensible manifold to which concepts are applied), pretty much like *phronesis* for Aristotle.[13]

As reflective, judgement serves the politician at a deeper and more important level. It constructs from the particulars of a given political condition new political forms that are as close as possible to the universal principles of right.[14] More precisely, it helps to adapt those principles to the degree of institutional progress a society has reached, thereby striking a balance between realism and ideality. Notice that in this case the task is not, as with determinant judgement, to apply pre-existing political concepts, but to find new ones. Much as in the cognitive domain, reflective judgement helps the formation of empirical concepts guided by the principle of the formal purposiveness of nature, in the political domain it delivers new political concepts guided by the presupposition that the political reality is amenable to the universal principle of right, although by progressive steps. Obviously, this adaptation can be done in clever and self-serving ways. The moralizing politician, for example, will certainly attempt to strike a balance that is not as ambitious as possible for the sake of the conservation of the status quo. For such a character, reality is *never* mature for change. But this does not affect the main point, namely that politics (in a Kantian perspective, at least) is about inventing its own rule depending on circumstances as much as it has to do with applying pre-existing laws borrowed from different domains (sociology, economics, anthropology and even right itself). If things are as suggested, reflective judgement is what enables politics to have its own, *peculiar* ability, irreducible to other forms of wisdom.

The political function of reflective judgement puts us on the right track to understand how politics is far from reducible to a science, let alone the mechanical application of formulae, rules established once for all and valid for all contexts. And yet, at the same time, it alerts us that (good) politics is never separable from a universal moment. We have learnt that the prudent politician never adopts immature means to realize justice. At the same time, the same politician will attempt to advance the universal principle of right *as much as possible*, and this presupposes a constant effort of creativity: the identification of that specific balance between reality and ideals that is neither too ambitious nor too conservative. To use once again the language of Rawls, it is ultimately judgement that, on the basis of the juridical and empirical laws already given, and the present circumstances, draws the boundaries of the realistic utopia.

6. The Primacy of Politics

If the interpretation here proposed is correct, politics for Kant is the most complex field of human activity. Good will is not enough to make a good politician, not even if that 'jewel' comes with solid and wide science. The moral and intellectual virtues of the politician remain in the best scenario sterile (and counterproductive in the worst) if they are not assisted by judgement. The task of the moral politician is thus harder than that of the honest human being. Leaving aside the problem that duties at times conflict, all the moral person needs to do is to obey the moral law, which, for Kant is known with perfect clarity in the soul of all rational beings. But the politician has an extra constraint, which is the prudent, 'judicious' definition of a realistic utopia.

To be sure, even in the ethical life – and for what matters in any compartment of human experience – judgement plays a role. The identification of which maxim, in given circumstances, is to be brought to the test of the Categorical Imperative is an operation that is by no means mechanical. *Phronesis* and an attitude very different from the automatic application of the moral law are necessary components of a successful moral life, even from a Kantian perspective.[15] In politics, however, the politician's judgement needs to be even more developed, because the task is more complex. While in the moral life the portion of reality touched by my action is relatively limited, in the case of politics the number of variables to be taken into account increases exponentially along with the number of empirical laws that need to be known and applied to reach the 'right' decision. In other words, if it is true that virtue and knowledge will not produce good politics without judgement, the converse also is correct. With no or only approximate knowledge of the reality for which our reforms are meant, judgement alone will not suffice to yield a good political decision. And here is probably the deepest point of differentiation with the moral case. In the moral life, at least in the overwhelming majority of cases, what duty requires is quite clear even to the least sophisticated and uncultivated understanding, as Kant in fact repeatedly affirms.

There is a final 'difficulty' politics faces that explains why good politicians are rare: judgement, unlike science, cannot be taught. As Kant puts it, we are dealing with 'a peculiar talent which can be practised only' (*KrV*, A133/B172). Judgement, like *phronesis*, cannot be taught because there cannot be a rule for the application of rules to concrete cases without an infinite regress. As Kant puts it,

> If [general logic] sought to give general instructions how we are to subsume under these rules, that is, to distinguish whether something does or does not come under them, that could only be by means of another rule. This in turn, for the very reason that it is a rule, again demands guidance from judgment. (*KrV*, A133/B172)

It follows that 'judgment is a peculiar talent which can be practiced only, and cannot be taught. It is the specific quality of the so-called mother-wit; and its lacks no school can make good' (*KrV*, A133/B172).

Right after this passage, Kant mentions three examples of activities that cannot be performed well unless the actor is endowed with that talent – judgement – which can be practised and yet not be taught. Interestingly, one of them is precisely the activity of the politician.

> A physician, a judge, a ruler (*Staatskundiger*) may have at his command many excellent pathological, legal, political rules, even to the degree that he may become a profound teacher of them, and yet, nonetheless, may easily stumble in their application (*KrV*, A134/B173).

In sum: science can be taught and the moral law is clear to everyone. But the lack of judgement, if Kant is right, has no remedy. At most, one can 'practise' judgement by exposing oneself to a series of good and bad examples of employment of that faculty, in the hope that one's natural talent will be stimulated by imitation. It is more likely to meet a good man than a good politician. And this is the case not only for the notorious tendency to dishonesty and corruption of all politics, but also, and perhaps more importantly, because a good politician needs to be a morally good, erudite and prudent person. *In foro interno* she must have assigned primacy to the moral law over self-love. This secures a firm adherence to the principles of right, an adherence 'for the right reasons', as Rawls would put it. She must have acquired solid and wide knowledge of the empirical laws relevant to her decisions, that is potentially all those of the social sciences plus history. She must be endowed by nature with a talent to know how and when scientific and moral norms of various kinds are to be applied. And she must have strengthened and refined this talent through practice. Not a little thing. Actually, a thing for very few.

Notes

Introduction

1 I use the English term 'right' to translate the German term '*Recht*', to conform with the translation by H. B. Nisbet. However, the reader should bear in mind that by *Recht*, Kant does not merely mean a subjective right, pertaining to individuals, but additionally the law that shapes national, international and global institutions. Thus *Weltbürgerrecht* is both a right that individuals can claim vis-à-vis the foreign countries they enter, and the central piece of the law that shapes the (yet to be constituted) world republic or federation of nations. In this last sense, *Weltbürgerrecht* contributes, with the other two parts of *Recht*, to defining a legal system articulated in domestic, international and cosmopolitan law.

Chapter 1: Kant's Theory of Human Rights

1 Recent work (e.g. Valentini 2012) has attempted to construct a Kant-inspired liberal account of human rights. Yet, this is not the same as offering Kant's own theory of human rights. The collective work *Kantian Theory and Human Rights* (Follesdal and Maliks 2014) offers different views on specific issues (Kant's holistic account of right, Kant and the human right to health care, Kantian metaphors and human rights jurisprudence, and so on), as opposed to a systematic reconstruction of an authentic Kantian account of human rights. Relevant also is Sciacca's analysis of Kant's idea of personality (Sciacca 2000).

2 Occurrences of these expressions are to be found in various works. In *To Perpetual Peace* the context is the relation between morality and politics. Kant claims: 'The rights of man [*Das Recht der Menschen*] must be held sacred. However great a sacrifice the ruling power may have to make' (*ZeF*, 8:380). In *Metaphysics of Morals* the phrases occur several times (*MS*, 6:236, 278, 304).

3 Some think that Kant's notorious exclusion of women and dependent workers from active citizenship (the right to vote) makes his theory incompatible with the principle of perfect formal equality as we

understand it today. However, there is room to interpret this exclusion as Kant's unfortunate attempt to defend the principle of equality, rather than violating it. I have offered an interpretation along these lines in Caranti (2012: 125–7). See also below, chapter 4.

4 In a recent essay, Pinzani (2017) notices that Kant does not talk of a right *to* (external) freedom, but indicates freedom itself as a right and argues that this is by itself problematic.

5 Since this 'right' is affirmed before the existence of the political structure needed to declare any right, it is to be understood as a moral entitlement, a legitimate claim each human can make to a certain form of treatment.

6 I have modified Mary Gregor's translation of the last phrase. Mary Gregor translates 'so long as they do not want to accept it'. I believe that 'even if' is compatible with Kant's text and makes more sense in this context.

7 I offer a critique of the Rawlsian account of human rights, as presented in *The Law of Peoples*, and as further refined by Joshua Cohen (2006), in Caranti (2011).

8 In their otherwise extremely detailed commentary on the *Rechtslehre* Byrd and Hruschka consider Kant's claim that we have an innate right to external freedom as an 'axiom' and ignore Kant's own ground for this right, namely our humanity. This is most puzzling given that they think (correctly) that Kant's entire system of right rests on our innate right to external freedom (Byrd and Hruschka 2010: 77–8).

9 One could say, albeit paradoxically, that heteronomous agency contains in it a quota of autonomy.

10 Although many commentators are inclined to identify practical freedom with autonomy, and the hermeneutical issue would deserve a long discussion, there are a variety of good reasons (historical, systematic, textual) to resist this tendency. The historical reason is that Kant introduced the notion of autonomy relatively late in his career, that is, after 1781. Until the first critique, in fact, Kant believes that all morality requires is practical freedom. And since practical freedom presupposes that some empirical end determines (without necessitating) my path of action, by Kant's own later standards, this moral theory would count as heteronomous. The systematic reason is that the distinction makes room for free (hence imputable) immoral behaviour, thus salvaging Kant from the usual charge of embracing the grotesque view that on his account only moral behaviour counts as free. The textual reasons are, quite simply, the definitions of autonomy, from the *Groundwork* on, that insist on the human will's capacity to be a law to itself independently of any sensuous inclinations (that is, without those empirical motives that determine practically free behaviour) as the hallmark of autonomous agency.

11 On this see my reply to Philippa Foot's thesis that moral agency remains mysterious in Kant because duty should be obeyed in the absence of any motivation (Allison and Caranti 2002: 63–95).
12 Höffe (2010: 85) takes it for granted that Kant has in mind autonomy as the ground for the innate right to freedom. This is probably because he thinks that the reference to a 'wholly supersensible' capacity or to the *homo noumenon* (*MS*, 6:239) is sufficiently univocal. Practical freedom, however, can be equally characterized as such, at least if one rejects from the beginning a compatibilistic account of Kant's theory of freedom. Moreover, Höffe does not seem to pay attention to the distinction between 'personality' and 'humanity'. Although Kant is not fully consistent in the use of the two terms, only 'personality' is always used to refer to humans' capacity to obey moral laws, which in turn grounds their worth and dignity. Therefore, when Kant speaks of an innate right that we have 'by virtue of our humanity' (not personality), it cannot be taken for granted that he means autonomy. It must be proved through arguments of the sort we have offered. See more on this in the next note.
13 Kant is not consistent in his use of the term 'humanity', especially in its distinction from personality. At times, as in the passages above, 'humanity' refers not only to the capacity to set ends, but also to the capacity to be ends in themselves, namely both to practical freedom and to autonomy. At other times, for example in *Religion* (*RGV*, 6:26–7) this latter capacity, that is, the capacity of moral agency, is attributed to personality. Likewise, at times Kant claims that humanity 'is a dignity' (*MS*, 6:462), and only a few lines later, as well as in many other passages, he claims that our dignity lies in our personality. This has led some commentators to believe that 'humanity', understood as mere rational capacity (practical freedom), is for Kant the source of our absolute objective worth, which in turn is the ground of morality (Wood 2008: 88). We cannot share this view. When Kant claims that humanity can be such a basis, he clearly takes the term in the broad sense that encompasses not only rational capacity (practical freedom) but also autonomy. Ultimately, as the passage quoted above shows beyond doubt, for Kant the source of our absolute worth is autonomy, or, what is the same, our capacity for moral agency.
14 I am indebted to Gunnar Beck for the list of authors who fall in the first group. See Beck 2006: 374–9.
15 I have slightly modified Mary Gregor's translation of this passage.
16 A similar point was made by Danto (1984: 2–30) against Gewirth's foundation of human rights. On this see more in chapter 2.
17 Incidentally, this is one of the features of autonomy that makes it attractive as a candidate for a foundation. Human rights are generally considered to spell out some prerogatives that pertain to humans

independently of the circumstances in which they live and, more interestingly, independently of what they have done. Human rights protect even the most heinous criminals, dictators, abusers; in a word, those who have done their best to remove any trace of decency from their lives. It is not by accident Amnesty International deplored the execution of Saddam Hussein (*https://www.amnesty.org.uk/press-releases/iraq-amnesty-international-deplores-execution-saddam-hussein*). Autonomy grounds a dignity that individuals could not alienate or compromise through immoral behaviour. For a view challenging the thesis that human rights should be fully independent of personal desert, see Nickel (2015).

18 In his book, Oliver Sensen (2010) seems to discourage any use of Kant's notion of dignity to ground contemporary human rights. In his opinion, four main differences between the contemporary and the traditional (Kantian) paradigm of dignity make the use of this notion unfit to play any grounding role (Sensen 2010: 312–13). The first two differences are particularly significant and deserve a quick treatment. Firstly, in the contemporary paradigm, which, among other things, shapes the preambles of the main human rights documents, dignity seem to be an absolute, non-relational property. By contrast, in the traditional Stoic conception, which Kant borrows according to Sensen, dignity is not an absolute value, but a relational one. Human beings possess dignity (by virtue of their reason) and are thus elevated above the natural world. Secondly, in the traditional Kantian paradigm human beings can lose or waste their dignity. We are all born with a capital of dignity, so to speak, which can be lost if we behave badly. In the contemporary paradigm, human dignity is precisely what one appeals to show that even the worst among us deserve some respect.

Regarding the first difference, the allegedly relational nature of the Kantian notion of dignity per se does not seem to diminish its foundational potential. It does not matter whether dignity confers on us an absolute or relational value. What matters is whether this value is enough to ground the normativity of contemporary human rights. Even granting, for the sake of argument, that our dignity is a relational property and as such 'merely' elevates us above the natural world, thereby calling for a protection of humans more extended than that reserved to other sentient beings, the crucial point is whether this higher dignity is sufficient to ground the extra rights we enjoy as humans. And I hold that even if there is no analytic inference from our autonomy-based dignity to the human rights that we have, one can hardly take seriously our capacity to follow the moral law and think that certain forms of degradation, precisely those that human rights are meant to avoid, are permissible.

The second alleged difference poses a more serious challenge. Here we intersect a criticism that the first edition of this book received from Alessandro Pinzani (2018). Pinzani reminds us that, for Kant, one can lose one's dignity as citizen upon breaking the law. Kant even makes room for the idea that criminals de-humanize themselves once they commit a crime. As such, they can even be owned by other persons, alienated, used as things. Since human rights are, among other things, meant to prevent this sort of degradation, what sense is there in starting from Kant to discover their foundation?

The first thing to say here is that what the subject loses, as Pinzani himself recognizes, is his dignity as a citizen, which is to be understood as a right to non-interference, rather than his dignity as a human being. Even if Kant does say that the criminal 'ceases to be a person", he cannot mean that the criminal loses everything that produces respect for him as a human being. In fact, Kant says that he can become an instrument in the hands of others, but they can never take the criminal's life or the parts of his body. If the criminal were reduced to the condition of an animal – that is, if the crime literally changed his nature, thereby degrading his *arbitrium* from *liberum* to *brutus* – then there would be no reason why free citizens could not take his life, as the lives of animals are taken for a variety of purposes.

This interpretation is reinforced by textual evidence, cited by Milene Consenso Tonetto (2018), another of my critics, against Sensen's interpretation of Kant's notion of dignity. In a passage of the *Doctrine of Virtue*, Kant says: 'I cannot deny all respect to even a vicious man as a human being; I cannot withdraw at least the respect that belongs to him in his quality as a human being, even though by his deeds he makes himself unworthy of it. So there can be disgraceful punishments that dishonour humanity itself (such as quartering a man, having him torn by dogs, cutting off his nose and ears' (TL AA: 06; 463). And Kant continues by saying that even the most vicious person is to be treated as a human being because he 'can never lose entirely his predisposition for the good' (TL AA: 06; 464). Even if we may lose our dignity as citizens, it seems that for Kant we may never lose our dignity as human beings. The latter is not contingent on how we behave. Finally, even if we grant for the sake of argument that Kant expressed a view on punishment that is at odds with his own notion of human dignity (let alone at odds with our contemporary understanding of human rights), this does not seem to me a sufficient ground to conclude that (a) one cannot have a foundation of human rights that rests on Kant's notion of autonomy, and (b) that this strategy is not a Kantian one. Since the notion of autonomy is so central for Kant's practical philosophy, while his comments on criminals are, to say the least, peripheral, I would say that my strategy still has a strong basis for being described as a Kantian one.

19 The last scholar (Baiasu 2016) who entered the debate between independentism and dependentism shares this view when he admits that the normativity of the universal principle of right follows from what Kant calls the moral law, as distinguished from and higher than the categorical imperative.

Chapter 2: Human Rights: the Contemporary Debate

1 For a debate on the relation between human rights, democracy and self-determination see Christiano (2015) and the reply by Peter (2015).
2 Tasioulas himself seems to realize that his account needs to say a bit more about dignity ('Of course, considerably more needs to be said about the content, and ontological basis, of human dignity'). But he thinks that it is enough to say that 'it is a presupposition [...] that human beings have the capacity to possess moral rights' or that they have 'intrinsic, non-derivative value'. In other words, it is presupposed that they have dignity. Ironically, Tasioulas here comes close to the circularity he elsewhere (Tasioulas 2013: 300) charges Nagel with. Similarly, in his attempt at a foundation, Schaber (2012) faces the crucial question of why being human should be a reason for having rights. But when he points to dignity for an answer he thinks that it is sufficient to find a reference to it in major human rights documents. Unfortunately, quoting what those documents say hardly amounts to a foundation.
3 Pogge (2008) thinks that governments of rich countries are the first addressees of the obligations generated by the human rights of the global poor, because those governments are directly responsible for shaping a world order that causes poverty.
4 This self-denial is part of a larger and fairly popular hermeneutical strategy that attempts to read the *Metaphysics of Morals* as independent of the truths about human beings Kant had already established in his moral writings, first and foremost the fact that they are autonomous. We have discussed the limits of this strategy in chapter 1.
5 Tasioulas (2012) includes Pogge in the political camp, at least before his 'change of heart' in the second edition of *World Poverty and Human Rights* (2008). The inclusion is due to Pogge's idea, mitigated in 2008, that an offence is not a violation of human rights unless it is perpetrated by representatives of a state or state-like entity. I doubt whether this suffices to make Pogge a representative of the political view. Holding that the addressees of human rights are only or mainly institutions (respectively Pogge's view in 2002 and 2008) is

compatible with an orthodox foundation. Quite simply, the question of what grounds human rights normativity is entirely independent of the question of who are the addressees of the obligations generated once that normativity is grounded. In fact, as far as I can see, Pogge is non-committal regarding the ultimate foundation of human rights. Similarly, I doubt that Dworkin's theory can be considered political simply because, like Pogge, Dworkin (2008) thinks that human rights are primarily rights against one's government.

Chapter 3: The Foundation of Human Rights: The Dignity Approach

1. Using a Kantian terminology, we could say that Pico's foundation of human dignity seems to rely more on *Willkür* than on *Wille*. By the former is meant the radical freedom to choose any pattern of action, including immoral ones, while the latter indicates what Kant considers as the highest form of freedom, that is, our capacity to discard those maxims that are incompatible with the moral law, and precisely for this reason.
2. According to Schiller, Kant privileges the 'dignity' of heroic self-denial over the 'grace' of the spontaneous harmony between reason and desire. As he famously put it, 'In Kantian moral philosophy, the idea of duty is presented with a severity which frightens all the Graces away' (Schiller 1793: 365). There are good reasons to believe that Schiller was wrong in this criticism, because nothing in Kant's system diminishes the value of the gracious harmony Schiller praised. Actually, Kant was well aware that we need to train our sensibility to remove possible obstacles to that harmony. As is well known, this is the main problem of Kant's moral anthropology which 'would deal only with the subjective conditions in human nature that hinder or help us in fulfilling the laws of the metaphysics of morals' (*MS* 6:217).
3. The Categorical Imperative, in all its formulations, and the Golden Rule are famously different. The latter basically says that you should not do what you are not prepared to receive from others. This is compatible with the possibility that you are prepared to treat others (and yourself) in immoral ways. Think of those who exploit others saying that this is part of human nature and therefore are prepared to receive the same treatment. By placing substantial limits on the way in which you are allowed to treat yourself as well as others (never as a mere means), the Categorical Imperative excludes this possibility.
4. It may prove useful to clarify whether the respect we have in mind is an instance of 'recognition respect' or of 'esteem respect', to use

Darwall's famous distinction (Darwall 1977). It will be recalled that recognition respect comes when we recognize a feature that dictates a certain disposition on the part of the agent. Thus, when we say that all human beings deserve respect, we are saying that we recognize in them a feature that dictates a certain appropriate behaviour. In contrast, appraisal or esteem respect is granted by virtue of the excellence some objects or persons have. We 'esteem respect' a great athlete, a great teacher, a great work of art and so on. Now autonomy interestingly seems to make us worthy both of recognition and of esteem respect. It is a feature we all have, but it is also an awe-generating characteristic of humans. After all, the distinction between recognition and esteem respect is not so sharp as Darwall may have thought, because recognition respect must rest on finding some 'excellence', or so it seems. When we respect persons we recognize an excellence different from that of a great athlete because everybody possesses it, but it still is a form of excellence, at least compared to the other species. Darwall argues that when we respect someone as a person we are not crediting him with anything. This, however, makes recognition respect mysterious. It is not clear why someone should restrict his actions in recognition of some feature possessed by the addressees (in this case people) unless one credits that feature as intrinsically valuable. We do not restrict our actions before an object merely by virtue of the fact that we recognize it as belonging to one class, not even if the characteristic is peculiar to that class. As Cranor puts it, 'the believed characteristic by virtue of which one respects a person must be believed to be a good-making characteristic of persons' (Cranor 1975: 312). On our theory, autonomy is that characteristic.

5   On the problem of the compatibility of the Golden Rule with perverse moral standpoints that formally respect the principle of reciprocity and the superiority of the Categorical Imperative in this regard see above, n. 3.

6   The conjecture that it is permissible to violate human rights of some in order to protect the human rights of a larger group is obviously controversial, and we do not need to take sides here. Michael Rosen (2011) cites the example of the German Constitutional court ruling on the German air safety law passed in the aftermath of the terrorist attacks of 9/11. The law allowed the German air force to shoot down an airplane hijacked by terrorists if there was overwhelming evidence that it would be used as a weapon to kill a large number of civilians. The constitutional court annulled the law with the consideration that the lives of the passengers could not be used as means for saving the lives of others. But this ruling is far from being non-controversial.

Rosen himself, despite his commitment to human dignity as a value that trumps other urgent moral consideration, wonders whether it makes sense to protect the lives of passengers (who would die anyway) at the cost of the lives of those on the ground targeted by the murderers.

7 Of course an ambiguity remained in the transition from the Enlightenment philosophical ideal of personhood to the first legal documents, that is the French Declaration and the US Bill of Rights, that affirmed the universality of the rights of men. In the terminology we introduce, is it mere practical freedom or (moral) autonomy that bestows dignity? When we try to show that moral autonomy is a better foundation, we are proposing a new philosophical grounding in the hope that this will translate in new and better legal documents.

8 What exact level of respect is due by virtue of this feature is a question here left unanswered, and we shall address it later. But notice that Rosen needs an answer as much as we do.

9 A different response to this charge against Kant is to be found in Hill (2013: 320–5).

10 The qualifications 'from the practical points of view' (*in praktischer Absicht*) or 'in a practical context' (*in praktischer Beziehung*) appear repeatedly in Kant's text. See for example *KprV* 5:42–57. They clarify that the affirmation that we are autonomous is not an epistemic truth, but only the view we are necessarily bound to adopt given the consciousness of the moral law as supremely authoritative for us – that is, given the fact of reason.

11 This example is used by Buchanan (2010).

12 This problem arises from a general difficulty already noticed by early critics of *The Law of Peoples* (Kok-Chor Tan 1998). Rawls's preference of peoples over individuals as authorized speakers in the ideal assembly defining the moral code of international affairs, combined with his toleration towards decent illiberal peoples, that by definition mirror the prevailing illiberal values of the majority, entails that liberal minorities or liberal individuals living inside a decent polity cannot legitimately demand the international community to redress possible discriminations.

13 I prefer not to use Huntington's term 'civilization' because I am convinced that Sen's criticism of this concept is correct. See respectively Huntington (1996) and Sen (2006).

14 Abdelwahab Meddeb (2008) is even more ambitious and suggests in his last work that the Muslim world can and should abandon a literal interpretation of the whole Qu'ran.

15 See for example Angle (2002, 2012). See also Chan (2007).

16 I owe both citations to Ferrara (2014).

17 Isaiah 49:6.

Chapter 4: The Kantian Model

1. Archibugi (1995) reminds us that from 1767 on, Kant gave twelve courses of lectures on natural law and often cited authors belonging to this school in his political writings. Moreover, in his 1786 review of Hufeland's 'Versuch über den Grundsatz des Naturrechts', Kant lists twenty-seven authors belonging to this school from Grotius to his contemporaries.
2. According to Bordiga (see Burgio 1991: 84), the expression is taken from the Bible (Job 16:2) and refers to the expression – *onerosos consolatores* – directed by Job to the friends who were trying to alleviate his suffering. The suggestion is plausible because both Kant's targets and Job's friends merely try to make evil less painful, instead of doing something radical to remove it.
3. This concern with the treatment of foreigners is obviously crucial for Kant's third definitive article.
4. The revolutionary import of Wolff's proposal did not go unnoticed among more conservative thinkers. In a treatise published nine years later, Emeric de Vattel, ambassador of the Saxon court in Berne, lamented precisely this aspect of Wolff's proposal. He found it unreasonable that the laws of nations should be derived from the idea of a supreme republic because, of all rights possessed by a nation, that of sovereignty is the most important, and therefore neither alienable nor open to limitation (Vattel 1916: 131).
5. This evolution is well reconstructed by Burgio (1991). If in the Middle Ages war was nothing but men's corruption of the celestial order – what Augustine (1900: 641) called *pax civitatis* and Aquinas (1884: 579) *perpetua pax*, in the Renaissance the picture changes only because Erasmus restricts the set of the corrupted individuals to that of the perverse princes. Their immoral disposition was considered the main cause of war. Given this premise, Erasmus could propose as an antidote to war a rather simple-minded hope for the moral regeneration of princes' souls. Compared to these pious hopes, Machiavelli's theorization of war seems a complete and positive breakthrough. For Machiavelli and perhaps any realist, war is the natural choice for the prince. It is actually the 'sole ability that one expects from the rulers' (Machiavelli 1967: 10). A prince is essentially committed to war because war is necessary for the state's creation, security and survival. Hence Machiavelli reorients the analysis of war from the allegedly corrupt psychological features of humankind (in particular, of the prince) to the material premises of war, that is, to the social, economic and, above all, institutional factors that cause it. War is embedded in the 'logic' of the state, or better, as Kant would later understand, in the

logic of certain kinds of states. Along these lines, Hobbes's analysis of seventeenth-century absolutism represents another stage of progress towards Kant's revolution. In fact, while Leviathan guarantees internal peace (this is its *raison d'être*), its absolute power gives the sovereign the opportunity to wage war whenever he desires. Hence, we could say, the philosopher who provided the strongest justification for the absolute state also helped us to discover its intrinsic bellicose tendency. As long as the absolute power of the state remained an unquestionable dogma, the only option left for a theory of peace was to think of political possibilities in which the powers of Europe could come to put aside their natural tendency to war. It is no accident that all projects of peace of the seventeenth and eighteenth centuries, among them that of Saint-Pierre, considered the possibility of perpetual peace as compatible with the conservation of the absolute power of the state. For these projects, peace will be achieved either if a most powerful state imposes its rule over the others (on the model of the pax Romana) or if the European sovereigns coalesce into a union against internal enemies (revolutionaries, rebels, liberals and so on). As we saw, Saint-Pierre proposes the union's right and duty to intervene in defence of sovereign when groups or individuals within a state threaten its authority. We are just one step away from Rousseau's lucid irony, which was – as in so many other cases – a source of inspiration for Kant. In his *Jugement sur le projet de paix perpétuelle*, Rousseau comments on how the Abbé Saint-Pierre simply fails to see that wars and despotism are tightly linked in an indissoluble causal nexus, and that the most efficient way to reach peace was to get rid of the *ancien régime*. This is precisely what Kant considers as the first of three steps necessary to reach perpetual peace.

6   In the Dialectic of Pure Reason Kant warns the reader that he uses 'idea' in 'its original signification' of an 'original' for which no real example is adequate, very much as Plato's ideas find no proper example in the sensible world. As Kant puts it in relation to the idea of virtue, 'This original is the idea of virtue, in respect to which the possible objects of experience may serve as examples (proofs that what the concept of reason commands is in a certain degree practicable), but not as an archetype. That no one of us will ever act in a way which is adequate to what is contained in the pure idea of virtue is far from proving this thought to be in any respect chimerical' (*KrV*, A315/B372). Hence ideas are neither fictions nor representations of something we can experience. They are not fictions because they do not express a fully chimerical reality. Rather, they set a standard that we recognize as something we can/should strive towards. They are not representations because in experience nothing perfectly corresponding to them could be found.

Both features of the term need to be kept in mind when Kant talks of an 'idea of a universal history with a cosmopolitan purpose'. One can never have an experience of a 'cosmopolitan purpose' in human affairs. Nonetheless the idea itself is not chimerical, because it expresses a standard for which we find many imperfect examples in history.

7 Kant does not call this constitution 'republican' yet. This may be used as evidence that the characterization of the good constitution as republican in the post-1789 writings is a homage to revolutionary France.

8 Besides Sen's famous thesis that freedom is development (Sen 1999), which entails that a restriction of freedom translates into a weakening of national economy, see also Giavazzi and Tabellini (2005).

9 On this reading, Kant's liberalism could not be considered, as Rawls does, as comprehensive.

10 According to Pinzani (2010) in *Idea* Kant had a view of human nature – man as a 'warped wood' and 'in need of master' (*IaG*, 8:23) – irremediably incompatible with moral progress. We believe that already in this essay Kant did not see human nature as fixed. Republican institutions are meant to curb the immoral tendency of human beings and therefore enable progress, even if this falls short of a complete moralization given what Kant would later call the 'radical' propensity to prioritize self-love over morality.

11 As we shall prove, Kant does not think that international institutions are to be established only among republics. The federation, at least in its initial stage, is thought of as composed of both republican and despotic countries. On this see below our discussion of the second definitive article of *To Perpetual Peace*.

12 Actually, *Idea* can be seen as an answer to Mendelssohn because *Jerusalem*, where Mendelssohn submits this remark, was published one year before Kant's 1784 essay.

13 Kant spots another contradiction between Mendelssohn's 'pessimism' regarding humanity's ability to progress and his restless intellectual activity aimed 'to promote the enlightenment and welfare of the nation to which he belonged' (*TP*, 8:308).

14 Kant does not explain what he has in mind; perhaps he means the affirmation of Enlightenment ideals and their institutional realization through the American and French Revolutions.

15 See *TP*, 8:310. Kant goes on to clarify that if the cosmopolitan stage turns out to be something worse than the previous stage (the condition of 'soulless despotism', as Kant calls it in *To Perpetual Peace*), then humanity will establish 'a lawful federation under a commonly accepted international right' (*TP*, 8:310).

16 As we said earlier, the plausibility of the first part of this twofold thesis rests on the consideration that no hegemonic power in history has kept

its leadership indefinitely. The declining role of the USA as sole hegemon in world affairs seems to prove, once again, the solidity of the thesis.

17 Kant's popularity in France was due to his having kept, in contrast with many other German intellectuals, a positive evaluation of the French Revolution even after the Terror.

18 Instructive is the case of Fichte, who moved from an initial enthusiasm, fuelled by his Jacobinism at the turn of the century, to a general rejection of Kant's cosmopolitanism in the context of his rediscovery of the metaphysical foundation of the state and, above all, of the nation. Schlegel, Görres, and Gentz also had similar trajectories. On this see Mori (2008: 52–3).

19 Since respect for the autonomy of peoples plays such a crucial role, one can understand why Kant introduces an exception to the general rule of non-interference stated in the fifth preliminary article. 'But it would be a different matter if a state, through internal discord, were to split into two parts, each of which set itself up as a separate state and claimed authority over the whole' (*ZeF*, 8:346) In this case, we have a condition of anarchy that removes the unity and the autonomy of the people in question. In other words, since there is no longer something like the identity (and therefore autonomy) of a people, there is also nothing to respect. Hence the rule of non-interference can be set aside.

20 We noticed above that Kant here makes the same point, almost word for word, made before by Voltaire.

21 Guyer (2006) rightly pointed out that Kant speaks the language of probabilities in this section.

22 In a reconsideration of his original theory, Doyle (1995: 101) recognizes that democracy, previously considered as a sufficient guarantee of inter-democratic peace, merely guarantees that the preferences of the average elector will influence the government, thus leaving completely indeterminate whether those are peaceful or bellicose.

23 See for example Archibugi and Beetham (1998: 81–3). Although Archibugi does not say explicitly that Kant shares this view, it is quite clear from the context that this his belief.

24 Michael Doyle is a significant exception. In his original 1983 essays as well as in his later reappraisals (1995, 2005, 2011) he has always stressed that Kant's recipe is made of three equally important ingredients. Similarly Bruce Russett (2001) insists that all three Kantian factors are crucial.

25 Byrd and Hruschka (2010: 176) hold that Kant's discussion of the forms of states in *To Perpetual Peace* is mainly about different forms of executive powers. I cannot share this view. When Kant distinguishes between despotic and republican *formae regiminis*, he is saying that a political system as a whole can either be despotic or republican. A

despotic government, for example, is not a system in which the executive is despotic, while possibly the legislative is not. It is a system in which power is exercised in a despotic manner because the two powers are not properly distinguished. It is no accident that the evidence cited by Byrd and Hruschka is dubious. The fact that Kant says that democracy necessarily founds [*gründet*] a (despotic) executive power does not mean that he reduces democracy (one of the three *formae imperii*) to an executive power. Kant seems to be saying that democracy, a necessarily despotic system as a whole, obviously yields a despotic executive power.

26 The contemporary literature on political representation is huge. Unfortunately, we cannot discuss it here. On the value of representation for democracy, for example, see Urbinati (2006).

27 Chris Brown (1992) and Cavallar (2001) also insist on the difference between the notion of liberal democracy assumed in DPT and Kant's notion of republic, albeit for reasons different from the ones here suggested.

28 Kant does not say in the first definitive article that a civic ethos is a significant peace-promoting factor. We inferred this thesis from the insufficiency of the dynamics of self-interest Kant explicitly alludes to. Elsewhere, though, Kant does say that the moralization of citizens is a condition necessary for a stable peace (*IaG*, 8:21, 8:26). Further evidence is indirectly available from the third definitive article. Kant does not seem to imagine an institution with the power to enforce cosmopolitan right. It follows that its application is left to the good will of individuals and peoples, that is, to their moral disposition. Not accidentally, Kant alludes to a common cosmopolitan conscience that rejects violations of the inherent rights of humans independently of where they occur (*ZeF*, 8:360). For a view similar to mine on this point, see Kleingeld (1995; 1999: 61). For a view that construes progress towards peace in legal but not in moral terms, see Höffe 1983: 244–5. A rich reading of Kant's republic similar to the one here suggested, with particular emphasis on the role of citizens' education, has been advocated by Ripstein (2009: 292–4).

29 *IaG*, 8:24.

30 It should be recognized that Kantian scholarship does not side unanimously with the broad reading. Norberto Bobbio for example favours the 'separate peace' reading (Bobbio 1983: xiv). Although Bobbio seems to take this reading for granted, he does provide an indirect reason that supports it. He argues that restricted access explains why Kant feels confident that the lack of coercive powers does not make the federation pointless: since republics have a pro-attitude towards peace, they can reasonably be expected to externalize this attitude towards other republics without coercion.

This is also Doyle's point that we criticized in our discussion of the second definitive article.

31 For a summary of Cavallar's and MacMillan's textual points see Doyle (2012: 209–10).

32 To be precise, Kant does not give up this ideal completely even in *The Metaphysics of Morals*. For example, he claims that 'all international rights [...] are purely provisional until the state of nature has been abandoned. Only within a universal *union of states* (analogous to the union through which a nation becomes a state) can such rights acquire peremptory validity and a true state of peace be attained' (*MS*, 6:350). If the union of states is to be analogous to that through which a mass of individuals become a people – no matter how limited and qualified this analogy may be – then this union cannot be the loose confederation Kant depicts elsewhere in the same work.

33 Pogge (2006) suggests that there is another – less explicit – reason that led Kant to this prudent result. For Pogge Kant adheres to the modern dogma of the indivisibility of sovereignty according to which a political authority can be said to be sovereign only if it holds full power. Hence Kant could not even conceive of a world republic with limited powers and competences.

34 Variations of the same reconciliatory line of interpretation can be found in Geismann (1996a, 1996b), Cavallar (1992), Lutz-Bachmann (1999) and Cheneval (2002).

35 Höffe (2006: 13–14) also notices how Kant introduces a reflection on cosmopolitan law when philosophers appeared interested only in the domestic dimension or (considerably less) in the international one.

36 Notice that Kant here and in other passages (e.g. *MS* 6:352) speaks of a community (*Gemeinschaft*) while in *To Perpetual Peace* he still describes peoples' right to enter into relations with other peoples in terms of a right to attempt to establish a new society, that is, *ein Besuchsrecht [...] sich zur Gesellschaft anzubieten* (*ZeF*, 8:358). To be sure, the term 'community' is not absent in this essay. Towards the end of the third definitive article Kant speaks of a 'universal community' that has developed up to a point that a violation of rights in one part of the world is felt everywhere. Only in *The Metaphysics of Morals*, though, is the idea that the right to visit serves the purpose of creating a universal community made explicit.

37 I have modified the translation here, because the connection between the code, as complemented by cosmopolitan right, and perpetual peace, is in my opinion not rendered clearly by Nisbet's choice to move the reference to perpetual peace to a new sentence.

38 Covell expresses a similar reading when he characterizes cosmopolitan law as 'the body of public international law that Kant saw as

constituting the juridical framework for the intercourse of men and states' (1998: 141–2). Covell however does not reduce cosmopolitan law to a legal framework for international trade.

39 It must be acknowledged that Doyle at times presents a theory broader than the one suggested by the passage above. For example in the same article he states, 'Hospitality does appear to include [...] the opportunity for citizens to exchange goods and ideas, without imposing the obligation of trade' (Doyle 1983: 227). Moreover, international trade is sometimes recognized as beneficial because it 'helps creating crosscutting transnational ties that serve as lobbies for mutual accommodation' (Doyle 2004). This suggests that he sees trade not as the final end, but as instrumental to the exchange of good and ideas and ultimately to 'accommodation' or 'peace'. The qualification is however of limited significance. To begin with, even the narrowest reading of the third definitive article acknowledges that the *final* end is 'accommodation' or 'peace', not trade. More importantly, what matters is whether one is ready to recognize (a) that cosmopolitan right enables (with or without the help of trade) the creation of a global moral conscience and (b) that *this* is the crucial and independent factor that leads to peace. As far as I can see, Doyle never finds in Kant anything along these lines. Finally, regarding the question of whether Kant intends any kind of trade as conducive to peace, or only trade practiced according to equal terms of cooperation, it is true that the discussion – in part II of the 1983 essay – of colonialism and imperialism shows a full awareness of how trade is not always 'good for peace'. But Doyle's diagnosis of why trade in those historical circumstances did not produce the desired effects is that the other two pillars of the theory (democracy and IGOs) were absent, not that unfair trade is in and of itself inefficient to promote peace. In fact, the sheer claim that all three pillars of the theory need to be in place to guarantee peace is fully compatible with considering any form of trade, even the most unfair one, as a powerful albeit in itself insufficient peace-promoting factor.

40 Kleingeld (2012: 136–7) mentions Hegewisch (1746–1812) as a naive believer in the quick and easy equation between trade and peace in order to highlight the distance between Hegewisch's views and Kant's. She also criticizes Rosen (1993: 74, 76, 211) and Fleischacker (1996: 385) for downplaying Kant's cosmopolitanism in favour of Adam Smith's view that free international trade and the market are intrinsic values as well as peace-promoting factors. Also Cavallar stresses that the interactions guaranteed by cosmopolitan right are not exclusively commercial ones (Cavallar 2002: 360). Although his recent book attacks the idea that Kant can be considered a cosmopolitan all

the way through, Cavallar still characterizes Kant's position as a form of 'thin moral cosmopolitanism' (Cavallar 2015: 2), which is already more than what the narrow reading is ready to concede.

41 See above, n. 36.

Chapter 5: Democratic Peace Theory

1 We do not distinguish at this stage between a monadic thesis (democracies are more peaceful in general) and the more popular dyadic thesis (democracies are peaceful only among themselves) because we believe that the distinction was not available before Mazzini first formulated the dyadic thesis with full clarity, as we shall demonstrate shortly.
2 <http://www.constitution.org/fed/federa04.htm>.
3 Despite a meritorious effort by Ossipow (2008), who noticed an abundance of similarities between *To Perpetual Peace* and the points made in Federalist papers, I do not think there is enough evidence to conclude that Kant was influenced by Madison or by the Federalists in general.
4 Babst later (1972) wrote a more accessible and popularized version in *Industrial Research*.
5 Data from Freedom House. See <http://www.freedomhouse.org/report/freedom/world/2016/maps-graphics>.
6 Doyle himself cites some controversial cases of inter-democratic conflicts that however, in his opinion, do not constitute true counter-examples: the Peru-Ecuador conflict (1941–2) was between young democracies (established less than three years before) – which would explain why the pacifying effects of liberalism were not activated; the Lebanon raid against Israel during the 1967 war could also be problematic because Lebanon, unlike all other neighbours of Israel, was a democratic state or on the verge of becoming one (the process was to be completed in 1975). For Doyle, however, the significance of this case is limited especially if one considers the frequency of the attacks by Israel's autocratic neighbours.
7 The possibility that capitalism must resort to war, among other things to open new markets, is compatible with DPT as long as the 'necessary' wars are not between democratic capitalist countries.
8 In fact, in *To Perpetual Peace* we find an unambiguous condemnation of the practices of 'colonial states'.
9 A fairly isolated voice has been Rummel (1975).
10 It should be admitted that, although the quotation is often attributed to Kissinger, none of the sources I have consulted indicates where and when he used these words. There is no doubt, though, that Nixon

and Kissinger helped the coup by Pinochet. This emerges from many declassified transcripts of their conversations.
11 Rousseau saw as a clear sign of decadence for a republic the professionalization of the army. Not only lawmaking activity, but also defence was not to be delegated. Kant in his third preliminary article invites the princes of his time to dismantle permanent armies constituted by mercenaries and professionals.
12 Although Rosato is not explicit about this, 'pacifist groups' should not be understood only as those opposed to all kinds of war, but should include citizens who oppose wars fought for the 'wrong reasons', that is, those incompatible with liberal, constitutional values.
13 In a private conversation Doyle described the OAS as a good example of the Kantian federation, as he understands it.
14 Small and Singer (1982: 205–6) give a definition, thereafter commonly adopted, that rests on two pillars: a minimum number of fatalities and the presence on both sides of organized armed forces. From this, the definition of war goes as follows: 'sustained combat, involving organized armed forces, resulting in a minimum of 1,000 battle-related fatalities', which Small and Singer would then qualify as '1,000 battle-related fatalities within a twelve-month period'.

Chapter 6: The Two Models Compared

1 *ZeF*, 8:350.
2 The non-interference rule of the fifth preliminary article allows one exception only: if the state in question is plagued by a civil war that brings it back to the state of nature. To the extent in which the barbaric state, discussed by Kant in the *Anthropology*, constitutes a case distinct form the state of nature, then force is permissible in this case too.

Chapter 7: Kant's Early Teleology in *Idea*

1 The example of weather predictions is along similar lines. We may not know whether next summer is going to be hotter, but we know that if we keep on polluting, the average temperature on our planet will increase.
2 In other words, in the beginning God created all species with their generic dispositions, but the development of an individual is left to nature, which has the power to generate new features out of the 'package' of generic pre-formed features implanted by God.

3   The shift from individual to specific pre-formation allows Kant to conceive of the development of reason (our chief capacity as determined by God) as occurring not in the limited time span of an individual life but in the succession of many individual lives occurring in the history of the species.
4   Species are not fixed entities in the contemporary paradigm, and alleged 'specific' dispositions are even less so.
5   In *To Perpetual Peace* nature does not 'push' to develop the pre-fixed disposition of the species, but enables humans to live in all areas of the world, then spreads them everywhere through war, and ultimately forces them to enter into (more or less legal) relationships.
6   One may think that a progressive teleology is justified by the fact that we need to assume it to make sense of our practical life. This, however, is not Kant's strategy in *Idea*, where this line of thought is never made explicit.
7   It is difficult because it rests on the fulfilment of three conditions: (a) a correct conception of the just constitution; (b) great experience tested in many affairs of the world (e.g. a comparative evaluation of the results brought about by republican and despotic regimes); (3) 'above all else a good will prepared to accept the findings of this experience' (*IaG*, 8:23).
8   In our case, admittedly a very complex one, that is the totality of human affairs.

Chapter 8: *To Perpetual Peace*: A Secular Guarantee of Progress?

1   In this work, we find the idea – already central in *Idea* and in *To Perpetual Peace* – that humans – out of self-interest – "will find themselves compelled to ensure that *war* [...] finally disappears as a mode of aggression" (*SF* 7:93). But we also find a new reason to look positively at the future in the sympathy bordering enthusiasm that the French Revolution aroused "in all spectators who are not themselves caught in it" (*SF* 7:85). This sympathy proves a human tendency in favour of justice and freedom constituting an extra reason – no longer objective but subjective – to believe that perpetual peace will be reached one day. In the same work Kant also makes the equally important point that if humans are set in the right objective circumstances, that is republican institutions at the domestic, international, and global level, they will not show the perverse and selfish tendencies they display under unjust governments (*SF* 7:93). This undermines scepticism about perpetual peace based on anthropological theses allegedly supported by experience.

2   An interesting account of the evolution of this thought is to be found in Mori (2008: 231–86).
3   *Ultra posse nemo obligatur* means that nobody can be obligated to do what is impossible, while *pro necessitate nemo obligatur* means that nobody can be obligated to promote what is necessarily going to happen.
4   One could add a sort of historical concern. From the vantage point of observers coming 200 years after Kant, one could say that history refutes Kant's rosy prediction, perhaps even in the weaker form of a guarantee of progress, continuous or discontinuous, linear or non-linear. Wars have been neither less frequent nor less cruel since the eighteenth century. If anything, the level of violence, especially in the 'short century', seems to have escalated. Moreover, war changed its nature: to use Clausewitz's categories, we could say that war – up to the nineteenth century – was fought by professionals, with a very precise political end (that of changing the will of the enemy), and basically considered and practised as politics by other means. The first world war changed all this: 'total mobilitazion' of entire peoples, the absence of a predetermined goal of war other than the annihilation of the enemy, the considerable loss of rationality in the fighting (and one could say also in the aftermath – just think of the heavy, probably unendurable conditions imposed on Germany after the First World War). An adequate reply to this concern, which cannot be provided here for sheer reasons of space, should look not just to the amount of violence that has occurred, but also and more importantly to the reasons why wars are fought today. Intuitively, the violence used to stop Nazism has a different moral status compared to the violence used for colonial wars. Hence any account that wishes to determine whether any progress has been made since Kant's time must investigate the 'quality' of wars, no matter how difficult this is to determine.
5   Remember the notion of *perpetual* peace.
6   In other words, the obstacles are just a question of coordination among agents, as opposed to insuperable blocks inherent to human nature.
7   The point that molecules do not have free will is to be dealt with in the following discussion of the anthropological concern.
8   In this regard, it is very instructive to take a look at Rawls's 'More precise idea of the democratic peace' (Rawls, 1999: 48–51). In this illuminating section of *The Law of Peoples* Rawls lists five conditions of socio-economic justice that are supposed to strengthen the mechanisms that contemporary scholars working in democratic peace theory appeal to.
9   Notice the empirical nature of the prediction and the cautious language. On a charitable reading, this means avoiding mercy for an

agent if this implies injustice to someone else (e.g. the injustice done to a victim if the state forgives the culprit).
10 On this reading, the status of the Guarantee Thesis would be that of a regulative yet transcendental principle similar to the principle of the purposiveness of nature described in the 1790 *Critique of Judgment* (*KU*, 5:181–6).

Chapter 9: Progress and Political Agency

1 For an excellent discussion of the difference between right and politics in Kant see Mori (2008: 165–230). When interpreters refer to the 'political philosophy' of Kant, however, it is quite common to understand by that his account of right. This is the case of interpreters such as Riley (1983), Williams (1983) and Shell (1980). There is obviously nothing wrong with that, provided that one keeps in mind that Kant's philosophy of politics is a different, albeit obviously not unrelated, story.
2 For an analysis of the characters of the moral terrorist and of the immoral noble see Cavallar 1994: 477–8.
3 We can assume the convergence between morality and happiness as a regulative ideal, but the latter cannot be made a condition of the former.
4 According to Ludwig (2006), the section on the guarantee of perpetual peace is meant precisely to counter this form of scepticism, which can easily be turned into an alibi for keeping the status quo.
5 One may object that this emphasis on the individual initiative to progress towards perpetual peace runs contrary to Kant's insistence on the possibility of complying perfectly with right with no consideration of one's intentions. In a Kantian framework one can perfectly discharge juridical obligations with no 'right intention', hence with no good will. In this context, however, the juridical system is not yet in force. Hence only a purely moral disposition (a good will) can push individuals to go beyond what their juridical system requires and modify it to make it more in line with the dictates of pure practical reason.
6 According to Saint-Pierre, sovereigns should adhere to the 'European Union' out of interest and not for a moral disposition. But it remains true that they should renounce their full and unbounded authority for the greater security of the state. As Rousseau would have pointed out in his *Jugement sur le projet de paix perpétuelle* (1980–96: 593), this presupposes the moral disposition to prioritize the state's interest over their personal interest, in particular their readiness to step down from their absolute power to declare war, which is a good portion of their

absolute power *tout court*. On this and on the radical novelty introduced by Kant in the tradition of peace projects see above, chapter 4.
7   Irrational because the advantages one pursues through aggression could be more efficiently reached through free trade in a context of international relations regulated by right.
8   On this famous motto and in general on the characters of the political moralist and of the moral politician see Marini (2001).
9   Kant says in this sense that we are unable to 'prophesy the future theoretically' (*ZeF*, 8:368).
10 For details on this see the preceding chapter.
11 Today, the signs that Kant's project has a certainly non-linear yet steady implementation are many: the spread of democracy in the world (from the 3 republics in Kant's time to the 123 democracies out of 195 in 2013, according to Freedom House), the global diffusion of the human rights culture, the strong stability and peacefulness of certain areas of the world capacity (the EU but more in general the whole democratic world), the Arab Spring with the wave of enthusiasm that it generated in global public opinion.
12 The faculty of understanding is the seat of a priori and empirical categories/concepts. Yet it does not provide rules for the application of its own rules (concepts). With an intuition that anticipates Wittgenstein, and in particular Kripke's reading of the *Philosophical Investigations*, Kant understands that subsuming the sensible manifold under concepts is not an operation that the mind can perform by applying a rule/concept of superior rank that specifies when this or that concept/rule fits the sensible manifold. In fact, in order to know when such a higher rule could be applied, we would need a further, higher rule. And this generates an infinite regress.
13 It is not by accident that in book 6 of the *Nicomachean Ethics* Aristotle associates *phronesis* with political ability.
14 Marini (2007) also thinks that judgement plays an important role for Kantian politics.
15 If by telling the truth I know there are concrete chances I am going to hurt a person so badly that she will fail an important exam, then I should probably abstain from 'sincerity', or even lie if necessary. In fact, in this case the maxim to be brought to the test is not 'lie any time the truth you are going to tell is going to hurt someone' but 'other things being equal, procrastinate the revelation of a truth until the damage for the person in question is minimum'. Identifying the 'right' maxim to guide our behaviour is a significant part of the ethical life and judgment plays a crucial role in this respect. On the relation between Kant and virtue ethics see Engstrom and Whiting (1996) and in particular Sherman (1997).

Bibliography

Al-Azm, S. 1970. *Critique of Religious Thought*. Beirut: Naqd al-Fikr al-Dini.
Allison, H., 1990. *Kant's Theory of Freedom*. Cambridge: Cambridge University Press.
Allison, H. and Caranti L. 2002. *Libertà Trascendentale ed Autorità della Morale in Kant*. Rome: Luiss Edizioni.
Anderson-Gold, S. 2006. 'Cosmopolitan Right Kant's Key to Perpetual Peace', in *Kant's Perpetual Peace. New Interpretative Essays*, ed. L. Caranti. Rome: Luiss University Press, pp. 137–47.
Angle, S. C. 2002. *Human Rights and Chinese Thought: A Cross-Cultural Inquiry*. New York: Cambridge University Press.
Angle, S. C. 2012. *Contemporary Confucian Political Philosophy: Toward Progressive Confucianism*. Cambridge: Polity Press.
An-Na'im, A. A. 1990a. *Toward an Islamic Reformation: Civic Liberties, Human Rights, and International Law*. Syracuse: Syracuse University Press.
An-Na'im, A. A. 1990b. 'Human Rights in the Muslim World, Socio-Political Conditions and Scriptural Imperatives', *Harvard Journal of Human Rights*. 3: 13–52.
An-Na'im, A. A. 2008. *Islam and the Secular State: Negotiating the Future of Shari'a*. Cambridge, MA: Harvard University Press.
Archibugi, D. 1995. 'Immanuel Kant, Cosmopolitan Law, and Peace', *European Journal of International Relations*, 1/4: 429–56.
Archibugi, D. 1997. 'So what if democracies don't fight each other?', *Peace Review*, 9/3: 379–84.
Archibugi, D. 2008. *The Global Commonwealth of Citizens: Toward Cosmopolitan Democracy*. Princeton: Princeton University Press.
Archibugi, D. and Beetham, D. 1998. *Diritti umani e democrazia cosmopolita*. Milan: Feltrinelli.
Archibugi, D. and Koenig-Archibugi, M. 2006. 'Che cosa c'è di democratico nella pace democratica?', *Quaderni di relazioni internazionali*, 2: 2–17.
Archibugi, D., Urbinati, N., Zürn, M., Marchetti, R., Macdonald, T. and Jacobs, D. 2010. 'Global Democracy: A Symposium on a New Political Hope', *New Political Science*, 32/1: 83–121.
Arendt, H. 1982. *Lectures on Kant's Political Philosophy*. Chicago: Chicago University Press.

Atkinson, A. and Brandolini, A. 2001. 'Promise and Pitfalls in the Use of "Secondary" Datasets: Income Inequality in OECD Countries', *Journal of Economic Literature*, 39/3: 771–800.

Babst, D. 1964. 'Elective Governments – A Force for Peace', *Wisconsin Sociologist*, 3: 9–14.

Babst, D. 1972. 'A Force for Peace', *Industrial Research*, 14/2: 55–8.

Baiasu, S. 2016. 'Right's Complex Relation to Ethics in Kant. The Limits of Independentism', *Kant Studien*, 107/1: 2–33.

Baiasu, S., Pihlstrom, S. and Williams, H. (eds). 2001. *Politics and Metaphysics in Kant*. Cardiff: University of Wales Press.

Barkawi, T. and Laffey, M. 2001. *Democracy, Liberalism, and War: Rethinking the Democratic Peace Debate*. Boulder: Lynne Rienner.

Bartal, Inbal Ben-Ami, Decety, Jean and Mason, Peggy. 2011. 'Empathy and Pro-Social Behavior in Rats', *Science*, 334: 1427–30.

Bauer, J. E. and Bell, D. A. 1999. *The East Asian Challenge for Human Rights*. Cambridge: Cambridge University Press.

Beck, G . 2006. 'Immanuel Kant's Theory of Rights', *Ratio Juris*, 19/4: 371–401.

Beetham, D., Carvalho, E., Landman T. and Weir, S. 2009. *Assessing the Quality of Democracy: A Practical Guide*. Stockholm: International IDEA.

Beitz, C. 1979. *Political Theory and International Relations* (Princeton: Princeton University Press).

Beitz, C. 2003. 'What Human Rights Mean', *Daedalus*, 132/1: 36–46.

Beitz, C. 2009. *The Idea of Human Rights*. Oxford: Oxford University Press.

Bekoff, M. and Pierce, J. 2009. *Wild Justice. The Moral Lives of Animals*. Chicago: University of Chicago Press.

Benoit, K. 1996. 'Democracies Really Are More Pacific (In General): Reexamining Regime Type and War Involvement', *Journal of Conflict Resolution*, 40/4: 636–57.

Bentham, J. 1927 [1786–9]. *Plan for an Universal and Perpetual Peace*. London: Sweet & Maxwell.

Besson, S. 2015. 'Human Rights and Constitutional Law: Patterns of Mutual Validation and Legitimation', in R. Cruft, M. S. Liao and M. Renzo, M. (eds), *Philosophical Foundations of Human Rights*. Oxford: Oxford University Press, pp. 279–99.

Besson, S. and Tasioulas, J. (eds). 2010. *The Philosophy of International Law*. Oxford: Oxford University Press.

Bielefeldt, H. 1997. 'Autonomy and Republicanism: Immanuel Kant's Philosophy of Freedom', *Political Theory*, 25: 524–58.

Bobbio, N. 1969. *Diritto e stato nel pensiero di Emanuele Kant*. Turin: Giappichelli.

Bobbio, N. 1985. 'Introduzione', in N. Merker (ed.), *Per la pace perpetua*. Rome: Editori riuniti, pp. vii–xxi.
Bobbio, N. 2005. *Il futuro della democrazia*. Turin: Einaudi.
Bohman, J. and Lutz-Bachman, M. 1996. *Frieden durch Recht*. Frankfurt: Suhrkamp.
Bohman, J. and Lutz-Bachman, M. 1997. *Perpetual Peace. Essays on Kant's Cosmopolitan Ideal*. Cambridge, MA: MIT Press.
Bordiga, R. 1991, 'Prefazione', in I. Kant, *Per la pace perpetua*. Milan: Feltrinelli.
Braumoeller, B. F. 1997. 'Deadly doves: Liberal nationalism and the democratic peace in the Soviet successor states', *International Studies Quarterly*, 41: 37–402.
Brown, G. W. 2009. *Grounding Cosmopolitanism: From Kant to the Idea of a Cosmopolitan Constitution*. Edinburgh: Edinburgh University Press.
Brown, M. E., Coté, O., Lynn-Jones, S. M. and Miller, S. E. (eds). 2011. *Do Democracies Win Their Wars?* Cambridge, MA: MIT Press.
Brown, M. E., Lynn-Jones, S. M. and Miller, S. E. (eds). 1996. *Debating the Democratic Peace*. Cambridge, MA: MIT Press.
Browning, G. 2011. *Global Theory from Kant to Hardt and Negri*. Basingstoke: Palgrave.
Buchanan, A. 2010. 'The Egalitarianism of Human Rights', *Ethics*, 120/4: 679–710.
Buchanan, A. 2013. *The Hearth of Human Rights*. Oxford: Oxford University Press.
Bueno de Mesquita, B., Morrow, J. D., Siverson, R. M. and Smith, A. 1999. 'An Institutional Explanation of the Democratic Peace', *American Political Science Review*, 93/4: 791–807.
Bueno de Mesquita, B. and Smith, A. 2011. *The Dictator's Handbook*. New York: Public Affairs.
Bueno de Mesquita, B., Smith, A., Siverson, R. M. and Morrow, J. D. 2003. *The Logic of Political Survival*. Cambridge, MA: MIT Press.
Burgio, A. 1991. 'Per una storia dell'idea di pace perpetua', in I. Kant, *Per la pace perpetua*. Milan: Feltrinelli. pp. 87–131.
Byrd, B. S. and Hruschka, J. 2010. *Kant's Doctrine of Right. A Commentary*. Cambridge: Cambridge University Press.
Caranti, L. 2006a. *Kant's Perpetual Peace: New Interpretative Essays*. Rome: Luiss University Press.
Caranti, L. 2006b. 'Perpetual War for Perpetual Peace? Reflections on the Realist Critique of Kant's Project', *Journal of Human Rights*, 18/3: 23–45.
Caranti, L. 2006c. 'One More Time Back to Kant: From the Democratic Peace to the Kantian Peace', in L. Caranti (ed.), *Kant's Perpetual Peace. New Interpretative Essays*. Rome: Luiss University Press, pp. 177–204.

Caranti, L. 2011. 'Human Rights and Democracy', in T. Cushman (ed.), *Handbook of Human Rights*. Abingdon: Routledge, pp. 85–99.

Caranti, L. 2011a. 'The One Possible Basis for the Proof of the Existence of the External World: Kant's Anti-Sceptical Argument in 1781 Fourth Paralogism', *Kant Studies Online*, 162–91.

Caranti, L. 2012. *La pace fraintesa. Kant e la teoria della pace democratica*. Soveria Mannelli: Rubbettino.

Caranti, L. 2013. 'What's Wrong with a Guarantee of Perpetual Peace?', in S. Bacin (ed.), *Kant und die Philosophie in weltbürgerlicher Absicht. Proceedings of the XI International Kant Congress*. Berlin: De Gruyter, pp. 611–22.

Caranti, L. 2014. 'The Guarantee of Perpetual Peace: Three Concerns', in A. Goldman, T. Patrone, and P. Formosa (eds), *Teleology and Politics in Kant*. Cardiff: University of Wales Press.

Caranti, L. 2018. *'Kant's Political Legacy*. Replies to Pinzani, Consani, Tonetto, Dos Santos, Barbieri, Dutra, Faggion, Klein', *Estudos kantianos*, 6/1: 117–29.

Carr, C . 1989 . 'Kant's Theory of Political Authority', *History of Political Thought*, 10: 719–31 .

Cavallar, G. 1992. *Pax kantiana*. Vienna: Böhlau.

Cavallar, G. 1994. 'Kant's Society of Nations: Free Federation or World Republic? *Journal of the History of Philosophy*, XXXII: 461–82.

Cavallar, G. 1999. *Kant and the Theory of Practice*. Vienna: Böhlau.

Cavallar, G. 2001. 'Kantian Perspectives on Democratic Peace: Alternatives to Doyle', *Review of International Studies*, 27: 229–48.

Cavallar, G. 2015 *Kant's Embedded Cosmopolitanism: History,. Philosophy and Education for World Citizens*. Berlin: De Gruyter.

Cederman, L.-E. 2001. 'Back to Kant: Reinterpreting the Democratic Peace as a Macrohistorical Learning Process', *American Political Science Review*, 95/1:15–31.

Chan, J. 2005a. 'Buddhism and Human Rights', in R. K. M. Smith and C. van den Anker (eds), *The Essentials of Human Rights*. London: Hodder Arnold, pp. 25–7.

Chan, J. 2005b. 'Confucianism and Human Rights', in R. K. M. Smith and C. van den Anker (eds), *The Essentials of Human Rights*. London: Hodder Arnold: pp. 55–7.

Chan, J. 2007. 'Democracy and Meritocracy: Toward a Confucian Perspective', *Journal of ChinesePhilosophy*, 34/2: 179–93.

Cheneval, F., 2002. *Philosophie in weltbürgerlicher Bedeutung: über die Entstehung und die philosophischen Grundlagen des supranationalen und kosmopolitischen Denkens der Moderne*, Basel: Schwabe.

Chiodi, G. M., Gatti, R. and Marini, G. (eds). 2001. *La filosofia politica di Kant: Seminario perugino per lo studio dei classici*. Milan: Angeli.

Christiano, T. 2011. 'An Instrumental Argument for a Human Right to Democracy', *Philosophy and Public Affairs*, 39/2: 142–76.
Christiano, T. 2015. 'Self-determination and the Human Right to Democracy', in R. Cruft, M. S. Liao and M. Renzo (eds), *Philosophical Foundations of Human Rights*. Oxford: Oxford University Press, pp. 459–80.
Clapham, A. 2006. *Human Rights Obligations of Non-State Actors*. Oxford: Oxford University Press.
Clark, K. A. and Stone, R. W. 2008. 'Democracy and the Logic of Political Survival', *American Political Science Review*, 102/3: 387–92.
Cobden, R. 1901. *Political Writings of Richard Cobden*. London: Ridgway.
Cohen, J. 2006. 'Is There a Human Right to Democracy?', in C. Sypnowich (ed.), *The Egalitarian Conscience: Essays in Honour of G. A. Cohen*. Oxford: Oxford University Press, pp. 226–48.
Cohen, J. 2008. 'Rethinking Human Rights, Democracy and Sovereignty in the Age of Globalization', *Political Theory*, 36/4: 578–606.
Confucius, 2003. *Confucius Analects, with Selections from Traditional Commentaries*, tr. Edward Slingerland. Indianapolis: Hackett.
Corradetti, C. 2009. *Relativism and Human Rights: A Theory of Pluralistic Universalism*. Dordrecht: Springer.
Covell, C. 1998. *Kant and the Law of Peace: A Study in the Philosophy of International Law and International Relations*. New York: Palgrave.
Cranor, C, 1975. 'Towards a Theory of Respect for Persons', *American Philosophical Quarterly*, 12: 303–19.
Cruft, R., Matthew Liao, M. S. and Renzo, M. (eds). 2015. *Philosophical Foundations of Human Rights*. Oxford: Oxford University Press.
Danto, A. 1984. 'Comment on Gewirth Constructing an Epistemology of Human Rights: A Pseudo Problem?', *Social Philosophy and Policy*, 1:25–30.
Darwall, S. 1977. 'Two Kinds of Respect', *Ethics*, 88/1: 36–49.
DeGrazia, D. 1996. *Taking Animals Seriously*. Cambridge: Cambridge University Press.
De Maistre, J. 1821.'Soirées de Saint-Pétersbourg', in *Oeuvres Complètes*. Lyon: Librairie générale catholique et classique: 1884–6.
De Waal, F. 2006. *Primates and Philosophers: How Morality Evolved*. Princeton: Princeton University Press.
De Waal, F. 2014. 'Natural Normativity: The "Is" and "Ought" of Animal Behavior', *Behaviour*, 151/2–3: 185–204.
Denis L (ed.). 2010. *Kant's Metaphysics of Morals: A Critical Guide*. Cambridge: Cambridge University Press.
Derrida, J. 2000. *Of Hospitality*. Stanford: Stanford University Press.

Dershowitz, A. 2005. *Rights from Wrongs: A Secular Theory of the Origin of Rights*. New York: Basic Books.

Dixon, W. 1994. 'Democracy and the Peaceful Settlement of International Conflict', *American Political Science Review*, 88/1: 14–32.

Doppelt, G. 1981. 'Rawls' System of Justice: A Criticism from the Left', *Nous*, XV/3: 259–307.

Doyle, M. W. 1983a, 1983b. 'Kant, Liberal Legacies, and Foreign Affairs', Parts I and II, *Philosophy and Public Affairs*, 12/3 and 12/4: 205–35, 323–53.

Doyle, M. W. 1986. 'Liberalism and World Politics', *American Political Science Review*, 80/4 (December): 1151–69.

Doyle, M. W. 1995. 'Liberalism and World Politics Revisited', in Charles W. Kegley (ed.), *Controversies in international relations theory: realism and the neoliberal challenge*. New York: St. Martin's Press, pp. 83–106.

Doyle, M. W. 2004. 'Liberal Internationalism. Peace, War, Democracy', <http://www.nobelprize.org/nobel_prizes/themes/peace/doyle/>.

Doyle, M. W. 2005. 'Three Pillars of the Liberal Peace', *American Political Science Review*, 99/3: 463–6.

Doyle, M. W. 2006. 'Kant and Liberal Internationalism', in P. Kleingeld (ed.),*To Perpetual Peace and other Writings on Politics, Peace, and History*. New Haven: Yale University Press, pp. 201–42.

Doyle, M. W. 2012. *Liberal Peace*. Abingdon and New York: Routledge.

Doyle, M. W. and Sambanis, N. 2006. *Making War and Building Peace: The United Nations after the Cold War*. Princeton: Princeton University Press.

Dworkin, R. 2013. *Justice for Hedgehogs*. Cambridge, MA: Harvard University Press.

El Fadl, K. A. 2003. 'Islam and the Challenge of Democracy', *Boston Review*, April/May.

Ellis, E. 2005. *Kant's Politics: Provisional Theory for an Uncertain World*. New Haven: Yale University Press.

Encarnation, O. G. 2006. 'Bush and the theory of the democratic peace', *Global Dialogue*, 8/3–4. Available at <http://www.worlddialogue.org/content.php?id=384>.

Engstrom, S. and Whiting, J. (eds). 1996. *Aristotle, Kant, and the Stoics*. Cambridge: Cambridge University Press.

Ernst, G. and Heilinger, J. C. (eds). 2012. *The Philosophy of Human Rights*. Berlin and Boston: De Gruyter.

Fagan, A. 2012. 'Philosophical Foundations of Human Rights', in *Handbook of Human Rights* London and New York: Routledge.

Fearon, J. D. 1994a. 'Domestic Political Audiences and the Escalation of International Disputes', *American Political Science Review*, 88/3: 577–92.

Fearon, J. D. 1994b. 'Signaling Versus the Balance of Power and Interests: An Empirical Test of the Crisis Bargaining Model', *Journal of Conflict Resolution*, 38/2: 236–69.
Fearon, J. D. 1995. 'Rationalist Explanations for War', *International Organization*, 49/3: 379–414.
Ferrara, A. 2008. *The Force of the Example. Explorations in the Paradigm of Judgment*. New York: Columbia University Press.
Ferrara, A. 2014. *The Democratic Horizon: Hyperpluralism and the Renewal of Political Liberalism*. Cambridge: Cambridge University Press.
Fiegle, T. 2014. 'Teleology in Kant's Philosophy of History and Political Philosophy', in A. Goldman, T. Patrone and P. Formosa (eds), *Politics and Teleology in Kant*. Cardiff: University of Wales Press, pp. 163–79.
Finnis, J. 1980. *Natural Law and Natural Rights*. Oxford: Clarendon Press.
Flach, W. 2005, 'Zu Kants geschichtsphilosophischem "Chiliasmus"', in *Phänomenologische Forschungen*, pp. 167–74.
Flach, W. 2006. 'Erreichung und Errichtung. Über die empiriologische Orientierung der Kantischen Geschichtsphilosophie', in R. Hiltscher, S. Klinger and D. Süß (eds), *Die Vollendung der Transzendentalphilosophie in der 'Kritik der Urteilskraft'*. Berlin: Duncker & Humboldt, pp. 183–9.
Fleischacker, S. 1996. 'Values behind the Market: Kant's Response to the Wealth of Nations', *History of Political Thought*, 57: 379–407.
Flikschuh, K. 2015. 'Human Rights in Kantian Mode: A Sketch', in R. Cruft, M. S. Liao and M. Renzo (eds), *Philosophical Foundations of Human Rights*. Oxford: Oxford University Press, pp. 653–70.
Follesdal, A. and Maliks, R. (eds) 2014. *Kantian Theory and Human Rights*. Abingdon: Routledge.
Forsythe, D. 1992. 'Democracy, War, and Covert Actions', *Journal of Peace Research*, 29/4: 385–95.
Fukuyama, F. 1992. *The End of History and the Last Man*. New York: Free Press.
Gandhi, M. K. 1924. *Young India 1919–1922*. Madras: The Huxley Press.
Garztke, E. 1998. 'Kant We All Just Get Along? Motive, Opportunity, and the Origins of the Democratic Peace', *American Journal of Political Science*, 42/4: 1–27.
Garztke, E. 2007. 'The Capitalist Peace', *American Journal of Political Science*, 51/1: 166–91.
Geiger, I. 2007. *The Founding Act of Modern Ethical Life: Hegel's Critique of Kant's Moral and Political Philosophy*. Palo Alto: Stanford University Press.
Geismann, G. 1996a. 'Kants Weg zum Frieden', in H. Oberer, *Kant. Analysen–Probleme–Kritik*. Würzburg: Königshausen & Neumann, pp. 333–63.

Geismann. G. 1996b. 'World Peace: Rational Idea and Reality. On the Principles of Kant's Political Philosophy', in H. Oberer, *Kant. Analysen–Probleme–Kritik*. Würzburg: Königshausen & Neumann, pp. 265–319.

Gewirth, A. 1984. 'The Epistemology of Human Rights', in E. F. Paul, F. D. Miller, Jr. and J. Paul (eds), *Human Rights*. Oxford: Blackwell, pp. 1–24.

Ghobarah, P. H. and Russett, B. 2004. 'The Comparative Political Economy of Human Misery and Well-Being', *International Studies Quarterly*, 48/1: 73–94.

Giavazzi, F. and Tabellini, G. 2005. 'Economic and political liberalizations', *Journal of Monetary Economics*, 52: 1297–1330.

Gleditsch, K. S. 2002. *All International Politics Is Local*. Ann Arbor: Universityof Michigan Press.

Gleditsch, N. P. and Hegre, H. 1997. 'Peace and democracy: Three levels of analysis', *Journal of Conflict Resolution*, 41: 283–310.

Goldman, A., Patrone, T.and Formosa, P. (eds). 2014. *Politics and Teleology in Kant*. Cardiff: University of Wales Press.

Gowa, J. 1999. *Ballots or Bullets? The Elusive Democratic Peace*. Princeton: Princeton University Press.

Gregor, M. 1963. *Laws of Freedom*. Oxford: Blackwell.

Griffin, J. 2001 'First Steps in an Account of Human Rights', *European Journal of Philosophy*, 9/3: 306–27.

Griffin, J. 2008. *On Human Rights*. Oxford: Oxford University Press.

Griffin, J. 2010. 'Human Rights and the Autonomy of International Law', in S. Besso and J. Tasioulas (eds), *The Philosophy of International Law*. Oxford: Oxford University Press, pp. 339–55.

Griffin, J. 2012. 'Human Rights: Questions of Aims and Approach', in G. Ernst and J. C. Heilinger (eds), *The Philosophy of Human Rights*. Berlin and Boston: De Gruyter, pp. 3–16.

Grotius, H. 1916 [1625]. *The Law of War and Peace*, trans. of IX edition by Kelsey, F. W. Washington: Carnegie Institution of Washington.

Guyer, P. 2000. *Kant on Freedom, Law, and Happiness*. Cambridge: Cambridge University Press.

Guyer, P. 2002. 'Kant's Deductions of the Principles of Right', in M. Timmons (ed.) *Kant's Metaphysics of Morals*. Oxford: Oxford University Press, pp. 23–64.

Guyer, P. 2006. 'The Possibility of Perpetual Peace', in L. Caranti (ed.), *Kant's Perpetual Peace: New Interpretative Essays*. Rome: Luiss University Press, pp. 143–63.

Habermas, J. 1996. *Between Facts and Norms. Contribution to a Discourse Theory of Law and Democracy*. Cambridge: MIT Press.

Habermas, J. 1997. 'Kants Idee des ewigen Friedens–aus dem historischen Abstand von 200 Jahren', in *Die Einbeziehung des Anderen: Studien zur politischen Theorie*. Frankfurt: Suhrkamp, pp. 192–236.
Hamilton, A., Madison, J. and Jay, J. 1788. *The Federalist*. New York: J. and A. McLean.
Hampton, M. 1998/9. 'Germany and The United States: Creating Positive Identities in Trans-Atlantia, *Security Studies*, 8/2–3: 235–69.
Harrison, E. 2002. 'Waltz, Kant and systemic approaches to international relations', *Review of International Studies*, 28/1: 143–62.
Hassouna, H. A. 1975. *The League of Arab States and Regional Disputes*. New York and Leiden, Oceana Publications.
Hayes, R. P. 1991 'Gotama Buddha and religious Pluralism', *Journal of Religious Pluralism*, 1: 72–7.
Henderson, E. 2002. *Democracy and War, the End of an Illusion?* Boulder: Lynne Reiner.
Herr, S. R. 2010. 'Confucian Philosophy and Equality', *Asian Philosophy: An International Journal of the Philosophical Traditions of the East*, 20/3: 261–82.
Hill, T. E., Jr. 2013. 'In Defence of Human Dignity: Comments on Kant and Rosen', in C. McCrudden (ed.), *Understanding Human Dignity*. Oxford: Oxford University Press, pp. 313–25.
Höffe, O. 1983. *Immanuel Kant*. München: Beck.
Höffe, O. (ed.). 1995. *Immanuel Kant: Zum ewigen Frieden*. Berlin: AkademieVerlag.
Höffe, O. 2006. *Kant's Cosmopolitan Theory of Law and Peace*. Cambridge and New York: Cambridge University Press.
Höffe, O., 2010. 'Kant's innate right as a rational criterion for human rights', in Lara Denis (ed.), *Kant's Metaphysics of Morals: A Critical Guide*. Cambridge: Cambridge University Press, pp. 71–92.
Howard, M. 1978. *War and the Liberal Conscience*. New Brunswick, NJ: Rutgers University Press.
Huntington, S. P. 1996. *The Clash of Civilizations and the Remaking of World Order*. New York: Touchstone.
Huntley, L. 1996. 'Kant's Third Image: Systemic Sources of the Liberal Peace', *International Studies Quarterly*, 40/1: 45–76.
Huth, P., and Allee, T. 2002. *The Democratic Peace and Territorial Conflict in the Twentieth Century*. Cambridge: Cambridge University Press.
Ignatieff, M. 2001. *Human Rights as Politics and Idolatry*. Princeton: Princeton University Press.
Institute for Economics and Peace. 2012. *Global Peace Index*. Sydney.
International Commission on Intervention and State Sovereignty (ed.). 2001. *The Responsibility to Protect: Report of the International*

Commission on Intervention and State Sovereignty. Ottawa: International Development Research Centre for ICISS.
Jacobi, F. H. 1825. *Fliegende Blätter*. Leipzig: Fleischer, vol. IV, pp. 1818–25.
Jayatilleke, K. N. 1975. *The Message of the Buddha*. London: George Allen and Unwin.
Johnson, M. G. and Janusz, S. 1998. *The Universal Declaration of Human Rights: A History of its Creation and Implementation, 1948–1998*. Paris: UNESCO.
Kahl, C. 1998/9. 'Constructing a separate peace: Constructivism, collective liberal identity, and democratic peace', *Security Studies*, 8/2–3: 94–144.
Kamm, F. M. 1989. 'Harming Some to Save Others', *Philosophical Studies*, 57: 251–6.
Kamm, F. M., 2007. *Intricate Ethics: Rights, Responsibilities, and Permissible Harm*. New York: Oxford University Press.
Kant, Immanuel. 1991. *Political Writings*, ed. Hans B. Nisbet. Cambridge: Cambridge University Press.
Kant, Immanuel. 1996. *The Metaphysics of Morals*, ed. and tr. Mary Gregor. Cambridge: Cambridge University Press.
Kateb, G. 2011. *Human Dignity*. Cambridge and London: Harvard University Press.
Kaulbach, F. 1975. 'Welchen Nutzen gibt Kant der Geschichtsphilosophie?' *Kant-Studien*, 66/1: 65–84.
Kersting, W. 1996. 'Weltfriedensordnung und globale Verteilungsgerechtigkeit. Kants Konzeption eines vollständigen Rechtsfriedens und die gegenwärtige politische Philosophie der internationalen Beziehungen', in R. Merkel and R. Wittmann (eds), *Zum ewigen Frieden: Grundlagen, Aktualität und Aussichten einer Idee von Immanuel Kant*. Frankfurt: Suhrkamp, pp. 172–212.
Kinsella, D. 2005 'No Rest for the Democratic Peace', *American Political Science Review*, 99/3: 453–7.
Kleingeld, P. 1995. *Fortschritt und Vernunft: zur Geschichtsphilosophie Kants*. Würzburg: Königshausen & Neumann.
Kleingeld, P. 2001. 'Nature or providence? On the theoretical and practical importance of Kant's philosophy of history', *American Catholic Philosophical Quarterly*, 75/2: 201–19.
Kleingeld, P., 2012. *Kant and Cosmopolitanism*. Cambridge: Cambridge University Press.
Kronowski(?) 1795. *Épitre du vieux cosmopolite Syrach à la Convention Nationale de France*. Paris(?): En Samartie.
Kuhn, T. 1962. *The Structure of Scientific Revolutions*. Chicago: University of Chicago Press.

Laberge, P., Lafrance, G. and Sumas, D. 1997. *L'année 1795. Kant. Essai sur la paix*. Paris: Librairie philosophique J. Vrin.
Lake, D. A. 1992. 'Powerful Pacifists: Democratic States and War', *American Political Science – Review*, 86: 24–37.
Layne, C. 1994. 'Kant or Cant: The Myth of the Democratic Peace', *International Security*, 19/2: 5–49.
Levy, J. 1988. 'Domestic Politics and War', *The Journal of Interdisciplinary History*, 18(4): 653–73 (doi: 10.2307/204819).
Lipson, C. 2005. *Reliable Partners: How Democracies Have Made a Separate Peace*. Princeton: Princeton University Press.
Loretoni, A. 1996. *Pace e progresso in Kant*. Naples: ESI.
Losurdo, D. 1983. *Autocensura e Compromesso nel Pensiero Politico di Kant*. Naples: Istituto Italiano per gli Studi Filosofici, Bibliopolis.
Louden, R. 1999. *Kant's Impure Ethics*. Oxford: Oxford University Press.
Ludwig, B. 2002. 'Whence Public Right? The Role of Theoretical and Practical Reasoning in Kant's Doctrine of Right', in M. Timmons (ed.), *Kant's Metaphysics of Morals: Interpretative Essays*. Oxford: Oxford University Press, pp. 159–83.
Ludwig, B. 2006. 'Condemned to Peace: What Does Nature Guarantee in Kant's Treatise of Eternal Peace?', in L. Caranti (ed.), *Kant's Perpetual Peace: New Interpretative Essays*. Rome: Luiss University Press. pp. 183–95.
Lutz-Bachmann, M. 1999. 'Kant's Idea of Peace and the Philosophical Conception of a World Republic', in J. Bohman and M. Lutz-Bachmann (eds), *Perpetual Peace: Essays on Kant's Cosmopolitan Ideal*. Cambridge, MA and London: MIT Press, pp. 59–78.
Maffettone, S. 2010. *Rawls: An Introduction*. Cambridge (UK) and Malden, MA: Polity Press.
Malik, R. 2014. *Kant's Politics in Context*. Oxford: Oxford University Press.
Mann, M. 2006. *The Dark Side of Democracy*. New York: Cambridge University Press.
Mansfield, E. D. and Pevehouse, J. C. 2000. 'Trade Blocs, Trade Flows, and International Conflict', *International Organization*, 54: 775–808.
Mansfield, E. D. and Pevehouse, J. C. 2003. 'Institutions, Interdependence, and International Conflict', in G. Schneider, K. Barbieri and N. P. Gleditsch (eds), *Globalization and Armed Conflict*. London: Routledge, pp. 233–50.
Mansfield, E. D. and Snyder, J. 2005. *Electing to Fight: Why Emerging Democracies Go to War*. Cambridge, MA: MIT Press.
Mansfield, E. D. and Snyder, J. 2009. 'Pathways to War in Democratic Transitions', *International Organization*, 63: 381–90.

Maoz, Z. 1998. 'Realist and Cultural Critiques of the Democratic Peace: A Theoretical and Empirical Re-assessment', *International Interactions*, 24: 3–89.

Maoz, Z. and Russett, B. 1993.'Normative and Structural Causes of the Democratic Peace, 1946–1986', *American Political Science Review*, 87/3: 624–38.

Marini, G. 1998. *Tre studi sul cosmopolitismo kantiano*. Pisa: Istituti poligrafici internazionali.

Marini, G. 2001. 'Per una repubblica federale mondiale', in G. M. Chiodi, R. Gatti and G. Marini (eds), *La filosofia politica di Kant: Seminario perugino per lo studio dei classici*. Milan: Angeli, pp. 19–34.

Marini, G. 2002. 'Implicazioni sistematiche dell'idea di repubblica in Kant', in (anon., ed.), *Raccolta di Scritti in Memoria di Antonio Villani*. Naples: Istituto Suor Orsola Benincasa: pp. 1539–51.

Marini, G. 2007. *La filosofia cosmopolitica di Kant*. Rome and Bari: Laterza.

McLaughlin Mitchell, S. 2002. 'A Kantian System. Democracy and Third Party Conflict Resolution', *American Journal of Political Science*, 46/4: 749–59.

McCrudden, C. (ed.). 2013. *Understanding Human Dignity*. Oxford: Oxford University Press.

Mearsheimer, J. 2001. *The Tragedy of Great Power Politics*. New York: Norton.

Meddeb, A. 2008. *Sortir de la malédiction. L'islam entre civilisation et barbarie*. Paris: Seuil.

Merkel, R. and Wittman, R. 1996. *Zum ewigen Frieden: Grundlagen, Aktualität und Aussichten einer Idee von Immanuel Kant*. Frankfurt: Suhrkamp.

Mill, J. S. 1973 [1859]. 'A Few Words on Nonintervention', in *Essays on Politics and Culture*, ed. G. Himmelfarb. Gloucester, MA: Peter Smith, pp. 368–84.

Miller, D. 2007. *National Responsibility and Global Justice*. Oxford: Oxford University Press.

Miller, D., 2012. 'Grounding Human Rights', *Critical Review of International Social and Political Philosophy*, 15: 407–27.

Mitra, K. 1982. 'Human Rights in Hinduism', in Arlene Swidler (ed.), *Human Rights in Religious Traditions*. New York: The Pilgrim Press pp. 77–84.

Molholland , L. S . 1990 . *Kant's System of Rights*. New York: Columbia University Press.

Moravcsik, A. 1997. 'Taking Preferences Seriously: A Liberal Theory of International Politics', *International Organization*, 51/4: 516–21.

Morgan, T. C. and Campbell, S. H. 1991. 'Domestic Structure, Decisional Constraints, and War: So Why Kant Democracies Fight?', *Journal of Conflict Resolution*, 35/2: 187–211.

Mori, M. 2008. *La pace e la ragione. Kant e le relazioni internazionali: diritto, politica, storia*. Bologna: Il Mulino.

Munck, G. L. 2009. *Measuring Democracy: A Bridge between Scholarship and Politics*. Baltimore: Johns Hopkins University Press.

Murti, T. R. V. 1980. *The Central Philosophy of Buddhism: a Study of the Madhyamika System*. London: Unwin.

Nagel, T. 1995. 'Personal Rights and Public Space', *Philosophy and Public Affairs*, 24/2, 83–107.

Narang, V. and Nelson, R. 2009. 'Who Are These Belligerent Democratizers? Reassessing the Impact of Democratization on War', *International Organization*, 63/2: 357–79.

Nickel, J. 2003 'Human Rights', in Edward N. Zalta, *The Stanford Encyclopedia of Philosophy*, <http://plato.stanford.edu/entries/rights-human/#GenIdeHumRig>.

Nickel, J. 2007. *Making Sense of Human Rights*. Malden, MA, Oxford and Carlton, Australia: Blackwell.

Nickel, J. 2015. 'Personal Deserts and Human Rights', in R. Cruft, M. S. Liao and M. Renzo (eds), *Philosophical Foundations of Human Rights*. Oxford: Oxford University Press, pp. 153–65.

Nordhaus, W., Oneal, J. R. and Russett, B. 2012. 'The Effects of the International Security Environment on National Military Expenditures', *International Organization*, 66/3: 491–513.

Nussbaum, M. 2001. *Women and Human Development: the Capabilities Approach*. Cambridge: Cambridge University Press.

Nussbaum, M., 2011. *Creating Capabilities: The Human Development Approach*. Cambridge, MA: Harvard University Press, 2011.

Nye, J. S. 2002. *The Paradox of American Power: Why the World's Only Superpower Can't Go It Alone*. Oxford: Oxford University Press.

Olson, M. and Zeckhauser, R. 1966. 'An Economic Theory of Alliances', *Review of Economics and Statistics*, 48/3: 269–79.

Oneal, J. R. 2006. 'Confirming the Liberal Peace with Analyses of Directed Dyads', in H. Starr (ed.), *Approaches, Levels, and Methods of Analysis in International Politics*. New York: Palgrave Macmillan, pp. 73–94.

Oneal, J. and Russett, B. 1997. 'The Classical Liberals Were Right: Democracy, Interdependence, and Conflict, 1950–1985'. *International Studies Quarterly*, 41/2: 267–94.

O'Neill, O. 2015. 'Response to John Tasioulas', in R. Cruft, M. S. Liao and M. Renzo (eds), *Philosophical Foundations of Human Rights*. Oxford: Oxford University Press, pp. 71–8.

Orend, B. 2000. *War and International Justice: A Kantian Perspective.* Waterloo, ON: Wilfrid Laurier University Press.

Ossipow, W. 2008. 'Kant's *Perpetual Peace* and Its Hidden Sources: A Textual Approach', *Swiss Political Science Review*, 14/2: 357–89.

Owen, J. M. 1997. *Liberal Peace, Liberal War: American Politics and International Security.* Ithaca and London: Cornell University Press.

Owen, J. M. 2004. 'Democratic Peace Research: Whence and Whither', *International Politics*, 41: 605–17.

Paul, E. F., Miller, F. D. Jr. and Paul, J. (eds). 1984. *Human Rights.* Oxford: Blackwell.

Peceny, M. 1999. *Democracy at the Point of Bayonets.* University Park: Pennsylvania State University Press.

Peceny, M. and Pickering, J. 2004. *Forging Democracy at Gunpoint.* Albuquerque: University of New Mexico.

Pendrick, G. J. (ed.). 2002. *Antiphon the Sophist: The Fragments.* Cambridge: Cambridge University Press.

Pennisi, A. 2012. 'Improving Economic Growth and Building Security: the Role of ASEAN in the Southeast Asian Region', *Warning*, 1.

Peter, F. 2015. 'A Human Right to Democracy?', in R. Cruft, M. S. Liao and M. Renzo (eds), *Philosophical Foundations of Human Rights.* Oxford: Oxford University Press, pp. 481–90.

Pevehouse, J. C. 2002. 'Democracy from the Outside-In? International Organizations and Democratization', *International Organization* 56/3: 515–49.

Pico (Gian Francesco Pico della Mirandola), 1948. 'Oration on the Dignity of Man', in Ernest Cassirer, et al., *The Renaissance Philosophy of Man.* Chicago: University of Chicago Press, pp. 223–55.

Pinzani, A. 2010. 'L'animale che ha bisogno di un padrone', in *Was ist der Mensch?/Que è o homen? – Antropologia, Estética e Teleologia em Kant.* Lesboa: CFUL, pp. 115–24.

Pinzani, A. 2017. 'Wie kann äussere Freiheit ein angeborenes Recht sein?', in C. Freiin von Villiez, J.-C. Merle (eds) *Aufsätze zu Kants Metaphysik der Sitten.* Berlin: De Gruyter (forthcoming).

Pinzani A. 2018. 'Uma fundamentação kantiana dos direitos humanos?' *Estudos kantianos* 6/1: 11–16.

Pogge, T. 2002. 'Is Kant's *Rechtslehre* a "Comprehensive Liberalism"?', in M. Timmons (ed.), *Kant's Metaphysics of Morals: Interpretative Essays.* Oxford: Oxford University Press, pp. 133–58.

Pogge, T. 2006. 'Kant's Vision, Europe, and a Global Federation', in L. Caranti (ed.), *Kant's Perpetual Peace. New Interpretative Essays.* Rome: LUISS University Press, pp. 75–96.

Pogge, T. 2008. *World Poverty and Human Rights. Cosmopolitan Responsibilities and Reforms.* Cambridge: Polity Press.

Pogge, T. 2009. 'Kant's Vision of a Just World Order', in T. E. Hill (ed.), *The Blackwell Guide to Kant's Ethics*. Oxford: Wiley-Blackwell.
Pritchard, D. M. 2010. *War, Democracy and Culture in Classical Athens*. Cambridge: Cambridge University Press.
Purdum, T. S. 2005. 'For Bush, a taste of vindication in Mideast', *New York Times*, 9 March. Available at <http://www.nytimes.com/2005/03/09/international/middleeast/09assess.html_r=0>.
Rauscher, F. 2001. 'The nature of "wholly empirical" history', in Volker Gerhard et al., *Kant und die Berliner Aufklärung. Akten des IX. Internationalen Kant-Kongress*, IV. Berlin and New York: Walter De Gruyter, 2001, pp. 44–51.
Rawls, J. 1999. *The Law of Peoples*. Cambridge, MA: Harvard University Press.
Ray, J. L. 2003. 'A Lakatosian View of the Democratic Peace Research Program', in C. Elman and M. F. Elman, *Progress in International Relations Theory: Appraising the Field*. Cambridge, MA: MIT Press, pp. 204–43.
Raz, J. 2010. 'Human Rights without Foundations', in S. Besson and J.Tasioulas (eds), *The Philosophy of International Law*. Oxford: Oxford University Press, pp. 321–38.
Recchia, S. and Urbinati, N. 2009. *A Cosmopolitanism of Nations: Giuseppe Mazzini's Writings on Democracy, Nation Building, and International Relations*. Princeton: Princeton University Press.
Reiter, D. and Stam, A. C. 2002. *Democracies at War*. Princeton: Princeton University Press.
Reiter, D. and Stam, A. C. 2003. 'Identifying the Culprit: Democracy, Dictatorship, and Dispute Initiation', *American Political Science Review*, 97/2: 333–7.
Riley, P. 1983. *Kant's Political Philosophy*. Totowa, NJ: Rowman and Littlefield.
Ripstein, A. 2009. *Force and Freedom*. Totowa, NJ: Rowman & Littlefield
Risse Kappen, T. 1995. 'Democratic Peace – Warlike Democracies? A Social Constructivist Interpretation of the Liberal Argument', *European Journal of International Relations*, 1: 491–517.
Robinson, E. 2001. 'Reading and Misreading the Ancient Evidence for Democratic Peace', *Journal of Peace Research*, 38: 593–608.
Robinson, E. 2006. 'Thucydides and Democratic Peace', *Journal of Military Ethics*, 5/4: 243–53.
Rock, Stephen R. 1997. 'Anglo-US Relations, 1845–1930: Did Shared Liberal Values and Democratic Institutions Keep the Peace?', in M. Fendius Elman (ed.), *Paths to Peace: Is Democracy the Answer?* Cambridge, MA: MIT Press, pp. 101–50.
Rodd, R. 1990. *Biology, Ethics, and Animals*. Oxford. Clarendon Press.

Rorty, R. 1993. 'Human Rights, Rationality, Sentimentality', in S. Shute and S. L. Hurley (eds), *On Human Rights: The Oxford Amnesty Lectures, 1993*. New York: Basic Books, pp. 111–34.

Rosato, S. 2003. 'The Flawed Logic of Democratic Peace Theory', *American Political Science Review*, 97/4: 585–602.

Rosato, S. 2005. 'Explaining the Democratic Peace', *American Political Science Review*, 99/3: 467–72.

Rosen, A. D. 1993. *Kant's Theory of Justice*. Ithaca: Cornell University Press.

Rosen, M. 2012. *Dignity: Its History and Meaning*. Cambridge, MA and London: Harvard University Press.

Rousseau, D. L. 2005. *Democracy and War: Institutions, Norms, and the Evolution of International Conflict*. Stanford: Stanford University Press.

Rousseau, J.-J. 1980–96. *Oeuvres Complètes*, ed. B. Gagnebin, M. Raymond et al. Paris: Gallimard.

Rummel, R. J. 1975. *Understanding Conflict and War*, vol. 4. Beverly Hills: Sage.

Russett, B. 1993. *Grasping the Democratic Peace. Principles for a Post-Cold War World*. Princeton: Princeton University Press.

Russett, B. 2005. 'Bushwhacking the Democratic Peace', *International Studies Perspectives*, 6/4: 395–408.

Russett, B. 2006. *Purpose and Policy in the Global Community*. New York. Palgrave Macmillan.

Russett, B. 2009. 'Democracy, War and Expansion through Historical Lenses', *European Journal of International Relations*, 15/1: 9–36.

Russett, B., Jackson, S., Snidal, D. and Sylvan, D. 1981. 'Health and Population Patterns as Indicators of Income Inequality', *Economic Development and Cultural Change*, 29/4: 759–79.

Russett, B. and Oneal, J. 1999. 'The Kantian Peace: The Pacific Benefits of Democracy, Interdependence, and International Organizations, 1885–1992', *World Politics*, 52: 1–37.

Russett, B. and Oneal, J. 2001. *Triangulating Peace: Democracy, Interdependence, and International Organizations*. New York: W. W. Norton.

Russett, B. and Pevehouse, J. 2006. 'Democratic International Governmental Organizations Promote Peace', *International Organization*, 60 (Fall): 969–1000.

Russett, B. and Starr, H. 2000. 'From Democratic Peace to Kantian Peace: Democracy and Conflict in the International System', in M. Midlarsky (ed.), *Handbook of War Studies*. 2nd edn. Ann Arbor: University of Michigan Press, pp. 93–128.

Saint-Pierre, Ch. I. Chastel de 1981 [1713]. *Projet pour rendre la paix perpétuelle en Europe*, ed. S. Goyard-Fabre. Paris: Garnier.

Sangiovanni, A. 2015. 'Why there cannot be a Truly Kantian Theory of Human Rights', in Cruft, R., Liao, M. S. and Renzo, M. (eds) *Philosophical Foundations of Human Rights*. Oxford: Oxford University Press, pp. 672–89.
Schaber, P. 2012. 'Human Rights Without Foundations?', in G. Ernst and J. C. Heilinger (eds), *The Philosophy of Human Rights*. Berlin and Boston: De Gruyter, pp. 61–72.
Sen, A., 1984. 'Rights and Capabilities', in *Resources, Values and Development*. Cambridge: Cambridge University Press, 1984, pp. 151–66.
Sen, A. 1999. *Development as Freedom*. New York: Anchor.
Sen, A., 2004. 'Elements of a Theory of Human Rights', *Philosophy and Public Affairs*, 32: 315–56.
Sen, A. 2006. *Identity and Violence: The Illusion of Destiny*. New York: W. W. Norton.
Sensen, Oliver. 2011. *Kant on Human Dignity*. Berlin: De Gruyter.
Schiller F. 1793. *On Grace and Dignity*, available at <http://www.schillerinstitute.org/educ/aesthetics/Schiller_On_Grace_and_Dignity.pdf>.
Schultz, K. 1999. *Democracy and Coercive Diplomacy*. Cambridge: Cambridge University Press.
Sciacca, F. 2000. *Il concetto di persona in Kant. Normatività e politica*. Milan: Giuffrè.
Shaw, M. 2005. *The New Western Way of War: Risk-Transfer War and its Crisis in Iraq*. Cambridge: Polity Press.
Shell, S. 1980. *The Rights of Reason: A Study of Kant's Philosophy and Politics*. Toronto: University of Toronto Press.
Sherman, N. 1997. *Making a Necessity of Virtue: Aristotle and Kant on Virtue*. Cambridge: Cambridge University Press.
Shue, H., 1980. *Basic Rights: Subsistence, Affluence, and U.S. Foreign Policy*. Princeton: Princeton University Press.
Simari, A. 1998. *Pace e guerra nel pensiero di Kant*. Milan: Giuffrè.
Singer, P. 1979. *Practical Ethics*. Cambridge: Cambridge University Press.
Small, M. and Singer, J. D. 1976. 'The War-Proneness of Liberal Regimes', *Jerusalem Journal of International Relations*, 1/1: 50–69.
Small, M. and Singer, J. D. 1982. *Resort to Arms: International and Civil War, 1816–1980*. Beverly Hills: Sage.
Smith, R. K. M. and van den Anker, C. (eds). 2005. *The Essentials of Human Rights*. London: Hodder Arnold.
Snyder, J. 1991. *Myths of Empire: Domestic Politics and International Ambition*. Ithaca: Cornell University Press.
Spiro, David E. 1994. 'The Insignificance of the Liberal Peace', *International Security*, 19/2: 50–86.
Stake, R. 1995. *The Art of Case Study Research*. Thousand Oaks, London and New Delhi: Sage.

Sukma, R. 2010. 'ASEAN and Regional Security in East Asia', in W. Hofmeister (ed.), *Security Politics in Asia and Europe*. Singapore: Konrad-Adenauer Stiftung, pp. 109–20.

Talbi, M. 1998. 'Religious Liberty', in C. Kurzman (ed.), *Liberal Islam*. Oxford: Oxford University Press, pp. 161–9.

Tan, K. C. 1998. 'Liberal Toleration in Rawls's *Law of Peoples*', *Ethics*, 108/2: 278–95.

Tan, S. 2004. *Confucian Democracy: A Deweyan Reconstruction*. Albany: State University of New York Press.

Taraborrelli, A. 2004. *Cosmopolitismo. Saggio su Kant*. Trieste: Asterios.

Taraborrelli, A. 2006. 'Reflections on Kant's Third Definitive Article of 'Perpetual Peace', in L. Caranti (ed.), *Kant's Perpetual Peace. New Interpretative Essays*. Rome: Luiss University Press, 133–42.

Tasioulas, J. 2012. 'On the Nature of Human Rights', in G. Ernst and J. C. Heilinger (eds), *The Philosophy of Human Rights*. Berlin and Boston: De Gruyter, pp. 17–59.

Tasioulas, J. 2013. 'Human Dignity and the Foundations of Human Rights', in C. McCrudden (ed.), *Understanding Human Dignity*. Oxford: Oxford University Press, pp. 291–312.

Tasioulas, J. 2015. 'On the Foundations of Human Rights', in R. Cruft, M. S. Liao and M. Renzo (eds), *Philosophical Foundations of Human Rights*. Oxford: Oxford University Press pp. 45–70.

Thompson, W. R. 1996. 'Democracy and peace: Putting the cart before the horse?', *International Organization*, 50/1: 141–74.

Tonetto Consenso M. 2018. 'Kant's Contribution to the Philosophy of Human Rights', *Estudos kantianos* 6/1: 29–38.

Tosel, A. 1999. *Kant Révolutionnaire. Droit et Politique*. Paris: Presses Universitaires de France.

Tundo, L. 1998. *Kant. Utopia e senso della storia. Progresso, cosmopoli, pace*. Bari: Dedalo.

Untersteiner, M. 1954. *The Sophists*. Oxford: Basil Blackwell.

Urbinati, N. 2006. *Representative Democracy: Principles and Genealogy*. Chicago: University of Chicago Press.

Valentini, L. 2012. 'Human Rights, Freedom, and Political Authority', *Political Theory*, 40: 573–601.

Vattel de, E. 1916. *The Law of Nations or the Principles of Natural Law* (1758), tr. Charles G. Fenwick. Washington: Carnegie Institution of Washington.

Voltaire 1821–3 [1769]. 'De la paix perpétuelle par le Docteur Goodheart', in *Oeuvres complètes*. Paris: Esneaux, vol. XIV.

Waldron, J. 2000. 'What is Cosmopolitan?', *Journal of Political Philosophy*, 8/2: 227–43.

Waldron, J. 2012. *Dignity, Rank, and Rights*. Oxford and New York: Oxford University Press.
Waltz, K. 1959. *Man, the State, and War*. New York: Columbia University Press.
Walzer, M. *Just and Unjust Wars: A Moral Argument with Historical Illustrations*. New York: Basic Books.
Weart, S. 1998. *Never at War: Why Democracies Will Not Fight One Another*. New Haven: Yale University Press.
Weinrib, E. J. 1992. 'Law as Idea of Reason', in H. Williams (ed.), *Essays on Kant's Political Philosophy*. Cardiff: University of Wales Press, pp. 15–49.
Wenar, L., 2005. 'The Value of Rights', in Joseph K. Campbell, Michael O'Rourke and David Shier (eds), *Law and Social Justice*. Cambridge, MA: MIT Press, pp. 179–209.
Wenar, L., 2008. 'Property Rights and the Resource Curse', *Philosophy & Public Affairs*, 36/1: 2–32.
Willaschek, M. 1997. 'Why the *Doctrine of Right* does not belong in the *Metaphysics of Morals*', *Jahrbuch für Recht und Ethik*, 5: 205–27.
Williams, H. 1983. *Kant's Political Philosophy*. New York: St. Martin's Press.
Williams, H. (ed.), *Essays on Kant's Political Philosophy*. Cardiff: University of Wales Press
Williams, M. C. 2001. 'The Discipline of the Democratic Peace: Kant, Liberalism and the Social Construction of Security Communities', *European Journal of International Relations*, 7/4: 525–53.
Wilson, W. 1986. *The Papers of Woodrow Wilson*, ed. A. S. Lind. Princeton: Princeton University Press, vol. 53.
Wolff, C. 1934 [1749]. *The Law of Nations Treated According to a Scientific Method*, tr. H. Drake. Oxford: Clarendon Press.
Wood, A. 2002. 'The Final Form of Kant's Practical Philosophy', in M. Timmons (ed.) *Kant's Metaphysics of Morals*. Oxford: Oxford University Press, pp. 1–22.
Wood, A. 2005. *Kant*. Malden, MA: Blackwell.
Wood, A. 2008. *Kantian Ethics*. Cambridge: Cambridge University Press.
Xiaorong, L. 2001. 'Tolerating the Intolerable: The Case of Female Genital Mutilation', *Philosophy and Public Policy Quarterly*, 21: 1–8.
Yitik, A. I. 2004. 'Does Qur'an Approve Religious Pluralism?, *Journal of Religious Culture/Journal für Religionskultur*. Frankfurt: Johann Wolfgang Goethe-Universität, 68/1: 1–5.
Yovel, Y. 1980. *Kant and the Philosophy of History*. Princeton: Princeton University Press.
Zayd, N. A. 2004. *Rethinking the Qur'an: Towards a Humanistic Hermeneutics*. Utrecht: University of Humanistics.

Index

A
acquired rights 19–20
Al-Azm, S. 98
Allison, H. 25–6, 259
animal rights 66
An-Na'im, A. 97
Archibugi, D. 8, 109, 113, 131–2, 164, 171, 174–5, 176, 177, 181, 266, 269
autocracy 108, 119, 131–2, 140, 147, 162, 165, 167, 171–3, 177, 179, 184–5, 187–8, 191, 196, 206, 252
autonomy 25–6, 84–5
  and active citizenship 140–2
  and humanity 27–8, 38–9
  and religion, 103–5
  and the moral law/morality 28, 58, 61, 64, 70
  and the spirit of democracy, 96–8
  as a universal, non-parochial value, 95–102
  basis of human dignity 2, 7, 19, 27–8, 38–9, 70
  basis of human rights 28–33, 61
  basis of the innate right to external freedom 26–8
  different from personhood, 58, 61, 71–3, 86–7
  different from practical freedom, 19, 23, 57, 61
  insufficient for determining the list of human rights 90–1
  proof of the reality of 81–5

B
Babst, D. 164–6, 273
Baiasu, S. 27, 262

Beck, G. 30–1, 259
Beitz, C. 50–1, 92
Bentham, J. 41–2, 66, 156, 161, 170
Bobbio, N. 120, 153, 270
Buchanan, A. 4, 36, 42, 48, 50, 265
Byrd, B. S. 153, 258, 270

C
Cavallar, G. 107, 143, 270–3, 277
Chan, J. 265
Christiano, T. 262
Cohen, J. 52, 92, 97, 258
Confucianism 95, 97, 99–103
cosmopolitan commonwealth 152; see also cosmopolitan constitution
cosmopolitan constitution 8–9, 115, 122–7, 152
cosmopolitanism 152, 269, 272, 273
Covell, C. 271, 272
Cruft, R. 43, 45, 48–9, 52, 54

D
Danto, A. 86, 259
Darwall, S. 264
De Waal, F. 68
DeGrazia, D. 68
Democracy 37–8
  and peace 160–5
  different from republic see republic
  the spirit of 96–7
democratic peace theory (DPT) 6–8, 164–9
  deterministic and probabilistic interpretations of 174–5

democratic peace theory (DPT) *continued*
   DPT and normative thinking 205–6
   dyadic and monadic interpretations of 171–4
   five versions of 170–1
   normative indications of 195–200
   rationalist and constructivist interpretations of 175–6
Derrida, J. 155
Dershowitz, A. 56, 95
dignity 5–7
   and esteem 55–6, 76, 86
   and the culture of human rights 52–3
   based on autonomy *see* autonomy
   basis of human rights 32–3, 36–9, 44–6, 51–3
   dignity approach 59–63
Doyle, M. 7–9, 107, 143–7, 154, 157, 162, 164–71, 173, 177–80, 183, 191–4, 195–8, 200, 206, 269, 271, 272, 273, 274
duty-based morality 7, 57
   not necessarily linked to the categorical imperative 63–5
Dworkin, R. 263

E
economic interdependence *see* international trade
El Fadl, K. 98–9
equality, 6–7, 18–19, 28, 32, 36–7, 96
   equal status 21, 45, 48, 50, 196, 200–1, 204
   right to formal 20–2, 133, 257
   value of 96–7, 102–3

F
federation/federalism 7, 110–11, 114–15, 117, 121, 126, 142, 161, 197, 199, 216, 232, 266, 267–70, 274
   restricted/unrestricted access to 143–8
   vs world government 148–51
Ferrara, A. 92, 96–7, 99–101, 265
Fiegle, T. 209
Flach, W. 209
Flikschuh, K. 33–5, 50
Foot, P. 259
foresight, 238–42
freedom
   external freedom, 19–20, 26–32, 34–5, 38–9, 50, 88, 136, 258
   practical freedom 19, 23–4, 26–8, 57, 72, 78, 84, 258–9, 265
   see also autonomy

G
Gewirth, A. 44, 49, 58, 85–6
global conscience 157–9, 202
Gregor, M. 29, 258, 259
Griffin, J. 7, 18, 42, 44, 58–9, 71–2, 81, 85–6, 89
Grotius, 109–11, 129, 266
guarantee thesis 11, 218–34, 243, 277
Guyer, P. 29, 209, 218, 221, 225, 229–30, 269

H
Habermas, J. 27, 151
Herr, S. 102
Hinduism 83, 95–6, 99–100, 103
history 10, 77
   and the foresight of the moral politician/political moralist 247–9
   as a system 217, 228–9
   end of 115, 220, 222
   metaphysics of 116, 123, 228
   methodology of universal 211
   progressive/teleological view of *see* progress
Höffe, O. 17, 21–2, 259, 270, 271

INDEX

Hruschka, J. 153, 258, 269, 270
human rights
  culture of 17, 41, 52–5, 73, 88,
    90–1, 98, 127, 230
  egalitarianism of 48
  foundation/justification of 1–2,
    4–7, 18, 32–3, 37, 43–4
    instrumental/reductive
      justification of 43–8
    justification deficit 4, 41–3
    non-instrumental/orthodox
      justification of 48–50
    practice based/political
      justification of 50–4
  list of 42–3, 49, 91
  nature of 42–3
  practice of 5, 50, 52–4, 71, 73,
    88–92, 96
human worth, 18–19, 27–33, 48, 55,
    57, 59–64, 67–70, 86, 90,
    95–6
  and passive citizenship 141
  basis of *see* autonomy
  equal among all individuals
    75–6
  higher than animal worth 66,
    74–5, 77–8
humanity
  as linked to autonomy *see*
    autonomy; personality
  definition of 23, 27
  different from personality 258,
    259
  duty towards 79
  ground of human rights 55, 76,
    80, 259
  ground of right to external
    freedom 5, 17, 19–26, 28–30
  intrinsically valuable 5
  (moral) progress of 115, 117,
    119, 123, 125–6, 221
  object/ground of respect 28, 79
  Recht-e der Menschen/Menschheit
    17
Hume, D. 67–8
Huntington, S. P. 265

I

Ignatieff, M. 95
individuality 96, 99, 101–2
innate rights 17, 20–3
  to freedom 2, 5, 17–20
Intergovernmental Organization
    (IGO) 10, 164, 193, 197–8;
  see also federation
international trade 9–11, 113, 153,
    154–9, 200, 202, 204, 220,
    272
Islam 83, 95–100

J

Judaism, 83, 97, 100–1
judgment (power of) 60, 250–4,
    277–8

K

Kamm, F. 5–7, 48
Kateb, G. 76–8
Kinsella, D. 191
Kissinger, H. 272
Kleingeld, P. 149, 151, 153, 155,
    209–11, 213, 215, 270, 272

L

Layne, C. 146, 176–7, 180–1, 187
Liao, M. S. 43, 45, 48–9, 52, 54
Liberalism 139, 161, 165–6, 176,
    183, 193, 203, 268, 273
Ludwig, B. 29, 31, 218, 221, 232, 277

M

Mann, M. 176
Maoz, Z. 170, 180–1
Marini, G. 154, 278
Mill, J. 163, 181, 193
Mitra, K. 103
moral law/morality
  ability to follow the 27, 31, 236–7
  consciousness of 82, 265

moral law/morality *continued*
  and politics *see* politics
    (autonomy of)
  different *formulae* of 63–5, 263
  in the animal world 68–70
  in the natural law tradition 109
  respect for *see* respect
moral politician 12, 237–8, 240–2, 244, 246–7, 249–51, 253, 278
moral sentimentalism 65, 67–8; *see also* Hume
moralizing politician 12, 238, 246, 249, 252
Mori, M. 107, 224, 233, 269, 276, 277
Murti, T. 100

N
Nagel, T. 1, 6, 48, 262
natural rights 17, 19, 52, 75, 103, 137, 157
Nickel, J. 37, 45, 49
Nussbaum, M. 44, 47

O
openness to diversity *see* pluralism

P
parochial objection 95
parochialism 17–8, 56, 59
peace
  democracy and 160–4
  democratic peace theory (DPT) 6–8, 164–9
    determinists and probabilists 174–5
    DPT and normative thinking 205–6
    dyadic and monadic interpretations 171–4
    five versions of 170–1
    normative indications of 195–200
    rationalists and constructivists 175–6
  guarantee of *see* guarantee thesis
  Kantian model of 115–60
    normative indications of 200–2
    origins of 108–15
  liberal *see* democratic peace Theory (DPT)
personality 17, 58, 66, 97, 257, 259; *see also* humanity
Pevehouse, J. 175, 193, 199
pluralism 18, 93, 97, 98–101
Pogge, T. 29–31, 50, 150, 199, 262, 263, 271
political moralist, 12, 234, 237–8, 241–2, 246–50, 278
politics
  autonomy of (from morality and right) 13, 235–9, 253
  impact of DPT on contemporary 169
  impact of Kant on contemporary 2–4
progress
  and political agency 235–54
  moral 120, 122–7, 268
  progressive/teleological view of 116–17, 127–8, 152, 159, 209–10, 213–17, 244
  see also teleological view of history
Pufendorf 109

R
Rawls, J. 1, 5, 14, 22, 50–1, 66, 92, 97, 143, 165, 198, 250, 253, 255, 258, 265, 268, 276
Raz, J. 5, 42, 50, 53, 59, 74–5, 78, 85–8, 91
reason
  practical 28, 47, 124, 242, 245
  as *ratio cognoscendi* of the moral law 251

pure 83, 116, 120, 149, 243, 245, 267, 277
public 54, 91–5
reflective equilibrium 54, 71, 89, 91–2
Renzo, M. 43, 45, 48–9, 52, 54
representation 136, 140, 165, 203
  burden of 136–40, 142
republic/republicanism 117, 120–2, 130, 133–6, 201
  different from liberal democracy/liberalism 9, 136–40, 203
  world republic 142, 148–50, 158
respect 5–6, 10, 17, 19, 26, 28, 32, 35, 55, 61–3, 71–2, 74, 86–8, 104
  equal respect 28, 32, 90
  for the moral law 26
right
  cosmopolitan 7, 17, 145–6, 147, 151–9
    and global conscience 157–8
    narrow vs broad readings of 153–7
    universal, of humanity 152
  international 152, 223, 268, 271; *see also* federation
  public 222–3, 244–5
  state 152; *see also* republic
  universal principle of 29–31, 34, 39, 252–3, 262
Ripstein, A. 154, 270
Rosato, S. 8, 176–8, 181–90, 194, 196, 200, 274
Rosen, A. 153, 272
Rosen, M. 73, 78–80
Rousseau, J. J. 111–13, 137, 161, 171, 211, 267, 274, 277
Rummel, R. J. 171, 273
Russett, B. 132, 143, 154, 170–1, 174, 179, 181, 185, 192–3, 197, 199, 205–6, 269

S
Saint-Pierre, Ch. 111–13, 161, 243, 267, 277
Sangiovanni, A. 31–9
Schaber, P. 72, 262
Schiller F. 263
Sen, A. 44–6, 94, 118, 265, 268
Spiro, D. 177, 180–1
Syrac 113–14

T
Talbi, M. 98
Tan, K. C. 265
Tan, S. 102
Tasioulas, J. 5–6, 43, 45–7, 49, 51, 72–3, 262
teleology, 115–21, 209–17; *see also* progress; progressive/teleological view of history
threshold objection 85, 86–91

U
utilitarianism 65–6

V
value/right conflation 85–6
Vattel de, E. 109, 129, 266
virtue ethics 65–7, 278

W
Waldron, J. 58, 73–6, 154
Walzer, M. 100, 173
Williams, H. 210, 215, 277
Wilson, W. 163–4
Wolff, C. 109–10, 112
world government *see* world republic

X
Xiaorong, L. 94